THE STRUCTURE
OF BEING

Studies in Neoplatonism:
   Ancient and Modern

Volume IV

R. BAINE HARRIS, GENERAL EDITOR

THE STRUCTURE OF BEING

A NEOPLATONIC APPROACH

EDITED BY

R. Baine Harris
OLD DOMINION UNIVERSITY

INTERNATIONAL SOCIETY FOR NEOPLATONIC STUDIES
Norfolk, Virginia

Published by
State University of New York Press, Albany

© 1982 International Society for Neoplatonic Studies

For information, address State University of New York
Press, State University Plaza, Albany, N.Y., 12246

Library of Congress Cataloging in Publication Data
Main entry under title:

The Structure of being.

    (Studies in Neoplatonism ; v. 4)
    Bibliography: p.
    Includes index.
    Contents: The logical peculiarities of Neo-
platonism / J.N. Findlay — On logical structure
and the Plotinic cosmos / R.M. Martin — Some
logical aspects of the concept of hypostasis in
Plotinus / John P. Anton — [etc.]
    1. Neoplatonism—Addresses, essays, lectures.
2. Ontology—Addresses, essays, lectures.
3. Plotinus—Addresses, essays, lectures.

I. Harris, R. Baine, 1927–   . II. International
Society for Neoplatonic Studies. III. Series.
B645.S83   186′.4   81-5627
ISBN 0-87395-532-3   AACR2
ISBN 0-87395-533-1 (pbk.)

CONTENTS

PREFACE

It would be a mistake to regard Neoplatonism as only a form of mysticism. Although it is a way of philosophizing that points to a form of knowing that is beyond dialectics, it does not have any mystical elements in its own dialectics. Its mysticism is to be found at the end of its philosophical progression and is not inherent in its epistemology. Philosophical knowledge, as well as scientific and artistic knowledge, are forms of discursive knowledge and, as such, have no mysticism whatsoever involved in them.

Neoplatonism also differs *logically* from the Platonism of the *Dialogues*. It could also be labeled "Aristotelian Platonism," since both Plotinus and Porphyry were highly influenced by Aristotle and his criticisms of Plato. Although Plotinus returned to the same main theme emphasized by Plato, he made major concessions to Aristotle, and especially to his logic. This tendency is even more pronounced in the writings of Porphyry, who was so enamored of Aristotle's logic that he emphasized it in his own writings and, in so doing, set the stage for the formation of another kind of Neoplatonism, namely, a type that focuses upon the logic and categories of Aristotle. A case could be made, I think, that there really have been two forms of Neoplatonism operative in the history of Western philosophy, namely, the Neoplatonism (or Plotinism) of Plotinus and the Neoplatonism of Porphyry; and, by and large, the latter has been far more influential than the former.

A close look at the history of Neoplatonism will reveal that hardly any later Neoplatonist followed Plotinus exactly. From Porphyry to Dean Inge, most "Neoplatonists" have been neo-Neoplatonists, deviants who have abandoned parts of Plotinus' system or departed to some extent from his logic or categories. Add to this the tendency of various Jewish, Islamic, and Christian writers to take only portions of his thought and combine it with their own to produce some hybrid variety of Neoplatonism, and we might be led to ask "What is normative in Neoplatonism?" To what degree must a follower of Plotinus remain true to his views in order correctly to be labeled a Neoplatonist? The answer, I believe, is to be found in the degree to which they follow his logic and epistemology. When they depart radically from either of them, they should no longer be labeled Neoplatonists.

In defense of the deviants, it might be noted that Plotinus was essentially a synthetic thinker, and synthetic thinkers are necessarily dated. His system was the product not only of his own philosophical methodology, but also of his own dated understanding of science, art, religion, and philosophy. Those in later times who have recognized his remarkable genius as an artist of metaphysics and have chosen to label themselves as his followers have usually sought to compliment him by complementing him. This they have done not by slavishly reproducing his own system, but by updating or correcting it or by producing their own versions of it. They have sought to duplicate his vision of the unity of being; and they have understood that this must occur as a synthetic function of their own thought and within their own intellectual and historical context. The disciple of Plotinus need not necessarily take Plotinus' own system per se as final, but one must emulate his logic and epistemology.

However tolerant we may wish to be toward the deviants in the Neoplatonic tradition, the fact remains that Neoplatonic logic is significant in determining what we now call "Neoplatonism." The nature of Platonism had been debated for six centuries prior to Plotinus and the Middle Platonists, and one of the major factors in the evolution of later Platonism was the accumulated impact of Aristotelian and Stoic logic. Distinctions can be made between the logic of Plato, the logic of Aristotle, the logic of Plotinus, and the logic of Porphyry. Neoplatonism, as a form of Aristotelianized Platonism, involves making certain important concessions to the logic of Aristotle. Plotinus rejected Aristotle's categories, substituting his own. He also rejected a portion of his logic. Porphyry, in turn, decided that Plotinus' categories and logic were inadequate and relied heavily on both Aristotle's categories and logic in his own thought, especially in dealing with the physical or sensible world. If the case can be made that there is a sufficient difference in the logic of Plato and Plotinus to justify the term "Neoplatonism," it can also be said, I think, that there is a sufficient difference in the logic of Plotinus and Porphyry to serve as the basis for defining and delineating the various historical types of Neoplatonism. At issue is whether there is only one prevailing Neoplatonic logic or two varieties.

The essays in this volume do not deal sufficiently with all the necessary questions entailed in a study of Neoplatonic logic, but they do provide a beginning for a consideration of some of them. They were not commissioned and are not products of single conference, but were presented at various meetings of the International Society for Neoplatonic Studies in the United States and Canada during the last four years. They have been selected because they focus, to some extent, upon the nature of Neoplatonic logic and methodology, broadly conceived.

The title, *The Structure of Being: A Neoplatonic Approach,* has been chosen in order to emphasize that Neoplatonism is but one among many efforts to suggest how being may be conceived to be structured. More precisely, Neoplatonism is an effort to suggest a logic of being, namely, how being might be conceived to be *logically* structured. Although some elements of it are highly speculative, the *logic on which Neoplatonism is based* is not. It is the aim of the editor of this volume to draw attention to the importance of Neoplatonic logic and methodology, both in the general definition of Neoplatonism and in determining the nature of particular historical instances of it. A very brief description of the fourteen essays now follows.

In the first essay J. N. Findlay suggests that the logical peculiarities of Neoplatonism still fit into the general logic of Platonism, but he indicates certain respects in which the logic of Plotinus goes much further. He insists that it cannot be viewed as an ordinary logic of propositional or functional calculus, but must be seen as a quite nonordinary type, which he describes to some extent. The second essay by Richard M. Martin contains a sketch of a formal logicometaphysical system that indicates some of the basic features of the system of Plotinus. The third essay by John P. Anton investigates the concept of hypostases in the *Enneads* and defends the position that the One is the first hypostasis, a view strongly denied by the late John N. Deck in the fourth essay. (Deck holds that the One is above hypostasis.)

The One is also the subject of the fifth essay by Eugene F. Bales. Bales notes that Plotinus uses three modes of discourse, (1) meontological, (2) ontological, and (3) paradoxical in discussing the One or the Good, and suggests that the view that the One radically transcends being is inadequate. In the sixth essay Michael F. Wagner explains Plotinus' theory of "Vertical Causation," namely, that the causes of bodies are not other bodies, but the Forms. He further illucidates Plotinus' position that real explanations appeal to forms rather than to interactions between bodies and that the Forms determine *the order of* our concepts. The seventh essay, by Christos Evangeliou, establishes the thesis that Plotinus' criticism of Aristotle's categories is based on ontological, and not logical, grounds.

The eighth essay, by John Fielder, is an analysis of the concept of self-predication as it applies to Plotinus, whereas the ninth essay, by Jonathan Scott Lee, is a study of participation (or eidetic causation) as it relates to omnipresence and monopsychism in the *Enneads.*

Professor Robert Brumbaugh, in the tenth essay, suggests that Neoplatonic philosophy is exactly what contemporary mathematicians are looking for in their discussion of the foundation of mathematics. He further indicates that Cantor's set theory fills a definite place in the Platonic curriculum suggested by Plato in *Republic* VII and developed further by later Platonists. He further opines that Proclus has more mathematical talent than he is usually credited with, especially in algebra.

The eleventh essay, by Carl R. Kordig, explores the mathematics of the mysticism of Plotinus and Proclus, concluding that the One must be said to have properties, but quite special ones, and not the ones we apply to ordinary, finite objects. He also concludes that the logic applicable to the One cannot be an ordinary logic. In the twelfth essay, Ronald Hathaway takes a close look at the logical anatomy of Proclus' proof and draws some conclusions about his general model of proof. Essay thirteen, by Evanghelos Moutsopoulos, focuses upon the idea of falsity as it occurs in Proclus, concluding that the main cause of falsehood is inherent to multiplicity and the conditions relating to it.

The fourteenth and final essay, by Leo Sweeney, contains an intensive analysis of the logical structure of being in Proclus' *Elements of Theology*. He suggests that in Proclus' cosmos two sorts of spontaneous and necessary causality are operative: participation, by which perfections come to be present in participants, which thereby are completed and perfected; secondly, a prior and nonparticipational process, by which the participated perfections themselves and their participants originate.

R. Baine Harris
Old Dominion University

The Logical Peculiarities of Neoplatonism

J. N. FINDLAY

I have chosen to address myself in this essay not to some historical or factual question, but to the philosophically important topic of the logical peculiarities of Neoplatonism. These logical peculiarities may be described in terms of pervasion and interpenetration, of sympathy and remote control, of multiple location, of elastic and variable identity, of iridescent variation of aspect, of differentiation without difference, and of potency more actual than act) Before, however, I go on to consider these peculiarities, I shall observe that the logical peculiarities of Neoplatonism are in large part simply the peculiarities of Platonism, and of the fundamental inversion, the "Eidetic Turn," as I may fashionably call it, in which Platonism consists. This inversion is one in which types and characters lose their predicative character, and are erected into the true substances or subjects of predicates, while their concrete instances are suddenly demoted from their substantial status into the new status of dependent instantiations or particularizations. We, in short, no longer take it that this individual or that is human and just, but that Manhood and Justice are "thisied" or "thatified," are "herified" or "therified," are "nowafied" or "thenified" in this or that case. By such an inversion, generic and specific features become the true and primary cases of identity, an identity unaffected by multiple location in space, or changing location in time, and which is capable of a persistence unmodified, or intrinsically unmixed with what is irrelevant, such as we never postulate in the case of instances.

It is, however, also an inversion that will permit us to make specific and generic natures as specific as we wish, so as to include whatever is discoverable and graspable in the individual, and also to leave our "natures" unsaturated in the Fregean sense, so that they permit saturation or completion in a number of alternative ways. It is further a logic in virtue of which universal types or patterns become, in a queerly inert, effortless manner, the "true causes" of their own instantiations, since it is by their "presence" in their instances, or by the "sharing" of their instances in them, that those instances are made what they are. Instances have in fact nothing that is intelligible and seizable, nothing that can be spoke of or pinned down, except for what they thus instantiate or exemplify. We try to dig down to their dark underlay of χώρα or spatiality, but can only do so by divesting ourselves of all conceptual lucidity, by deluding ourselves with a spurious argument to the effect that whatever exists must be somewhere, with the "somewhere" being only the indefinite possibility of instantiation that we feel must be there if instances are to have any basis at all.

Neoplatonism further takes over from Platonism the marriage between general patterns and cases of the Good or the Intelligible: the true substances of logical subjects are all special forms of Goodness, cases involving no mere congeries of elements but an ordered, unified pattern in which diversity is wholly subordinated to unity, and the tendency to exceed or fall short is so hemmed or curbed that a single set of measures works everywhere. This belief in well-ordered μετριότής further obtains whether we are dealing with the natural numbers, the harmonic proportions, or the regular geometrical figures—the solids or patterns of movement—until we rise to the self-moving patterns of living creatures in which substantial reality goes hand in hand with beauty. Neoplatonism in fact goes further than Platonism in its close marriage of substantial being with value, for while Plato is willing to accord some sort of parasitic, secondary status to a παρέκβασις or a negation, Neoplatonism is inclined to attribute all deviation, privation, or factitious combination to the inherent defects of instantiation, and to the "matter" that is the ultimate wall of darkness in which the eidetic illumination terminates.

Neoplatonism further takes over from Platonism the view of there being, in the higher cases of self-movement, an inherent affinity, not merely with the specific life patterns that the instance embodies, but also with the whole range of the Eide which, as Soul-instances, they can know. Each higher case of Soul is therefore also an instance of Mind, and, as such, shares imperfectly in the changelessness of the total eidetic system, persisting throughout the whole flux of instances since it is unable to step out of flux altogether.

In all these respects Neoplatonism simply takes over the logic of Platonism, and we may commend it for freeing us from all the anxieties and perils of particularism: the impossibility of justifying our search for unifying patterns in the welter of particular cases and our faith in their continued presence in further cases, and our faith, also, in a general trend in things towards well-ordered integration, which is not only presupposed by all scientific research, but also underlies all self-restraint, all courage, and all justice. To believe that principles of order are the mere dependencies of what happens to exist, rather than the source and guiding force of the latter, is to surrender oneself to the boundless demoralization of the typically modern outlook, which stands as pathetically helpless as Saint Sebastian while the arrows of chance afflict it from every side. These arrows now stem from scientific laboratories rather than from faithless men.

I do not, however, wish to dwell on the general merits of Platonic logic, but to consider the respects in which Neoplatonism goes further than it does. This it does in stressing the *unbroken continuity* of the eidetic system, from its most generic to its most specific phases, and from what is most powerfully positive in it to what is most shadowy and negative, and also from what is most definitely this or that in it, to what is most definitely something quite different. The stress on eidetic continuity is, also to be found in Plato. The *Phaedrus* compares a genus to a living body that can be cut at many places indefinitely, though there are always some cutting points that are natural and right. The *Republic* tells us of an eidetic system in which all relations will be as eidetic as the terms that they connect, while the *Parmenides* provides a specimen of an indefinite multiplicity nesting within the most absolute simplicity and unity. But in Neoplatonism we operate throughout with hypostases that shade into other hypostases, that in fact *are* other hypostases operating in a slightly different medium or manner, or that are said, with a final access of approximation, to be separated from other hypostases by nothing but difference, as if this were the most inconsequential sort of separation that there could conceivably be. Yet this stress on continuity goes together with a profound recognition of gulfs and distances: the higher hypostasis has a self-sufficiency and an independence from the lower hypostasis that the lower hypostasis never can share. In being a dependent offshoot of the higher hypostasis, it is separated by an ontological gulf from that of which it is the offshoot. And, likewise, in including other forms of being as its necessary context, it also excludes them from the intrinsic nucleus that makes it what it is. The structure which results is one where everything shades into everything, yet nothing is blurred: it realizes among Eide that essential mystery of motion in which positions never can be in touch with other positions, and yet there is no such thing as a break or division among them. The mathematical theory of Real Numbers is something that *could* have been Neoplatonically conceived: as it stands, it only reveals the complete powerlessness of separative thought.

I should, however, like to elucidate my view of the Neoplatonic continuum by trying to set forth a typical account of Neoplatonism that would lend itself to picture-thought, and that soon turns into a strange fable. On this account the Neoplatonists were silly enough to treat Unity—the most abstract of categorial attributes that implies only that something is something and not nothing—as if it were not merely something highly positive, but also a peculiar instance of itself, having no other attribute but being purely and resolutely single. This self-existent singularity and uniqueness had no awareness of itself or of anything else, and it had not the slightest tendency to seek relief from its single state by the smallest exercise in self-duplication or differentiation. Nonetheless, by some strange necessity that had nothing to do with a need, its very needlessness precipitated the existence of something which was more than resolutely single, which was inherently prone to distinguish itself as subject from something else as object, and to do this over and over again, so that it was confronted with a whole offspring of distinct phases, which were in fact infinite in number and embraced all that could *be* or be conceived. This spawning of a kaleidoscope is in fact the substitute for a vain effort to penetrate the One as object. The Second Hypostasis tries to conceive the One in its unity, but can only succeed in splintering it into a host of ones, whose participation in the One makes them an organized complex whole, but which, in being organized and complex, are also everlastingly and absolutely separate from the One itself. The Second Hypostasis is accordingly a seeing, intellective one, a *Nous* or Intelligence, and what it sees is the hierarchically arrayed Eide, its coeval companions. In seeing them it becomes a seer, and as such capable of seeing itself in them, and them in itself. The life of the Intelligence is then described in phrases of great literary beauty which, seen in the sort of logic that we are now using, is no more than a Gandavyūha, a very lovely fairy tale. In the heavenly regions there are many distinct νόες or νοῖ, one for each of us and for the celestial agents as well, but they are all eyes and vision, and see each other as such: the situation rather resembles a nightmare I had when I was a child—I awoke to see millions of shining eyes looking at me from every direction. And in this heavenly region every eidetic shape carries the whole eidetic system in itself, while emphasizing its own peculiar contribution to that system. The νοῖ in that region vainly attempt something like locomotion, but the earth on which they tread is rather terrifyingly alive, and they carry their starting point with them wherever they journey. The condition in which they subsist is described in terms so superlative that one feels rather like someone staying in some snow-white Alpine hotel surrounded by scenery similarly snowy. It is, in short, as free from the suffering, the patience, and the labor of the negative as are the much admired writings of Benedetto Croce. Heracles (up there) remembers nothing of his labors, so that there is little reason for him to retain his peculiar corner in the poetic mansions. I do not, however, wish to cast ridicule on some of the most brilliantly beautiful tractates in human literature, but only to stress a single point: that it can be read as an extraordinary travelogue or piece of science fiction, and that the question then emerges whether we really want to believe in such an ecstatic intellectual state, whether we really want such a beatifically blurred condition to exist. Would it not be preferable to be in one of Fra Angelico's heavenly assemblies, with their bright-cheeked saints and angels and golden trumpets, or in the select group of the upper 400 to whom Beatrice presents Dante? It is the feeling that what Plotinus describes so ecstatically is no more than a myth or a fairy tale that leads people to think that he is not worth studying, exactly what Prince Eugene and the court ladies may have felt when they read Leibniz's charming treatises about the Monads.

The so-called process of emanation, which I prefer to call Irradiation or περίλαμψις, and which has led from the One to the *Nous,* can also be seen as a magical but factual process. There is the famous passage where Plotinus exploits its analogy with the way in which fire radiates warmth to environing objects, or in which odorous objects diffuse scent into the surrounding air, and so on, which suggest that it is merely a marvellous fact that hypostases should shed or drop exhalations about them which try to resemble them but which also necessarily fall short of them. And while this exuberant burgeoning seems vaguely exciting, the fact that it always results in something inferior is vaguely depressing: it is as if one's children were always smaller and stupider than oneself, until all generation ended up in producing dwarfish idiots. One is inclined to echo Plotinus's occasional regret: how much nicer it would have been had there been no such declining procession, if only everything had remained in its first primitive condition. And what a pity that there is this strange ontological necessity that corresponds to no need, but which gives rise to such deep need in the lower hypostases. The doctrine becomes even stranger when we are told that the submission to this necessity was also perfectly free. What, we are inclined to ask, possessed the One to let anything derive from itself?

The procession does not cease to excite questions as we go on to its next stage, the procession of the World Soul. Here the decline is to succession, the piecemeal running through items that were previously given together, and the use of λογισμοί, reasonings, where previously all was accomplished sight. It is not clear what advantage is secured by falling out of eternity into time, and how such a dismantled state as one that involves change and flux could have sprung from the all-togetherness of eternity. The Third Hypostasis, however, exhibits further declensions than the merely temporal: it proceeds to a certain limit and not further, and there is confronted by an ambient darkness which is merely the shadow cast by its own light. But it is not content to circulate happily within this limit: it yearns to go forth and build empires in the shadow, to shed the light of its missionary countenance in the darkest Africa which calls itself Matter. This darkest Africa has, moreover, a strange aptitude or ἐπιτηδειότης for extension, bulk, or division into parts: it yields in a short time a colonial diaspora to which copies of eidetic originals are exported, and a whole set of complexly organized structures built up. Among these structures will be the organized bodies of men and animals, and to these structures certain less-enlightened sorts of soul will be strangely attracted, desiring audaciously to have something they can count as their very own, and that they can manage with considerable departures from the august patterns laid up at higher levels. The rest of the story involves the sinking of many souls into deplorable states of defect and excess, and their close identification with their perishable bodies, until they become wholly forgetful of their superb sister the World Soul, who runs the heavens so suavely and so masterfully, and even more forgetful of the perfect Intelligence and the supreme Unity from which she springs. The sad process of decline, however, can be reversed: earthly beauties can lead souls on to the beauties of laws and virtues and institutions, these on to the beauties of intelligible patterns, until the soul, completely absorbed into its *Nous,* and united with every other *Nous* and with every object, can divest itself of the last traces of specificity and individuality, and can come into coincidence with the partless One, to which it owes every vestige of its being, its character, and its organized unity. There is, however, something very dubiously σεμνόν, glorious, or sacred in this last ἔνωσις or ἅπλωσις: it seems a fine goal to strive for, but is it at all fine to get there? Personally I find the full wheel of πρόοδος and ἐπιστροφή, when conceived in the fabulous manner I have just described, a little more depressing than the celebrated Buddhist wheel of birth and death: the latter at least goes on to perpetual novelty, while the former merely cancels out its original, inexplicable mistake. The depression I am describing was one that I myself experienced in my early years of adolescent mysticism: it rather put me off mysticism for a large part of my later life.

I wish to suggest, however, that there is something deeply and fundamentally wrong about the picture of Neoplatonism that I have just sketched, and that what is wrong about it is the *logic* with which it has operated, which is the logic of the propositional calculus and the functional calculus, especially when these are restricted extensionally and avoid all modalities and quantifications over functions, and so on. The logic I have used in it is, in fact, the logic of ordinary talk about concrete individual things and persons and what they are like, how they stand to one another, or what they do to one another. It is the logic to which classical expression was given in Wittgenstein's *Tractatus,* with who can say what sense-destroying results. It is also the logic of some of the less-inspired utterances of Plotinus, as when he talks nostalgically of a return to the One, or more extremely, of the wise refusal to leave the parental home altogether, or as when he treats matter and body as positive, malefic agencies that we must try to foil or circumvent. In this bad logic there are, first of all, individual bodily or psychic things which are neither conceived as being more or less optionally and variably carved out of the totality of being, nor as capable of fission or coalescence, nor of combination or resolution into unities as genuine as they are. And these instantial things are then sorted out into classes by certain common characters, and arranged into patterns by dependent relations, while all the time all real agency in the world is a function of the instantial things in question. The picture is irresistible: it is what the philosopher sees when he looks at his own hands and the objects arranged all over his desk, or what the housewife sees when she overlooks the various bottles and packages in her crowded food cupboard. To treat Neoplatonism as some exponents have treated it is to apply just such a logic to it, to describe it as a series of shelves and layers in some decayed pantry, with strange juices dripping down from the upper shelves to the lower, and a concurrent rising of strange effluences and odors from the lower shelves to the higher. This may be what the universe is like, but what, one is inclined to ask, is the reason to suppose it is so? And what reason have we to be pleased that this is the way it is?

The logic with which we have to understand Neoplatonism is, however, a totally different logic from the ordinary. It must be a logic in which substantiality and agency reside in the generic or specific pattern and never in the poor instance, and it is, moreover, a logic in which the hierarchical rise from the more specific to the more generic; though it may lessen determinateness, it also deepens and widens *power*. The true genus, which is, of course, not any and every factitious general concept dreamt up by some arbitrary classifier, contains all its subordinate species δυνάμει or in power, and holds together in a rich unity what must necessarily fall apart in the species and the instance. It is infinitely more substantial and more concrete than its species or its instances. And the Neoplatonists, while they sometimes defer to the Aristotelian subordination of potency to act, really invert Aristotle altogether, as every eidetic philosophy must do. The potency of the genus, we may say, in a rather Irish fashion, must have a higher degree of actuality than the one-sided, limited, so-called actual instance. To be Justice itself or Life itself is to be a richer, more various, more enduring thing than to be a just act or man, or a living organism that endures for a season. There is, of course, a potency that connotes defect or privation, and this is the potency above all possessed by the poor dead lady Matter, who is nothing at all except insofar as she gets decked out with costume jewellery imitated from eidetic originals. And there are similar negative potencies in the stupidity or ignorance or confusion of souls functioning at much higher levels of being. But true δύναμις is also true ἐνέργεια, and a higher ἐνέργεια than the limited ἐνέργεια of the species or instance.

This according of power to the genus, of course, reaches a maximum when we climb to the supreme transcendental, the One or Good. *It* may not be any determinate sort of good thing, and *It* may not be an existent instance of any sort whatsoever, but it is the unlimited power of all specification and all instantiation, and so more momentously and conceivably actual than the most remarkable species or individual that we can possibly conceive. And we may note further, that the One of Neoplatonism not only *can* exercise its boundless power, but also *has* exercised it in the countless species and instances that have streamed forth from it, and so has in a sense given proof of its infinite intrinsic riches. And the exercise of this power, though corresponding to no inner stirring of need, and though free and not compelled, is also ontologically necessary. The One could not be the all-sufficient principle of Unity that it is unless it could specify itself in countless eidetic shapes, and unless these in their turn could instantiate themselves in the countless more-or-less imperfect cases that we encounter in this world. And we may note further that, although the complete vision of the ordered eidetic shapes (and the soul's unending endeavor to arrive at this vision) always falls short of envisaging Unity itself, they in effect know it as perfectly and as concretely as could be desired. They achieve everything except arriving at the terminal obelisk in which the whole park of being centers, but they know that and what it is, and where it lies in relation to the whole well-laid-out estate. They know it as the Cantorian transfinitist knows what Aleph is in knowing that it is the number *of* all the finite cardinals—the number of a clearly conceived, rationally ordered series of numbers—which is, nonetheless, not one *of* their number. There is, therefore, reason in saying that although the One does nothing at all, it in a sense does everything that anything else only seems to do, and that although it is not aware of itself or of anything else, it knows itself in all the minds and souls that know anything at all, and that all these only unfold the infinite possibilities that lie locked up in itself. And of what these minds and souls do not conceive or know, the One has knowledge in their dim sense of something beyond all their conceptions, and in *being* what they cannot even dimly conceive.

There are similar interpretative changes necessary if we are to understand the procession of the Soul from the *Nous*. If we think of the *Nous* as some actual mind that eternally envisages everything, we have changed it from being Mind itself into being *a* mind—an individual or personal intelligence—and if it is such, it has simply become identical with some sort of a World-Soul of a curious timeless type. In such a supreme thinking unity we could not share: it would be a superior mind from which we could perhaps learn, but not an intelligence in which we could participate. The correct interpretation of the *Nous* is not, I am sure, that it is *a* very special, timeless intelligence, but that it is Very Intelligence Itself and, as such, a power present in all souls. These souls in their concentrated insights and argumentative ratiocinations are the limited actualizations of its eternal vision, while it, as their power, has a higher actuality than any thinker or activity of thought. It is the eternal pattern towards which active thinking only strives. Its instantiation in souls and their intellectual activities, including those of the supreme Soul of the cosmos, is therefore an ontological necessity, though not a need, in its nature. In the World Soul and in our inferior souls and minds, it shows forth its substantial riches, and thinks itself—not in and for itself, but in and for them. Its unthinkingness is, however, merely a consequence of its being Thinking itself, and not a particular thinker or case of thinking. It can only be in the World Soul or in our souls that it can actually think itself.

Now I know that the Eckhartian and Hegelian propositions that I am affirming are not clearly asserted by Plotinus, any more than Christian orthodoxy has ever adopted a view according to which the Father and Son fulfill themselves in the Holy Spirit, though I think this may have been in the mind of Jesus when he saw the supreme sin in the rejection of the Holy Spirit. What I am, saying, however, is that the Neoplatonist picture only makes complete sense if it is filled in the manner I have suggested, which alone conforms to its peculiar logic. That peculiar logic will also demand that we cease to divide the noetic cosmos into the rigid genera and species favored by antique classification: the eidetic realm involves complex unities of a loosely affiliated and a closely affiliated kind, of a richly substantial and of a highly abstracted sort, of a remotely disjoined and scattered as well as of an eidetically neighboring sort. It has, in short, all the open texture and variability of alignment that occurs in ordinary discourse. Plato shows some awareness of these differing types of eidetic pervasion in some key passages in the *Sophist,* and Plotinus and other Neoplatonists probably did much the same. The eidetic realm may have many crisscross divisions and alignments imprinted upon it, and the same applies to the cases and classes of cases in which it is instantiated.

If I now turn to Soul and souls, it is here that I think the various ravishing descriptions of Plotinus have their appropriate place. There are no thrills or journeys in the world of the *Nous*, since this world can find no place for so temporal a thing as a thrill or a journey. The excitements of intelligible beauty are the excitements of the soul functioning noetically: it is only the soul that can experience noetic enlargements. I imagine that every scientist or artist has these noetic excitements. In the same way the ecstatic experience of approach to the supreme Unity and of the retreat from the same are experiences in the life of Soul, and it is in souls that Soul is thus ecstatic. Even if there are experiences at the point of union, they are *qua* experiences, soul-states, and it is for the soul that they are something σεμνόν, awe-inspiring: *qua* conditions of the One there can be nothing wonderful or sacred about them, if indeed it is fit to talk about them at all. Saint Teresa and Saint John of the Cross have recorded experiences that were certainly soul-states, since in them there was still something that was the small bucket lost in the larger volume of water or the lesser flame lost in the greater. The Upanishadic description of a man united with Brahman as resembling the state of a man in the embrace of a beloved wife obviously describes a soul-state: there is certainly a residual duality in the conjugal embrace. And the descriptions of Nirvana as an island, a refuge, and so on, obviously describe some soul-state: they are descriptions of a happy arrival, not of what happens when one gets there. I am forced, however, to believe that, with the vanishing of Soul or Ahankara, Brahman himself will cease to be Cit and Ānanda, though he may very well continue to be Sat. I need not document the lower regions of psychic activity. It is in the enlargements of experience precipitated by the vision of beauty, by insights gained into eidetic relations, by the deep love that enables us to see another as if he were ourselves, that we rise to the threshold of *Nous* and the more august threshold of the One.

I wish to conclude this paper on what you will think an unexpected note. I am unable to believe in the World Soul of Neoplatonism because Copernicus and his successors, as well as the recent results of planetary exploration, have undermined the foundations of any astral theology. The starry heavens are very far from declaring the glory of God, and if we desire evidences of his presence, I fear we must seek them in the moral law within, or in the aesthetic and intellectual laws that are likewise within. I believe, however, in the Holy Spirit or blessed otherworldly Soul, which is beyond personal difference, and which carries within itself as transcendental regulators both the Noetic Order and the Unity beyond it, and which, while active in space and time, brings the One and the *Nous* to bear upon everything. In saying this, it must not be imagined that I am becoming a humanist or a relativist of some sort: I believe in the austere sovereignty of the Eide and in That which is beyond eidetic difference. And in making these principles regulators of Soul, I am not demoting them to some inferior status—I believe that to be regulative is to enjoy a higher ontological status than to be what is called constitutive, and that while the supreme Hypostases are beyond the imperfect realm of existence and actuality, they are the infinitely powerful and perfect source of the latter, and so more real and important than anything instantial. The sort of mysticism that I think follows from a true understanding of the logic of Neoplatonism, accordingly, is a mysticism that only seeks to ascend to the noetic and supranoetic heights in order to return from them, and which sees those heights as sources from which transcendent light streams, and to which light one can render oneself pervious and transparent, rather than as regions where it is at all desirable to go or stay, except when one is finally handing over the task of existence to others, having made one's own final contribution to it. I believe that the positions I am advocating accord with the teachings of Jesus and Paul, though there is much in Mahayana Buddhism that accords with them also, for example, the belief in a realm of essence which is also down here, in a Nirvana which to accomplished insight is identical with Samsara, and in the interpenetration of all natures in Buddha Vairocana, who is very much the sort of highly charged guiding Spirit in whom I should like to believe. I hope in conclusion that you will look kindly on my many heresies and syncretisms, and that I may perhaps help you to frame your own viable and inspiring interpretation of Neoplatonism instead of a merely mythical and pictorial one.

On Logical Structure and the Plotinic Cosmos

R. M. MARTIN

The primary aim of this paper is to attempt to bring what in essentials is the great cosmological vision of Plotinus into harmony with contemporary science, including logic and mathematics. The brief sketch of a logicometaphysical system to be presented is thus thought to provide an at least rough approximation to some of the basic features of the Plotinic system. We need not worry as to how exact the fit is. No doubt it is very loose in some respects and perhaps too tight in others. Enough will be shown, it is hoped, to suggest that with suitable emendations and extensions, however, the approximativeness may be lessened and the fit made more comfortable throughout.

To attempt to get the exact fit, incidentally, is eminently "dialectical" in the Platonic—and no doubt Plotinic—sense. A. E. Taylor commented many years ago that "what the *Republic* calls "dialectic" is, in principle, simply the rigorous and unremitting task of steady scrutiny of the indefinables and indemonstrables of the sciences, and that in particular . . . [Plato's] . . . ideal, so far as the sciences with which he is directly concerned goes, is just that reduction of mathematics to rigorous deduction from expressly formulated logical premises by exactly specified logical methods of which the work of Peano, Frege, Whitehead, and Russell has given us a magnificent example,"[1] It is thus eminently dialectical to apply Plato's ideal to the Plotinic system itself. Recall also Plotinus' own comment (*Enneads* I.3.5–6) that dialectic is "the precious part of philosophy: in its study of the laws of the universe, Philosophy draws on Dialectic much as other studies and crafts use Arithmetic, though, of course, the alliance between Philosophy and Dialectic is closer."[2] Of course we must not force the letter of logical theory construction upon either Plato or Plotinus, so much as note similarity of spirit across the centuries. Recall also the remarkable comment in I.8.1 where Plotinus writes: "Our intelligence is nourished on the proposition of logic, is skilled in following discussions, works by reasonings, examines links of demonstration, and comes to know the world of Being also by the steps of logical process, having no prior grasp of Reality but remaining empty, all Intelligence though it be, until it has put itself to school." Well, let us put ourselves to school on what is, in essentials, the Plotinic system.

Let "One" be a proper name for the Plotinic One or Unity, and "AllSoul" for the Psyche or the All-Soul. And let "Int" be a one-place predicate so that "Int x" expresses that x is a form or a member of the Intelligible Realm of *Nous*. And let "Obj x" express that x is an object of the lower Cosmos, of the lower world of Nature or of the Sensibles, among which are included human bodies. Roughly, then, we have these four expressions for the four Plotinic levels; two of them, note, are proper names and two of them are predicates. The proper names are for the primary unities, and the predicates are for multiplicities, which, however, also have a kind of unity—a secondary unity, let us say. With this notation in mind, let us reflect now upon (1) the logic of emanation; (2) the role of modern set theory with sets construed as elements in the Intelligible Realm; (3) how the lower souls may be construed modally as constructs in terms of "AllSoul"; (4) the character of the "Plan contained in the Reason-Principle" whereby the All is governed; and, finally, (5) the notion of the return to the One, the flight of the alone to the Alone.

Let us consider first the logic of emanation, which is no doubt best construed in terms of a dyadic relation. Let "x Em y" express that x emanates into y or that y is an emanation from x. The exact behavior of this relation is, of course, where we wish to focus our inquiry. Let us first specify a few very simple principles (*Pr*) concerning emanation. First, the relation Em is presumably *totally irreflexive, asymmetric,* and *transitive.* Thus

> *Pr1.* $\vdash (x) \sim x$ Em x,
> *Pr2.* $\vdash (x)(y)(x$ Em $y \supset \sim y$ Em x),

and

> *Pr3.* $\vdash (x)(y)(z)((x$ Em $y \cdot y$ Em $z) \supset x$ Em z).

Also the four realms clearly are *mutually exclusive,* in the sense that

> *Pr4.* $\vdash \sim$ Int One $\cdot \sim$ One $=$ AllSoul $\cdot \sim$ Obj One $\cdot \sim$ Int AllSoul
> $\cdot \sim$ Obj AllSoul $\cdot \sim (Ex)($Int $x \cdot$ Obj x).

And all four domains *exist* in appropriate senses, so that

Pr5.   ⊢ E!One · (E*x*)Int *x* · E!AllSoul · (E*x*)Obj *x*.

Concerning the One we have some special principles as follows:

Pr6.   ⊢ (*x*)(∼ *x* = One ⊃ One Em *x*);

Pr7.   ⊢ ∼(E*x*)(∼ *x* = One · (*y*)(∼ *y* = One ⊃ *x* Em *y*)).

Pr6 states that everything other than the One is an emanation from the One, and *Pr7* that there is nothing other than the One from which everything other than the One emanates.

Some immediate consequences of these principles are that

Pr8.   ⊢ (*x*)(Int *x* ⊃ One Em *x*).

Pr9.   ⊢ One Em AllSoul,

and

Pr10.   ⊢ (*x*)(Obj *x* ⊃ One Em *x*).

But the following also hold:

Pr11.   ⊢ (*x*)(Int *x* ⊃ *x* Em AllSoul)

and

Pr12.   ⊢ (*x*)(Obj *x* ⊃ AllSoul Em *x*).

Every intelligible emanates into the AllSoul and the AllSoul into every object. No object, however, emanates into anything, so that

Pr13.   ⊢ (*x*)(Obj *x* ⊃ ∼ (E*y*)*x* Em *y*).

Concerning the One, very little can be truly said or not said in terms of Em! Thus

Pr14.   ' ⊢ ∼ **F** One '

for most predicates **F** not containing Em. Of course in a fuller discussion we shall have to be more specific here about the **F**'s, how they are constructed, and so on.

Concerning the intelligible realm, however, a good deal can be said, and it may be of interest to try to view it in terms, partly at least, of modern set theory. Sets are thought by many contemporary theorists to constitute par excellence the very prototype of intelligible entities. Some even go so far as to say that they are the *only* such objects, but this contention might seem somewhat extreme. Let us require here only that sets are *included* among the intelligibles but perhaps do not exhaust them.

Clarification is in order. Note that in including sets among the intelligibles, we are not *using* the notions of set theory in the underlying logic of the theory of emanation. For this latter we are using only the familiar first-order quantification theory with identity. The domain of individuals is taken to consist of all the entities of the four Plotinic realms, including now sets in the intelligible realm. To specify all this we take ε for the membership relation and Λ for the null set as primitive. We may then define (D)

D1.   "Set x" as "$(x = \Lambda \text{ v } (Ey)y \text{ ε } x)$",

and stipulate that

Pr15. $\vdash (x)(\text{Set } x \supset \text{Int } x)$.

We also need to specify what the members of sets are to be allowed to be. Clearly the members are to be just the inhabitants of the lowest realm, sets of such, and so on, but not the One nor the AllSoul. If these were allowed membership, we should then be *using* set theory to formulate the Plotinic theory, rather than merely allowing sets their proper place in the intelligible realm. Thus we have as additional principles that

Pr16. $\vdash \sim (Ex)\text{One ε } x \cdot \sim (Ex)\text{AllSoul ε } x \cdot \sim (Ex)(\text{Int } x \cdot \sim$
Set $x \cdot (Ey)x \text{ ε } y)$,

and, more generally, that

Pr17. $\vdash (x)(y)(x \text{ ε } y \supset (\text{Set } x \text{ v Obj } x))$,

and hence, of course, that

Pr18. $\vdash (y)((\text{Set } y \cdot \sim y = \Lambda) \supset (Ex)(x \text{ ε } y \cdot (\text{Set } x \text{ v Obj } x)))$.

It was remarked that the One and the AllSoul are given primary unity, and that the intelligible realm and the cosmos are multiplicities and have only secondary unity. How then do we handle the individual souls, and the oneness of these realms? To attempt to answer the first question, let us bring in the human body. Let "HB x" express that x is a human body. What then is the human person or individual soul? If we allow ourselves the logical devices of the calculus of individuals (Leśniewski's *mereology*)—which we shall surely wish to do at some point—in addition to quantification theory with identity, we may proceed as follows. Let $(x \cup y)$ be the compound or sum individual consisting of x and y together, and let us suppose that we can form the sum of any two entities from the whole Plotinic universe. Also we let "x Ens y" express that x ensouls y, that is, that x enters into or affects y in the appropriate manner. We then may identify the living human person or individual soul-*cum*-body (LPer) as merely the compound entity (AllSoul $\cup x$) where x is an HB ensouled by the AllSoul. Thus we may define

D2.   "LPer x" as "$(Ey)(\text{HB } y \cdot x = (\text{AllSoul } \cup y) \cdot \text{AllSoul Ens } y)$".

Then clearly we have that

Pr19. $\vdash (x)(y)(z)((\text{HB } y \cdot x = (\text{AllSoul } \cup y) \cdot \text{AllSoul Ens } y \cdot$
HB $z \cdot x = (\text{AllSoul } \cup z) \cdot \text{AllSoul Ens } z) \supset y = z)$,

and of course, where "P" is the part-whole relation between individuals, that

Pr20. $\vdash (x)(y)(\text{LPer } x \cdot \text{LPer } y \cdot (Ez)(\text{HB } z \cdot z \text{ P } x \cdot z \text{ P } y)) \supset x = y)$.

Note that *Pr19* and *Pr20* are merely logical truths, showing the one-to-one correspondence between living persons and ensouled human bodies. Also clearly

Pr21. ⊢ $(x)(\text{HB } x \supset \text{Obj } x)$,

but

Pr22. ⊢ ~ $(Ex)(\text{HPer } x \cdot \text{Obj } x)$.

The use of "Ens" here for the relation of ensoulment is a desirable extension of our vocabulary. Plotinus explicitly states, in IV. 3. 9, that "if we are to explain and to be clear, we are obliged to use such words as 'entry' and 'ensoulment,' though never was . . . [the] All unsouled, never did body subsist with soul away, never was there Matter unelaborate; we separate, the better to understand; there is nothing illegitimate in the verbal and mental sundering of things which must in face be co-existent."

Now let us consider the unity of the realm of the intelligibles. This may be taken in terms of the notion of the *fusion* of a class in the sense of the calculus of individuals. Thus we may identify *Nous* with this fusion. More formally, we may let

D3. "*Nous*" abbreviate "Fu'Int".

Where i_1, i_2, · · · is the nondenumerably infinite array of intelligibles, the entity *Nous* is merely $(i_1 \cup i_2 \cup \cdots)$. Of course we can never carry out an enumeration of these intelligibles, their cardinality presumably being beyond all bounds even among the transfinite cardinals.

With the notion of *Nous* available as a collective term, so to speak, we may emend *Pr11* above. It might appear too strong to say that each and every intelligible individually emanates into the AllSoul. A weaker and perhaps more acceptable statement is that *Nous*, as a whole, does; that is, that the intelligibles *collectively* emanate into the AllSoul. Thus in place of *Pr11* we might better require that

Pr11'. ⊢ *Nous* Em AllSoul.

Let us try now to justify some of these principles, to some extent at least, on the basis of the actual text.

That there is a multiplicity of ideal forms is discussed at some length in VI.7, and in II.4.4 it is commented that

> there must be some character common to all [forms] and equally some peculiar character in each keeping them distinct. This peculiar characteristic, this distinguishing difference, is the individual shape. But if shape, then there is the shaped, that in which the difference is lodged. There is, therefore, a Matter accepting the shape, a permanent substratum. Further, admitting that there is an Intelligible Realm beyond, of which this world is an image, then, since this World-Compound is based on Matter, there must be Matter there too.

The feature common to the forms is no doubt that they are instantiable or inhere in something else. This feature is "there," then as characterizing the entities in the intelligible realm. Where there is an "individual shape" or character, there also is implicitly that which is shaped or characterized. There is then "intelligible matter" in the ideal realm in just this sense. And note how natural it seems to include sets in the intelligible realm, sets above all having this property of having members—except the null set, which is somewhat adscititious anyway. It is very interesting to note that Plotinus, in II.4.5, comments that "we discover these two—Matter and Idea—by sheer force of our reasoning which distinguishes continually in pursuit of the simplex, the irreducible, working on, until it can go no further, towards the ultimate in the subject of inquiry." The irreducible in any inquiry are the notions characterized in primitive terms in just such and such a way, much as subjects (proper names or variables) and predicates, together, of course, with the basic logical ingredients, are irreducible elements in language systems.

The definition *D2* is in close harmony with I.1.3–5. Plotinus states that

> we may treat of the Soul as in the body—whether it be set above it or actually within it—since the association of the two constitute the one thing called the living organism, the Animate. . . . Now this Animate might be merely the body as having life: it might be the Couplement of Soul and body: it might be a third and different entity formed from both.

Or, we can add, it might be all three. "The truth lies," Plotinus contends, "in the consideration that the Couplement subsists by virtue of the Soul's presence." Plotinus seems to come out here by saying that whatever we wish to say concerning the Animate, we can say in terms of the ensouled Couplement. A most natural interpretation of these remarks is thus in terms of logical sums, as in *D2*. Recall also, in I. 7. 3, that "life is a partnership of Soul and body; death is the dissolution; in either life or death, then, the Soul will feel itself at home." The AllSoul is clearly "at home" in both itself and any of its couplements.

That a proper name should be taken for the Soul is amply justified in IV.9, in which it is argued that there is but one Soul, although there is a sense in which we may speak of your soul, my soul, and so on. "We are not asserting the unity of soul in the sense of a complete negation of multiplicity—only of the Supreme can that be affirmed—we are thinking of soul as simultaneously one and many, participant in the nature divided in body, but at the same time a unity by virtue of belonging to that Order that suffers no division. . . . These reflections show that there is nothing strange in that reduction of all souls to one. But it is still necessary to inquire into the *mode* and *conditions* [italics added] of the unity," as well, of course, into the perhaps merely verbal partition of the All-Soul into the celestial and lower souls. This all can be done, however, it would seem, on the basis of the foregoing logical reconstruction, as we shall see in a moment.

Incidentally, the remarkable passage in II.3.13 no doubt gives the key to what remains to be done.

> The gist of the whole matter lies in the consideration that Soul governs this All by *the plan contained in the Reason-Principle* [italics added] and plays in the All

exactly the part of the particular principle which in every living-thing forms the members of the organism and adjusts them to the unity of which they are portions; the entire force of the Soul is represented in the All but, in the parts, Soul is present only in proportion to the degree of essential reality held by each of such partial objects.

How Whiteheadian this sounds, the "degree of essential reality" being akin to the degree of ingression of an eternal object into an actual occasion, and to the extent to which any occasion acts in accord with the vision of it in the primordial nature of God. Should we introduce a numerical measure here? It is tempting to do so, just as it is in the discussion of Whitehead.[3] We might let "x Em^i y" be taken primitively to express that x emanates into y only to degree i. A much more elaborate theory would result. However, let us not introduce here complications beyond necessity.

The cosmic plan contained in the Reason-Principle will be discussed in a moment.

In IV.3, Plotinus argues "against those who maintain our souls to be offshoots from the Soul of the universe (parts and not an identity *modally parted* [italics added])." On the contrary, "there is one identical soul, *every separate manifestion being that soul complete* [italics added]." Plotinus is sensitive to divergent meanings of "part," and regards it as false that individual souls are "parts" of the AllSoul in most senses of that word. However, there is one sense that he does seem to allow. There is the sense of "part" in which we speak of a theorem as being a part of the entire science to which it belongs. "The theorem is separate, but the science stands as one undivided thing, the separation into theorems being simply the act of making each constituent notion explicit and efficient: this is partition without severance; each item potentially includes the whole science, which itself remains an unbroken total." How now are we to handle the multiplicity of souls so as to assure that there is only one identical soul, "every separate manifestation being that soul complete?" The key notion here is that the individual souls are only "modally parted" from the AllSoul—*intentionally* so, we might say—but not actually so.

To handle intentionality, let us adopt Frege's notion of the *Art des Gegebenseins,* or mode or manner of linguistic presentation. Let us consider first the embodied AllSoul as taken under this or that predicate. Let "F_0" by a predicate-description of entities capable of *intellection,* of intuiting entities of the intelligible realm. Let "G_0" be a predicate-description of entities capable of *reasoning* in the ordinary sense, and "H_0" for unreasoning entities (or animals). We can then consider human and animal bodies under these three different predicates, which give, as it were, the three characteristic acts of the lower souls. To provide for the first two, the intellective and reasoning human souls, we form ordered couples of human persons with "F_0" and "G_0." Thus $\langle x, F_0 \rangle$ becomes identified with the intellective soul (IntSoul) of person x, and $\langle x, G_0 \rangle$ with x's reasoning soul (ReasSoul). Thus, in general, we may let

D4a. "IntSoul $\langle x,$ "F_0"$\rangle$" abbreviate "(HPer $x \cdot$ "F_0" "Den x)", where "Den" stands for the relation of multiple denotation between the one-place predicates of the language and whatever objects that language is concerned with. And similarly

> *D4b.*   "ReasSoul $\langle x,$ "G_0"$\rangle$" for "(HPer $x \cdot$ "G_0" "Den x)".

And similarly for Unreasoning Souls, *mut. mat.* (*D4c*).

Note that the principle of individuation for the multiplicity of intelligible and reasoning souls is the human body, and for the unreasoning souls, the animal body. This would surely seem to accord with Plotinus' intent.

Note the need for the intentional treatment of the lower souls. It might well obtain factually that

$$\vdash (x)(F_0 x \equiv \text{Repr } x),$$

for some "Repr" expressing, say, that x reproduces its kind by sexual union. But we would not wish then to regard $\langle x,$ Repr$\rangle$ or $\langle x,$ Repr$\rangle$ as an intellective soul. Hence the use of the predicate "F_0" rather than the property (or class) F_0 as the second item in the couple, which use prevents the replacement of "F_0" by its factual equivalent "Repr." And clearly we would not be tempted to replace the *name* of "F_0" by the name of "Repr," these being very different names.

Now "nothing of Real Being is ever annulled." There is no "bodily partition" among the intelligibles, "no passing of each separate phase into a distinct unity; every such phase remains in full possession of that identical being. It is exactly so with the souls." Recall that definitions *D4a* to *D4c* make of "bodily partition" the principle of individuation for the separate souls. Even so, each separate soul remains in "full possession" of the AllSoul. Note also that, although the whole human person is regarded here as capable of intellection and reasoning, it is only the person *under the given predicate-description* that is regarded as a soul. In this way an intentional multiplicity of individual souls is achieved, so to speak, but with the unity of the AllSoul preserved. All of the lower souls involve, in a suitable way, the whole of the AllSoul, as we see from the definitions. There is thus no actual partition of the AllSoul into a multiplicity, only a modal or intentional one.

No doubt we should distinguish here between embodied and unembodied souls. *D4a* to *D4c* are concerned, of course, with embodied souls, and it is they to which the predicates "F_0," "G_0," and "H_0" are regarded as applicable. Analogous definitions could be given taking the AllSoul itself under these descriptions. There would then be just three such unembodied souls. The multiplicity can be achieved, however, by taking "F_0," "G_0," and "H_0" more narrowly as descriptive of just the intellective, rational, and unrational capacities and/or activities *of the various individual souls*. We would then have as many "F_0"s as intellective souls. Let "$F\frac{a}{0}$" be the intellective predicate for the AllSoul as ensouling human person a, "$F\frac{b}{0}$" for the AllSoul as ensouling human person b, and so on. Then

> *D5a.*   'UnIntSoul $\langle$AllSoul,$EF\frac{a}{0}\rangle$' may abbreviate '(HPer **a** $\cdot$ $EF\frac{a}{0}$ Den **a**)'

where '$EF\frac{a}{0}$' is the structural description of the predicate '$F\frac{a}{0}$'. And similarly for the other two, *mut. mat.* (*D5b–D5c*). According to these definitions, it is, of course, the AllSoul that performs intellection or reasoning through or by means of a human person, so to speak.

In this way, then, "the world of unembodied souls" is provided, as well as those "in our world" that "have entered body and undergone bodily division" (IV.1.1). Recall that "soul, there wthout distinction or partition, has yet a nature lending itself to divisional existence; its division is secession, entry into body." Also "the secession is not of the Soul entire; something of it holds its ground, that in it which recoils from separate existence." Thus, although AllSoul occurs essentially in the expansions into primitive terms of the *definientia* of *D4a–D4c*, it is only certain very special "phases" of AllSoul that are considered, not all phases, not all properties ascribable to it. "Thus it is that, entering this realm, it [the AllSoul] possesses still the vision inherent to that superior phase in virtue of which it unchangingly maintains its integral nature. Even here [in the world] it is not exclusively the partible soul: it is still the impartible as well: what in it knows partition is parted without partibility; undivided as giving itself to the entire body, a whole to a whole, it is divided as being effective in every part"—of the body, we should add, as well as being effective in every part of every body.

Again, in IV.2.1., it is noted very explicitly that

> the bodies are separate and the Ideal-Form [AllSoul] which enters into them is correspondingly sundered while, still, it is present as one whole in each of its severed parts, since amid that multiplicity in which complete individuality has entailed complete partition, there is a permanent identity; . . . In whatsoever bodies it occupies— even the vastest of all, that in which the entire universe is included—it gives itself to the whole without abdicating its unity. . . . Itself devoid of mass, it is present to all mass: it exists here [in distinct phases (?)] and yet is there, and this [there] not in distinct phases but with unsundered identity: thus it is "parted and not parted," or, better, it has never known partition, never become a parted thing, but remains a self-gathered integral, and is "parted among bodies" merely in the sense that bodies, in virtue of their own sundered existence, cannot receive it unless in some partitive mode; the partition, in other words, is an occurrence in body, not in soul.

Enough discussion now—perhaps too much—on the AllSoul and its various phases or partitions, but not yet enough about its role as the Demiourgos and the Cosmic Plan. How are we to handle this latter? Clearly the AllSoul *orders* every object and every intelligible whether that object partakes of that intelligible or not. The Soul governs the All by the plan contained in the Reason-Principle, as was noted in II.3.13. And in IV.3.13, we are told that "The Ineluctable, the Cosmic Law, is . . . rooted in a natural principle under which each several entity is overruled to go, duly and in order, towards that place and Kind to which it characteristically tends, that is, towards the image of its primal choice and constitution." Are we to regard the Plan, then, as including items provided by metaphysical principles such as *Pr1–Pr22,* and so on, or are we to think of it as having to do only with the objects of the lower cosmos? The former (*Pr1–Pr22*) are already provided for and stipulate the way the world is, where "world" is taken in the widest possible sense. And one of the ways the world is, of course, is that the AllSoul plans how "each several entity," including the lower souls, goes "duly and in order to that place and Kind" to which it properly belongs. Thus the Plan seems to have to do primarily with the lower Cosmos, and with the intelligibles only in their relevance, so to speak, to the lower Cosmos. The AllSoul "looks towards its higher and has intellection; towards itself, and orders, administers, governs its lower" (IV.8.3).

The Plan here, incidentally, has some affinity with the primordial valuations constituting Whitehead's primordial nature of God. These are fixed once and for all and concern each and every actual occasion with respect to the ingression in it of each and every eternal object.

Let "Order" be a new primitive for the dyadic relation of ordering in just the sense that the AllSoul is to be regarded as ordering the lower cosmos. Syntactically speaking, the AllSoul orders that such-and-such sentences obtain. Some of these sentences are to the effect that

$$x \ \varepsilon \ y,$$

where x is an object and y is a set of objects. Others of these sentences concern the lower souls, which in the foregoing treatment are regarded as entities taken under a given linguistic description or *Art des Gegebenseins*. Thus the theory concerning Order will be in the *metametalanguage* of that in which sentences concerning the lower souls occur. This is harmless enough, merely a fact to be noted.

A word more is in order concerning the syntactical structure of the sentences concerning the lower souls. Because we are not using set theory here as part of the basic logic of the entire scheme, the ordered couples used for handling the lower souls are merely *virtual*. The notation for them is thus wholly eliminable in favor of a primitive notation in which no ordered couples are values for variables.[4] And the bringing in of an *Art des Gegebenseins* carries us into the metalanguage, enabling us to speak of the AllSoul in its various modal or intentional phases. Expressions for the lower souls are thus significant only contextually; more specifically, in contexts in which the AllSoul (in its entirety, so to speak) is taken under different linguistic descriptions. Any sentence (in primitive terms) of this kind let us call an *LS-statement,* a statement ascribing to or denying something or other of the lower souls. Similarly let us call *Obj-statements* sentences of the form

$$` \ x \ \varepsilon \ y \ `$$

where **x** is a constant for an object and **y** for a set. (Note the legitimacy here of using set theory in speaking about *objects*.) Now the Plan is concerned in part surely with LS- and Obj-statements, as we shall see in a moment.

As metametalinguistic principles concerning the Plan, we have then the following:

Pr23. $\vdash (x)(a)(x \ \text{Order} \ a \supset (x = \text{AllSoul} \cdot \text{Sent} \ a))$

and

Pr24. $\vdash (a)(\text{AllSoul Order} \ a \supset \text{Tr} \ a),$

where "Tr a" expresses that a is a truth of the metalanguage. *Pr23* here is a *Limitation Principle,* according to which only the AllSoul orders anything, and whatever it orders is a sentence of the metalanguage. *Pr24*, a *Principle of Cosmic Obedience*, we might call it, is to the effect that whatever is ordered is true. We may assume also a *Completeness Principle*, that the AllSoul orders all logical consequences (LogConseq) of what it orders.

Pr25.   ⊢ (*a*)(*b*)((AllSoul Order *a* · *b* LogConseq *a*) ⊃ AllSoul Order *b*).

Having built set theory into the lower cosmos, we need to allow the AllSoul to provide for its axioms, and no doubt for basic scientific law also. Let "SetAx *a*" express that *a* is an axiom of the set theory assumed, and "ScL *a*" that *a* is an acceptable scientific law. Then also a *Principle of Scientific Law* obtains:

Pr26.   ⊢ (*a*)((SetAx *a* v ScL *a*) ⊃ AllSoul Order *a*).

Provision must also be made for laws governing intelligibles that are not sets. Let "IntL *a*" express that *a* is such a law. Then also a *Principle of the Intelligible Realm* obtains:

Pr27.   ⊢ (*a*)(IntL *a* ⊃ AllSoul Order *a*).

That this principle is needed is evident from IV.3.13, where it is said that "even the Intellectual-Principle, which is before all the Cosmos, has it also, its destiny, that of abiding intact above, and of giving downwards; what it sends down is the particular whose existence is implied in the law (or decreed system) of the universal."

Finally, surely, the AllSoul orders all (factually) true LS- and Obj-statements.

Pr28.   ⊢ (*a*)(((LSSent *a* v ObjSent *a*) · Tr *a*) ⊃ AllSoul Order *a*).

This is the *Principle of Factuality*.

Note that *Pr24* provides only that truth is a necessary condition, not a sufficient one, for what is ordered. The preceding principles *Pr1–Pr22* (or rather their translations within the metalanguage) are themselves true but not ordered. Note also that all of the principles, including the Plan principles *Pr23–Pr28*, are timeless, all being stated in what Frege called the "tense of timelessness." Time, space, and the like, being relevant only for objects of the lower cosmos, are provided in what is ordered, not in the ordering, so to speak.

Another point is perhaps worth making. In taking an entity under a linguistic description, we can, of course, allow for equivalent descriptions in various ways: in terms of *L-equivalence,* in terms of some suitably defined notion of *synonymy,* or in terms of the linguists' relations of *paraphrase* or *translation*. An entity taken under any paraphrastic description is just as good, like a rose by any other name. This point would be scarcely worth the making were it not so frequently misunderstood.

The multiplicity, but not the unity, of the lower cosmos has been commented on. How can we handle the unity? Merely as the fusion of the realm of objects. Thus

D6.   "LCosmos" is short for "Fu'Obj".

This definition is of course analogous to *D3,* above of "Nous," and makes use of Leśniewski's mereology just as that definition does.

It should be recalled from II.3.13, that the "Soul governs this All by the plan *contained in the Reason-Principle* [italics added]." Reasoning has to do with statements—or propositions if you like—whereas intellection has to do only with the pure apprehension of the intelligibles. Intellection is thus not propositional, whereas reasoning is. The Plan is thus given by the AllSoul in its capacity for reasoning, and is stated in terms of statements. It is only statements that are ordered. Of course, reasoning presumably presupposes intellection of that which is reasoned about, just as statements must contain in an essential way names or other expressions for the intelligibles.

A further remark or two now about the One. "That awesome Prior, The Unity, is not a being [in the sense of being an intelligible, the AllSoul, or any object of the lower cosmos] . . . : strictly, no name is apt to it, but *since name it we must* [italics added] there is a certain rough fitness in designating it as unity [or "One" as above] with the understanding that it is not the unity of some other thing" (VI.9.5.). Without a name for it, any systematic discourse concerning it would presumably be impossible. We could not even state our metaphysical scheme. And although *Pr14*—that very few interesting properties can be ascribed to the One—does proceed by a kind of *via negativa,* still there is much to say concerning the One as the ultimate source of emanation and as the object of aspiration "There"—for "There only is our veritable love and There we may unite with it, not holding it in some fleshly embrace but possessing it in all its verity" (VI.9.9).

In all talk of the return to the One, "the flight of the alone to the alone," the converse of the relation Em (ˇEm) is no doubt the fundamental one. Consider *Pr6–Pr10,* rewritten now in terms of "ˇEm." These indicate that everything other than the One bears ˇEm to it—no second thing does—and thus every intelligible does, the AllSoul does, and every object does. We can read "ˇE" as "aspires to the condition of," "desires to return to the purity of," or the like. Note that by *Pr11',* the AllSoul bears ˇEm to *Nous*; by *Pr12,* every object bears ˇEm to the AllSoul; and by *Pr13,* nothing bears ˇEm to any object. All this seems as it should be. Note the analogue of *Pr11'* here rather than that of *Pr11.* Rather than to say that the AllSoul bears ˇEm to each intelligible, we require only that the AllSoul bears ˇEm to *Nous* itself, that is, to the intelligibles taken collectively, to the Divine Mind. The appropriateness of this gives support to using *Pr11'* in place of *Pr11.* . . . . Of course there is much more to be said about the return to the One, the flight of the alone to the Alone, but essential in all such discourse, it would seem, is the relation ˇEm.

It was suggested above that it might be of interest to introduce a numerical degree for emanation, so that "x Em^i y" would express that x emanates to y to just the degree i. ("y ˇEm^i x" would then express that y aspires to x to just degree i.) The same may be said for the relation Ens for ensoulment. The need for this may be seen as follows. In IV.4.36 we are told explicitly that "we cannot think of the world as a soulless habitation, however vast and varied, a thing of materials easily read off, kind by kind—wood and stone and whatever else there may be, all blending into a cosmos: [on the contrary,] it must be alert throughout, every member living by its own life." Plotinus allows "grades of living within the whole, grades to some of which we deny life only because they are not perceptibly self-moved; in truth, all of these have a hidden life; and the thing whose life is patent to sense is made up of things which do not live to sense, but, nonetheless, confer upon their resultant wonderful powers towards living."

To provide for this "hidden life," let "x Ens^i y" express that x ensouls y to just the degree i. If $i = 1$, there is total ensoulment. But we would presumably have as a principle that every object is ensouled by AllSoul to a degree, however small, greater than 0:

> *Pr29.* $\vdash (x)(\text{Obj } x \supset (Ei)(i > 0 \cdot \text{AllSoul Ens}^i x))$.

We can then rephrase *D2*, the definition of "LPer" for living persons, in such a way as to require the ensoulment to be high. If a body is ensouled to a high degree, then and only then is it living. But even dead bodies are ensouled to some very small degree. *Pr29* is, thus, a kind of *Principle of Panpsychism.*

A few final comments. The foregoing contains a sketch of the barest beginnings of the Plotinic system. Additional primitives, of course, are needed, many further principles, much further elaboration. Only the barest logical maquette, so to speak, has been given here. Enough has been shown, however, it is hoped, to enable us to see that the system could be further developed in such a way as to throw more and more light on the full logic of the All-Soul and of the accompanying metaphysical theory. Further, this can be done in such a way, as here, as to bring it into harmony with contemporary scientific theory, both in mathematics and in the empirical sciences. There should be no fundamental conflict, it is contended, between the great Plotinic vision and modern science. But the latter should not be disregarded in our attempt to understand the former. Hence the presence here of set theory and of scientific law as having their proper roles in the entire system.

Also it is interesting that in the delineation of the lower souls, an intentional kind of metalogic is needed, and that in the delineation of the Plan, the semantical truth concept. Without these resources, including of course quantification theory, it is unthinkable that the liaison here could take place. Perhaps this is the reason no one has attempted it heretofore—apparently the resources were simply not available. In any case, it is hoped that the foregoing helps to show the usefulness of modern logic as a tool of philosophical analysis. Logic should not be seen only as a subject apart, a *logica docens,* having to do just with abstract metamathematical structures, but also as a *logica utens,* helping out not only in the clarification of philosophical problems, but in the analysis of the great historical texts as well.

Some Logical Aspects of the Concept of Hypostasis in Plotinus

JOHN P. ANTON

Recent studies on the philosophy of Plotinus have drawn attention to the complex problems interpreters face when discussing the number of *hypostases*,[1] or what the term means in the case of the One, the *Nous,* and the Soul. The full exploration of these broad topics, especially in the light of Plotinus' theory of "production" and his critique of the alternative views other Neoplatonists held, falls outside the scope of this paper. Since Plotinus' answer to the question "What criteria must X satisfy to qualify as a *hypostasis*?" is given in the relevant texts,[2] and as such may be treated as a separate issue, the present paper assumes familiarity with the related doctrines in order to consider in some detail certain logical aspects of the One qua hypostasis.

Source: Reprinted from *The Review of Metaphysics* 31:2 (December, 1977), pp. 258–271. Reprinted by permission. Originally presented at the Second International Congress of the International Society for Neoplatonic Studies, Brock University, October 23, 1976; and in revised version at the joint session of the Society for the Study of the History of Philosophy with the American Philosophical Association, Pacific Division, Portland, Oregon, March 25, 1977.

Plotinus believes that it is impossible that contradictory statements are forthcoming when we speak correctly about the One. Though the One is beyond οὐσία (ἐπέκεινα τῆς οὐσίας) and thus beyond predication, it is still the case that he makes it the object of discourse. The thesis that contradictions are not possible when we speak of Being or of that which truly is, is common to both Plato and Aristotle. In the realm of higher dialectic, only true statements are possible, and *epistēmē,* as a system of true statements, is free of contradictions. This thesis is fundamental to all classical ontology.

Given that according to Plotinus we can discourse about the One and that we must learn how to speak "correctly" when referring to the One, the issue is to decide whether his own discourse on the One qua hypostasis is tainted with even *seemingly* contradictory statements. Thus what is needed is to examine the logical status of certain statements on hypostasis as it pertains to the One. The issue has been raised by John N. Deck in his book on Plotinus.[3] Though he has ably defended Plotinus against the charge of contradiction, the solution he offers casts a doubt on whether the One can be said to be or have hypostasis in the fullest sense. It will be shown, however, that his solution is misleading and unwarranted. The textual evidence does not support it.

II

Deck writes:

> The One or Good, was demonstrated by the need of Nous for a principle and a good. The Nous is other than the Good; the caused is other than the cause. The One is thus a distinct hypostasis, a distinct "nature."[4]

In a long footnote (fn. 5) on the same page, Deck notes that "hypostasis" "is not for Plotinus himself a common designation of the One." This may be so, but it matters little how common the designation is or how frequently the term occurs in the text. The important thing is that Plotinus uses it in significant ways and that he frequently employs the verbal form ὑφίσταται and its derivative expressions to discuss fundamental aspects of the One as well as *Nous* and Soul. The discussion which follows is restricted solely to the One qua hypostasis.

Deck admits that he has been able "to find only one place where he [Plotinus] calls the One in so many words "the first hypostasis,'" and cites *Enneads* VI.8. 15.30, where the expression ὑπόστασις δὲ πρώτη occurs, and then proceeds to give a list of the following related passages:

(i) VI.6.3.11: the One as *"having* hypostasis."
(ii) VI.8.13.43–44: "the hypostasis *of* the Good."
(iii) VI.8.7.47: *"its* quasi-hypostasis" (οἷον ὑπόστασις αὐτοῦ).

What Deck says in the rest of this important footnote is worth quoting in full.

> It would seem that the designation of the One as an hypostasis in systematic accounts of Plotinus' philosophy is based on the title of VI, 1. which treatise is an elementary outline of the doctrine of the One, the Nous and the Soul: "About the Three Hypos-

tases Which Are Principles (περὶ τῶν τριῶν ἀρχικῶν ὑποστάσεων)." This title, however, like all the titles of Plotinus' treatises, is not Plotinus' own (Porphyry, ch. 4, lines 16–18). In speaking of the One, the Nous and the Soul in this treatise, Plotinus calls them "these three" (V.1.10.5) or "the three natures" (V.1.8.27).

Several critical observations and reservations are in order:

1. The passage V.1.10.5. regarding the expression "these three," has no direct bearing on Deck's point. The text reads: Ὥσπερ δὲ ἐν τῇ φύσει τριττὰ ταῦτά ἐστι τὰ εἰρημένα, οὕτω χρὴ νομίζειν καὶ παρ᾽ ἡμῖν ταῦτα εἶναι. The expression "these three" is used in a collective sense and refers in the text to (a) the One beyond being, ἐπέκεινα τοῦ ὄντος ἕν . . . , (b) Nous, νοῦς . . . , (c) the nature of the Soul, τῆς ψυχῆς φύσις.

2. The expression "the three natures," ταῖς φύσεσι ταῖς τρισίν, is made with reference to Plato's *Parmenides* in order to show agreement on these three natures. Therefore, we must not take it for granted that "natures," as used here, is part of Plotinus' stock terminology, nor are we allowed to infer that "nature" is used synonymously with "hypostases." Furthermore, there is no reason to insist that what the passage says may serve as evidence for or against the thesis that the One is a hypostasis. Just the same, Deck holds that "nature can mean hypostasis."[5]

3. Deck goes beyond the question of whether this passage supports an interpretation which permits us to count the One among "the three hypostases." Thus he proceeds to dismiss "systematic accounts of Plotinus' philosophy" that favor this view and even has reservations about appealing to words used in Porphyry's titles. However, Deck offers no decisive argument to show that Porphyry had taken liberties when editing the master's works.[6]

Deck admits that he has been able to find only one place (VI.8.15.30) where Plotinus "calls the One in so many words 'the first hypostasis.'" However, he does not consider this passage decisive enough to concede, as we shall see, that the One is one of the primary hypostasis; rather, as he argues, its status is no more and no less than that of a "quasi-hypostasis." But before we examine the grounds for his thesis, we must first take a careful look at what Plotinus says in the passage to which Deck refers the reader in order to decide its relevance to Deck's initial point that Plotinus is in fact identifying on this sole occasion the One and the first hypostasis rather than presupposing it. The real question is whether Plotinus is discussing the point which Deck claims. When line 30 is read in context, we obtain a different picture. First we need to note that *Enneads* VI. 8, deals with the topic "On Free Will and the Will of the One."[7] Now, the text where line 30 comes reads:

Ὑπόστασις δὲ πρώτη οὐκ ἐν ἀψύχῳ οὐδ᾽ ἐν ζωῇ ἀλόγῳ   30
ἀσθενὴς γὰρ εἰς τὸ εἶναι καὶ αὕτη σκέδασις οὖσα λόγου
καὶ ἀοριστία· ἀλλ᾽ ὅσῳ πρόεισιν εἰς λόγον, ἀπολείπει
τύχην· τὸ γὰρ κατὰ λόγον οὐ τύχη.[8]

Translation:

Moreover, the first hypostasis cannot consist of something inanimate or of life irrational; for such a life [or state] is weak in respect of being, and itself a skattering of reason and indetermination. However, to the extent that it advances toward reason, it abandons chance; for what is in accordance with reason, is not subject to chance.

Strictly speaking, line 30 in this passage does not say what the first hypostasis is; it presupposes reference to the One. Taken in isolation, as we shall see, its meaning becomes ambiguous. To illustrate this point we need to go back to the opening lines of chapter 15, especially 4–10, where the term "hypostasis" occurs in a way that fixes the context for what lines 30–34 mean to convey.

Εἰ δὲ τὸ συνὸν τῷ ᾧ σύνεστιν ἓν καὶ τὸ οἷον ἐφιέμενον τῷ ἐφετῷ 5
ἕν, τὸ δὲ ἐφετὸν κατὰ τὴν ὑπόστασιν καὶ οἷον ὑποκείμενον, πάλιν αὖ ἡμῖν ἀνεφάνη ταὐτὸ ἡ ἔφεσις καὶ ἡ
οὐσία. Εἰ δὲ τοῦτο, πάλιν αὖ αὐτός ἐστιν οὗτος ὁ ποιῶν
ἑαυτὸν καὶ κύριος ἑαυτοῦ καὶ οὐχ ὥς τι ἕτερον ἠθέλησε
γενόμενος, ἀλλ' ὡς θέλει οὗτός. 10

MacKenna's translation, itself not free from misinterpretations, reads as follows:

Since in the Supreme "associated" and "associating" are one, secker and sought one, the sought serving as Hypostasis and substrate of the seeker—once more God's being and his seeking are identical; once more, then, the Supreme is the self-producing, sovran of Himself, not coming to be as some extern willed but existing as wills it.[9]

It is important to see why MacKenna's translation is misleading. Plotinus' argument takes the form: "If so and so is the case, on the basis of what the interrelated terms a and b, and c and d, mean with reference to the One, then it should be clear that certain identities follow." The theorem, so to speak, he is about to prove in this chapter is that love (*eros*) and the beloved (*erasmion*) are identical in the One as love of itself. Thus, if the copresent, the *synon,* and that in which it is copresent (*tò en ō synestin*) are one, and if the desiring and the desired (*ephiemenon tò ephetō*) are one, in which case the desired is in the fashion of hypostasis and as though *hypokeimenon,* then it becomes clear to us that desire (*ephesis*) and *ousia* are identical. The context in which the argument occurs makes it evident that Plotinus is not purporting to prove here that the One is a hypostasis; rather, his point is that the concept of hypostasis can help us understand how it is that the One is the ideal case of self-love. The argument starts with distinctions and comparisons in order to collapse the meanings of the terms involved, with the assistance of the mode of hypostasis. If so, it is not correct to say that "hypostasis" here is a substitute for the One, which is what MacKenna's translation "serving as Hypostasis" implies.

The passage to which Deck appeals comes only twenty lines later, 3 f., where the expression "first hypostasis" occurs. However, the word "first," in order to support his claim, should have normally come in line 6, where the collapsing of the correlative terms is defended. Instead, Plotinus avoided using it there, and for good reasons. In lines 30 and following, we suddenly have a new unit of thought which contains a negative particle, to tell us in what things the first hypostasis is not to be sought: inanimate things and irrational life. Nothing explicit is said about what this first hypostasis is as such. Are we then to suppose that it is to be found in something animate and in instances of rational life? No such conclusion follows. Yet its nature remains unidentified, and the passage ends on advice as to how to ascend to that which is not just logos but more beautiful (*kallion*) than logos.

But now we have a new question: What is that which is more beautiful than logos? The answer to this is suggested in what the next sentence says: whatever qualifies as the root of reason (*riza tou logou*), which is of itself and that in which everything terminates (*eis touto ta panta lēgei*). Unless the reader is already familiar with the preceding chapters, it is difficult to decide whether the "root" means the One or *Nous*. Either can meet this requirement in certain ways, though not both of the word "everything" or "all" is taken in the most inclusive and absolute sense, which would then include *Nous* itself. Without these qualifications, *Nous* can conceivably be regarded as the "first hypostasis." Strictly speaking, Plotinus offers no unequivocal answer in these lines of the passage under consideration, and that is why it is misleading to quote out of context, thus forcing the passage to say what it does not. Instead of a direct answer, Plotinus resorts to a simile: this "root of reason"[10] is "like the principle and ground of a greatest plant, living according to logos, while the principle itself remaining by itself, giving the being which the plant received according to logos" (translation supplied). The text reads:

'Ρίζα γὰρ λόγου παρ' αὐτῆς καὶ εἰς   35
τοῦτο λήγει τὰ πάντα, ὥσπερ φυτοῦ μεγίστου κατὰ λόγον
ζῶντος ἀρχὴ καὶ βάσις μένουσα αὐτὴ ἐφ' ἑαυτῆς,
διδοῦσα δὲ κατὰ λόγον τῷ φυτῷ, ὃν ἔλαβεν, εἶναι.

As chapter 15 draws to a close, the issue remains unsettled. The question which still lingers in the reader's mind is not whether Plotinus intends to identify the One as the first hypostasis, but whether the argument is one which aims to establish this identity. This is so because the main emphasis is on what is eros and what self-love means in the ultimate sense of the word. Probably Plotinus could have settled the issue and dispensed with the ambiguity if instead of the expression "root of reason" he said "root of *Nous*." The difficulty can no doubt be removed by borrowing freely from the texts, but it would be a different solution. Hence, if the One is the first hypostasis, which it is, we must look for further textual evidence. Had Deck made use of the difficulty in lines 30–38, he probably could have made a stronger case for his "quasihypostasis" thesis. However, since he considers chapter 18 to have provided a clear statement for what the first hypostasis is, he finds it necessary to seek the countervening evidence elsewhere.

III

In discussing Plotinus' tactic in philosophizing about the One, Deck observes, and correctly so, that Plotinus employs "dualistic phrases, but usually to correct them, usually to remind his hearers that these phrases must be purged of dualism to apply to the One" (p. 10). Deck also draws attention to Plotinus' awareness of "speaking incorrectly" (οὐκ ὀρθῶς) in VI.8.13–18, and of resorting to "words which must depart from the rigor of knowledge (παρανοητέον ἐν τοῖς λόγοις)" (VI.8.13.1–5; 47–50).

Thus, according to Deck, such "incorrect speaking" of the One occurs in a number of cases, which are reproduced below.

    (i) The One is from itself, from itself and through itself: παρ' αὐτοῦ, VI.8.14.42; ἐφ' αὐτοῦ, VI.8.11.33.

    (ii) It is towards itself: πρὸς αὐτὸν καὶ ἐς αὐτόν, VI.8.17.26; πρὸς αὐτό, V.3.10.51.

    (iii) It wills itself, VI.8.13.38–40.

    (iv) It makes or constitutes itself as cause of itself: αἴτιον ἑαυτοῦ, VI.8.14.42.

    (v) It made itself to subsist: αὐτὸς ἄρα ὑπέστησεν αὐτόν, VI.8.16.30.

    (vi) It is self-sufficient (qua good): ἱκανὸν ἑαυτῷ I.8.2.4–5.

Of these six select instances of "incorrect speaking," so named on the ground that the expressions are dual and hence misleading, the crucial one for the purposes of this paper is (v): "it made itself to subsist."

Since the One needs nothing (I.8.2.4–5; VI.9.6.18), Deck argues that:

> It does not need subsistence, entity, act or life. If it needed any of these it would not be the first: some other principle, toward which it tended, would supply them to it (cf. III.8.11.38–44). Nor does it *have* them. For in having them, it would be two: itself, and that which it had. Neither needing nor having them, but the source from which they proceed, the One is beyond subsistence, beyond entity, beyond act (pp. 10–11).

Now we come to another crucial expression in Plotinus, in Deck's list:

    (vii) The One is before subsistence: πρὸ τῆς ὑποστάσεως, VI.8.10.37.

Hence:

    (vii) The One does not subsist: οὐδὲ ὑπέστη, VI.8.10.35–38; τὸ μὴ ὑποστάν, VI.8.11.1–5.

Of course, Deck is careful to note that "Plotinus is not contradicting himself. The One is or has all these [viz., substance, entity, act, life, self-sufficiency], to the extent that neither they nor the being or having of them involves duality" (p. 11).

The real issue for Deck is not so much whether Plotinus is contradicting himself, but whether the One is a hypostasis, and if so how are we to understand it qua hypostasis. He absolves Plotinus of the charge of contradiction by saying that "Plotinus applies negative formulae to the One, not to deny positivity of it, but to deny duality." And he continues, further down, to say:

> Thus positive formulae can be applied to the One, provided that they be qualified to remove the taint of duality: the One has quais-subsistence, quasi-entity, quasi-life, which are identical with itself (p. 11).

Deck cites VI.8.7.46–54 and renders Plotinus' expression οἷον[11] ὑπόστασις αὐτοῦ as "quasi-subsistence." Now, it may be objected that the charge of contradiction need not be raised at all, notwithstanding Deck's defense against it; nor is it correct, as will be shown, to attribute to Plotinus a doctrine of "quasi-subsistence." In pursuing his analysis, Deck is (a) inventing an issue which is cast in the form of a rhetorical question: "Does Plotinus contradict himself?" and (b) dismissing the issue by forcing an interpretation which the text does not justify, namely that the meaning of "hypostasis" in the case of the One is that of "quasi-subsistence." Contrary to Deck's view, the text requires that the term "subsistence" be kept intact, and that it means "hypostasis par excellence." This meaning can be best understood in the context of αὐτεξούσιον "in control of itself."

A. The "quasi-subsistence" problem: οἷον ὑπόστασις. The passage to which Deck appeals comes immediately after Plotinus has stated that it would be most absurd to take away "self-control" from the Good, for it neither needs anything nor moves towards any of the things which move towards it, and he continues in lines 46–54:

> ῞Οταν δὲ
> δὴ ἡ οἷον ὑπόστασις αὐτοῦ ἡ οἷον ἐνέργεια ᾖ (οὐ γὰρ ἡ
> μὲν ἕτερον, ἡ δ' ἕτερόν ἐστιν, εἴ γε μηδὲ ἐπὶ τοῦ νοῦ
> τοῦτο) οὔτι μᾶλλον κατὰ τὸ εἶναι ἡ ἐνέργεια ἢ κατὰ, τὴν
> ἐνέργειαν τὸ εἶναι· ὥστε οὐκ ἔχει τὸ ὡς πέφυκεν ἐνεργεῖν,   50
> οὐδὲ ἡ ἐνέργεια καὶ ἡ οἷον ζωὴ ἀνενεχθήσεται εἰς τὴν
> οἷον οὐσίαν, ἀλλ' ἡ οἷον οὐσία συνοῦσα καὶ οἷον συγγε-
> νομένη ἐξ ἀιδίου τῇ ἐνεργείᾳ ἐξ ἀμφοῖν αὐτὸ αὑτὸ ποιεῖ
> καὶ ἑαυτοῦ καὶ οὐδενός.

Translation:

> When the hypostasis of the Good, such as this can be,[12] is regarded as actuality (for these are not two different things, not even in the case of Nous), it is no more the case that actuality is determined by being than being is by actuality. Therefore, "to act," as originated by nature, does not apply here, nor can actuality and what is like (its) life be reduced to what is like (its) *ousia;* rather, *ousia,* such as it may be in this case, as copresent and as being born together with actuality since eternity, is what the Good makes itself from itself and nothing else.

If the above rendition is close to Plotinus' meaning, then "hypostasis" in the case of the One-Good must be used in the fullest sense of the term. Hence, it seems rather baffling to call it "quasi-hypostasis." The text makes it clear that Plotinus means to correlate the concepts of "hypostasis" and *"energeia"* with the help of "being," *"ousia,"* and "life." The words συνοῦσα, συγγενομένη, and ἀμφοῖν support this view. If so, the "incorrect way of speaking" has been cleared of its difficulties by the time Plotinus has ended each chapter.

B. The issue of contradiction. We need now to turn to those passages in which Plotinus is allegedly denying hypostasis of the One. The difficulty begins to emerge when we try to understand the sense in which the One is "before subsistence" (πρὸ τῆς ὑποστάσεως) and such that "it made itself to subsist" (αὐτὸς ἄρα ὑπέστησεν αὑτόν). Let us consider the text. The expression πρὸ τῆς ὑποστάσεως occurs in VI.8.10.37. The main question which chapter 10 raises in this connection is whether "chance" can have any place in a philosophical account of the One qua *archē*. Thus, Plotinus asks:

Τὴν δὴ ἀρχὴν παντὸς λόγου τε καὶ τάξεως
καὶ ὅρου τῶς ἄν τις τὴν τούτου ὑπόστασιν ἀναφείη τύχη;

Translation:

> When we ask about that which is the origin of every logos and order and limit, how can one ascribe its hypostasis to chance?

The answer is that we cannot. Now, since the One is also the *first*, we must stop there and say nothing more. We may inquire into the things generated from it, but not into the origins of that which is truly ungenerated. At this point Plotinus finds it necessary to raise a question about the meaning which the expression "to give hypostasis to X" can have in the case of the One. In this connection, Deck is right when he says that Plotinus must remove from his exposition of the One "the taint of duality." Thus, Plotinus needs to correlate two things: (a) what it means *to give hypostasis* and (b) what it is *to be ungenerated*. It is the former that presents a problem of possible duality. What he concludes in lines 22–38, in complicated "question and answer" language, is that the One is at once ungenerated and by necessity, that is, "using itself such as it is." "Being master of its own *ousia*," nothing made the One subsist. The One gave itself its own subsistence and necessarily so. The expression οὐχ ὑποστήσας ἑαυτόν appears to contradict the expression πρὸ τῆς ὑποστάσεως only because the text is complicated. The misunderstanding can be removed without much difficulty with the aid of two recommendations: the first is editorial, the second calling for careful contextual reading.

(1) Textual emendation.

Lines 22–25 must be read as a series of *three interconnected questions*, and not as a simple passage consisting of one question ending on the word *kurios* (1. 23), and the rest as a quasi-question in the *hypothesis-apodosis* syntactical mode. Seen in this way, the intent of the passage can be more faithfully rendered, and thus the expression οὐχ ὑποστήσας ἑαυτόν falls in line with the thesis which pervades the entire tractate. By placing a question mark rather than a period at the end of line 25, the passage would translate:

> But then, can we say that, if the One is ungenerated and while being such as it is, that is not master of its own *ousia*? And can we say that, if not master of it, while being such as it is, that *it did not cause itself to subsist* (οὐχ ὑποστάσας ἑαυτόν) by using itself such as it is, and that this is so by necessity and could not be otherwise?

(2) Contextual reading.

Given that the One is master of its own *ousia*, it is inherently necessary that it be conceived as causing itself to be its own subsistence. Ten lines later, after he has explained why the One has "fullness of power" (ὑπερβολὴν τῆς δυνάμεως) and it is thus impossible for it to "arrive at what is worse" (ἐλθεῖν πρὸς τὸ χεῖρον), he returns to the issue of hypostasis. The context of these lines permits us to see what Plotinus means by the expression οὐδε ὑπέστη.

Since the aspect of necessity (ἀνάγκη) had already been discussed in previous chapters of VI.8., where it was established that the necessity of the One is different from other necessities, it makes no sense in the present context of chapter 10 to say that there is such a thing as a necessity and also the One, as if this is a real duality. Since the One is not subject to necessity but rather is itself the ground of all other necessities, of being and law, the question, rhetorical to be sure, is "How could one, then, say that it is necessity which causes the One's subsisting (ὑπέστησεν), especially if the One is understood as having fullness of power?"

Obviously, Plotinus must insist that this is not the way to talk about the One qua hypostasis, for it is not the case that it is thus that it came to subsist (ὑπέστη); nor can it be that it is *this necessity* that afforded subsistence to the other subsistents (ὑποστάντων) that came after it and because of it. Given that the One has no source other than itself for its hypostasis, such as it may be, it is evident that *qua* One, it is prior to all cases of subsistence. Now the concluding question, which already contains the answer, becomes: "How can it then be that what is admittedly prior to hypostasis, attains subsistence (ὑπέστη) by virtue of something else, unless it did so by itself?" Therefore the place of the subject of the verb ὑφιστάναι cannot be occupied by the word "necessity."

Since the One is the only thing that is (i) πρὸ τῆς ὑποστάσεως and (ii) the ὑποστήσας ἑαυτόν, it is also the only thing which is at once (iii) a hypostasis underived from another hypostasis. These considerations set the context for the opening question of chapter 11: 'Αλλὰ τὸ μὴ ὑποστὰν τοῦτο τι; "But what is this One which is 'not subsisting'?" The dialectical discussion which follows holds no surprise for the reader. Logically enough, Plotinus returns to the aspect of subsistence to restate that the One "attained its own subsistence from itself before any other" (ἐφ' αὐτοῦ γὰρ καὶ ὑφέστηκε, πρὶν ἄλλο).

IV

The preceding analysis was not directed against a position Deck obviously does not hold, namely that Plotinus is in fact open to the charge of contradiction. Rather, the purpose was to show that the issue of contradiction does not even arise in any significant way, not even as a preliminary difficulty. However, there is one residual problem in Deck's interpretation, namely his contention that, in the case of the One, we can only speak of its being a "quasi-hypostasis." This, as has been argued, is a mistaken interpretation. In addition to what has been said in the discussion of the relevant texts, further support may be adduced from VI.8.13, lines 50–52 and 55–59, where Plotinus clearly speaks of the Good in connection with an argument to show that it is possible to bring will and being together (συνακτέον εἰς ἓν τὴν βούλησιν καὶ τὴν οὐσίαν).

Εἰ γὰρ ἡ βούλησις 55
παρ' αὐτοῦ καὶ οἷον ἔργον αὐτοῦ, αὕτη δὲ ταὐτὸν τῇ
ὑποστάσει αὐτοῦ, αὐτὸς ἂν οὕτως ὑποστήσας ἂν εἴη
αὐτόν· ὥστε οὐχ ὅπερ ἔτυχέν ἐστιν, ἀλλ' ὅπερ ἠβουλήφη
αὐτός.

Translation:

> For if will is from Him and like His work, while His will is identical with his
> hypostasis, He himself can thus come to subsist (οὕτως ὑποστήσας) as is possible
> for Him. Therefore, this did not occur by chance but precisely as He willed.

There is no reason, therefore, to call this a quasi-hypostasis. In fact, it seems
evident that Plotinus has anticipated such reservations as Deck has expressed. If
we were to ask what a quasi-hypostasis would amount to, most certainly it would
have to be one which is not deserving of the One, for it would be lacking in
something. One could conceive of no stronger instance than the case of hypostasis
which is lacking in *energeia*. Quite likely Deck would resist this imputation on his
view, but let us consider the case. Plotinus would most definitely reject it as
inadmissible and disown it outright on the basis of what he states in VI.8.20, lines
11–15:

Εἰ δὲ ὑόστασιν ἄνευ ἐνεργείας τις
θεῖτο, ἐλλιπὴς ἡ ἀρχὴ καὶ ἀτελὴς ἡ τελειοτάτη πασῶν
ἔσται. Καὶ εἰ προσθείη ἐνέργειαν, οὐχ ἓν τηρεῖ. Εἰ οὖν
τελειότερον ἡ ἐνέργεια τῆς οὐσίας, τελειότατον δὲ τὸ
πρῶτον, πρῶτον ἂν ἐνέργεια εἴη.   15

Translation:

> If one posits hypostasis without *energeia*, the *Archē*, which is the most perfect of all
> principles, would be incomplete and imperfect. And if one would make *energia*
> something composite, then he could not preserve the One. Thus, if *energeia* is more
> perfect than *ousia*, and that which is first is most perfect, it must be that *energeia* is
> the first.

The argument leads to the fundamental thesis that hypostasis calls for more
than the mere addition of *energeia*. What makes the concept of hypostasis intelligible and actual is the original activity of the One, which is presupposed by its
ousia. Given these ontic restrictions, it is difficult to see how we can speak of a
"quasi-hypostasis" in the case of the One. In fact, it cannot be other than the *first
hypostasis*. This is what "correct discourse" about the One demands.

The One, or God, Is Not Properly *"Hypostasis"*:
A Reply to Professor John P. Anton

JOHN N. DECK

As someone who essays to be a contemporary Christian Neoplatonist, I have been very much alive to the perennial problem of the articulation of the "negative theology" of the One with the more positive indications of the divine nature to be found in the Judaeo-Christian tradition.

Meanwhile, to be sure, the "negative theology" itself requires careful and continuous consideration because Plotinus also allows himself, in a way, to predicate something of the One.

When, then, someone is found to argue that the One is, for Plotinus, literally and without correctives a "hypostasis," the "first hypostasis," there is involved first of all a simple problem in Plotinian interpretation; but beyond that, the philosophico-theological question of what can and cannot be said of the First, the Source, God—what can and cannot be said, and *how* it can be said or not said.

Professor John P. Anton's paper, "Some Logical Aspects of the Concept of Hypostasis in Plotinus,"[1] adopts precisely these positions. And it is devoted almost exclusively to a criticism of certain remarks I had made in *Nature, Contemplation and the One* (*NCO*)[2] concerning the appropriateness (or inappropriateness) of des-

ignating the Plotinian One an "hypostasis." In replying to it I will expose Plotinus' doctrine again, and also, by implication at least, indicate what I as a philosopher think can*not* be said of the One, or of God.

Professor Anton correctly discerns that I interpreted Plotinus as *not* taking the
One to be hypostasis in an unqualified sense, but his route to this intuition is a
somewhat surprising one: He picks up his indications from a rather bland footnote
and a few phrases used some pages beyond it. He treats these materials as though
they were a fully articulated argument, with odd results.

The "bland footnote" (*NCO*, p. 19, n. 5) in question was to annotate the
mention of the One in the text of *NCO* as "a distinct hypostasis, a distinct
'nature.'" I had remarked only that "Hypostasis is not, for Plotinus himself, a
common designation of the One." Professor Anton does not deny this (Anton, p.
25. I had said that I had "been able to find only one place where Plotinus calls
the One, in so many words, the 'first hypostasis.'" The place was *Ennead*
VI.8.30.

Parturiunt montes. In a discussion stretching over four pages (Anton, pp. 26–
30), replete with phrases like "Deck's initial point," "whether Plotinus is discussing the point which Deck claims," "the passage to which Deck appeals," and
so on, Anton argues, in brief, that the mention of "the first hypostasis" in this text
must be taken in the context of a rather long section to see that it is indeed the One
which is so designated. If a person did not read rather far back and rather far
ahead, he might take "the first hypostasis" to refer to something else. But according to Anton, "the first hypostasis" here *does* refer to the One. So?

But meanwhile, Professor Anton seems to have guessed that if I *had* written
an *exprofesso* tractate on "The Plotinian One—A Hypostasis?" I would have tried
to make much of Plotinus' phrases "before hypostasis?" (πρὸ τῆς ὑποστάσεως)
and "quasi-hypostasis" (οἷον ὑπόστασις)—but he does not understand *why* I
would have done so. Possibly because of his concentration on a footnote, he fails
to see, in the few pages of *NCO* (pp. 9–11) to which we are both referring, the
outline of a full-scale argument which shows why the One absolutely cannot be,
for Plotinus, without qualifications a hypostasis. This argument is contained in
these pages and, in fact, displayed in their visible structure.

I wish to take this opportunity to present that argument before making further
replies to Professor Anton's critique.

At the beginning of my systematized presentation of Plotinus' One—talk, I
had written:

> Plotinus is at once in difficulty when he begins to describe the One. He sees that
> for him the One must be ineffable. Even the name "One," *if* taken as a positive
> designation, is not suitable (V.5.6.28–30). To add a predicate to the One, or even to
> say that it *is,* would be to make it two—"One" and "is"—and therefore, [make] the
> "one which is" the second nature and not the first.

Not I wish to make it clear that I regarded, and do regard, this as Plotinus
most profound doctrine of the One. It is to be taken as absolutely definitive—as

absolutely qualifying *any* statements he may make elsewhere which predicate *anything* of the One, with or without cautions or qualifying words or phrases. In short, I am saying that *he means it*—if he means anything. My insistence on this is perhaps affected by my own philosophic adhesion to it, as also by the "logical precedence" that it obviously must enjoy when it is taken in full seriousness. *Strictly speaking, the One is absolutely without predicates.*[3]

I went on to show that for Plotinus even "the Good"—which, indeed, he uses often enough as a virtual synonym for the One—is not, strictly speaking, a proper designation. It is the good for the others, but it is *not good for itself*—"good for itself" involves a duality.

This led to another point. The One is in no way whatever dual. Hence any predicate that displays or implies duality would be doubly wrong in its application to the One. Wrong because it is a predicate and wrong because it is in itself dual. For example, the One wills itself, that is, the One is a (or the) self-willer.[4]

Nevertheless, Plotinus uses the dualistic words. He "must" use them. As I put it in *NCO*:

> And yet the very simplicity of the first principle can be expressed, unless we are merely to repeat endlessly "the One," only by words and phrases which in themselves connote duality. Plotinus is fully aware of this. His tactic is to employ the dualistic phrases, but usually to correct them, usually to remind his hearers that these phrases must be purged of dualism to apply to the One.

A little further on I mentioned several of these phrases, which Plotinus himself uses in the long passage (VI.8.13–18) where he cautions us at the outset that he is speaking incorrectly (οὐκ ὀρθῶς): from itself and through itself, wills itself, makes or constitutes (ποιεῖ) itself. These are dualistic phrases, they would give the One two "sides" or two aspects (e.g., the maker and the made).

Writing now, I would go even further and at least suggest that *any* phrase taken, as it must be taken, from the world of being (which, we will recall, is for Plotinus dualistic through-and-through, the world of Knower-Known or, as some like to say, Intelligence-Intelligible)—*any* word or phrase, with the possible exception of "the One"—is at least implicitly dual.

What about "hypostasis"? I think it should at any rate be examined for internal duality, which in all probability will show up. It is dual at least in its primitive meaning, "a standing-under." That which in its own nature "stands-under" requires, as its dialectic partner, that under which it stands. This two-sided meaning does seem sometimes to be Plotinus', meaning notably in a text from which both Professor Anton and I quote (VI.8.20) (see page 38). But whether this duality and/or other dualities are involved in other cases where Plotinus uses the word is a large and unexplored question.

Now since *no* predicate, taken as it is from the realm of being, can, for these two reasons, be applied in an utterly proper sense to the One, the application of *any* predicate must be qualified by a denial. This situation naturally results when one applies the language of being to that which is above being.[5] Thus in *NCO* (p.

11) I lined up texts in which Plotinus (a) affirms and (b) denies the subsistence, act, freedom, and life of the One. I proceeded:

> Plotinus is not contradicting himself. The One is or has all these, to the extent that neither they nor the being or having of them involves duality. When Plotinus denies an attribute of the One he does so to affirm the simplicity of the One; when he affirms an attribute he shows that the One, though simple, is not negative.

Out of this, Anton gets no more than "Deck is inventing an issue which is cast in the form of a rhetorical question: 'Does Plotinus contradict himself?'" (Anton, p. 30), and then devotes two-and-one-half pages (pp.31–33 to "the issue of contradiction."

I suggest that the contradictory formulas cited would raise the question of contradiction in almost anyone's mind, when it is operating on a certain level. But, in point of fact, I was neither inventing this "issue" nor making much of it. I moved at once to something much more vital: *how* Plotinus uses the negative formulas, *how* he uses the positive. I was guided here again by the realization that (a) *neither* type is quite right, and (b) that he "must" use both.

And again, in the knowledge that Plotinus cannot properly predicate *anything* of the One, I was attracted in *NCO* (p. 11) to a text in which he apparently qualifies several predications, among them hypostasis. This text is VI.8.7.49 54. Professor Anton objects to my translation of οἷον in this text by *quasi*, and offers his own translation:

> When the hypostasis of the Good, *such as this can be,* is regarded as actuality (for these are not two different things, not even in the case of *Nous*), it is no more the case that actuality is determined by being than being is by actuality. Therefore, "to act," as originated by nature, does not apply here, nor can actuality and what is *like* (its) life be reduced to what is *like* (its) *ousia*; rather, *ousia, such as it may be in this case,* as copresent and as being born together with actuality since eternity, is what the Good makes itself from itself and nothing else (Anton, p. 30).

I have italicized the words he uses to translate οἷον (and to avoid saying "quasi"). Now I submit that even his translation could easily be read as meaning quasi-hypostasis, and so on. I can see that he is trying to attach another shade of meaning to "such as this can be," "such as may be in this case," but it is far from clear what that shade may be. "Like" seems awfully like "quasi." I do not wish to labor this argument: Anton's new translation simply has not made his point.

At the very end of his article, Professor Anton returns to the "quasi-hypostasis" question. He seems to have no notion of why I "pounced" on the expression οἷον ὑπόστασις in the first place:

> If we were to ask what a quasi-hypostasis would amount to, most certainly it would have to be one which is not deserving of the One, for it would be lacking in something (Anton, p. 33).

Why? Why should quasi-hypostasis be taken "most certainly" as necessarily less than hypostasis? Why not as *more than hypostasis*? Even a cursory reading of

NCO should have conveyed this meaning. On page 11 I had closely connected the phrase πρὸ τῆς ὑποστάσεως *before* hypostasis with the characteristic Plotinian doctrine (derived from Plato) that the One is beyond; is the sense of *above*; *ousia*: ἐπέκεινα τῆς οὐσίας. The One is before, prior to, above hypostasis *and for this reason* is called quasi-hypostasis.

But in pursing the ill-conceived notion that a quasi-hypostasis is lacking in something, Professor Anton considers the case: maybe it is lacking in *energeia* (act). Then he finds a text in which the word "hypostasis" occurs, and which says that the One is act (or rather, that act is the first). This is used for a triumphant vindication of the One as the "first hypostasis."

Now in the text in question Plotinus is saying that the One and its producing of itself are the same. The preferred word for this seems here to be the Aristotelian *"energeia,"* and it would be interesting to dilate, both textually and philosophically, on the appropriateness and inappropriateness of calling the One *"energeia,"* or of substituting *"energeia"* for "One."

Professor Anton, however, does not see this, nor does he notice that the to-him-obnoxious phrase οἷον ὑπόστασις occurs again in the line just above the first line he quotes. In fuller rendition:

> We must not fear to posit the first act without entity, but we must posit this itself [the first act] as a quasi-hypostasis. If we were to posit a hypostasis without act, the *Arché* would be lacking and the most perfect of all would be imperfect. And if we *added* act, we would not preserve the One. Now if act is more perfect than entity, and the first is the most perfect, the first will be act (VI.8.20.9–15, trans. Deck).

The notion here seems to be that the One is a self-subsistent act. The nuance of "quasi-hypostasis" is slightly different here, but the meaning comes through again that the quasi-hypostasis being spoken of is "more than" hypostasis: The act (which is the One) is a *quasi* hypostasis because it does not have a subject or substratum in which it inheres, but is, as it were, its own subject or substratum— or, better yet, "gets by" without a substratum.

As I remarked above, Professor Anton leaves out the first sentence. So, with reference to this very text, he says "it is difficult to see how we can speak of a quasi-hypostasis in the case of the One." The text itself, when read with the first sentence, makes it impossible *not* to speak of the act-which-is-the-One as quasi-hypostasis.

If I may be permitted to mention what I think is just under the surface in Professor Anton's article, I would say that he is attempting to impose a logic on Plotinus that is not Plotinus' own and which is not philosophically productive. Hypostasis is not a "big word" for Plotinus,[6] "the One" is. But hypostasis *is* a big word—an important "concept"—for Professor Anton, and in this sense it is no accident that he called his paper "Some Logical Aspects of the Concept of Hypostasis."

But does he find a logic of hypostasis in our philosopher? In note 2 (p. 158), Prof. Anton proposes to refer us to "key passages" in the *Enneads* which give "the basic features of hypostasis." For "infinite and nonspatial," he cites VI.3.8. 35ff.

The doctrine is not there at all; hypostasis is not mentioned; the text contrasts sensible with true *ousia* but not in terms of infinite-finite or spatial-nonspatial. The other text he cites in this connection (VI.9.6.10–12) contains the often-discussed doctrine that the One is infinite in power. The text (and the whole context) concerns the One; hypostasis is not mentioned. For "undiminished giving," he cites texts that display the *Nous* (III.8.8.46–48) and the One (III.8.10.1–19) as "undiminished givers." For "the One qua *hypostasis* [italics Anton's] transcends knowledge altogether," he cites VI.7.39.19–33. "Hypostasis" does not occur either in the texts or the contexts, and so forth.[7]

He is simply taking texts about the One, the *Nous,* and Soul or souls, and, because he is certain that hypostasis is an overarching concept applied to the One, *Nous,* and Soul, giving it out that these texts are "Plotinus' answer to the question 'What criteria must X satisfy to quality as a *hypostasis*?' " (Anton, p. 24). *Plotinus has neither the question nor the answer.*

Thus, if an interpreter's question may be allowed to arise, "Is the One an hypostasis?," the answer is to be found, not in the "logical aspects of the concept to hypostasis," not, that is, in the logic of hypostasis, but in the "logic," so to speak, of the One. Indeed, any "concept" (better, any entity) has its proper home at the level of *Nous.* It must be adjusted downward to "apply" below the level of *Nous,* and adjusted upward to "apply" to the One. And this is what seems to happen with hypostasis. The hypostasis, in the fullest sense, is the *Nous.* The inferior hypostasis, Soul, is less-as-a-hypostasis. The One is above hypostasis and is best described, when the word "hypostasis" is used at all, as quasi-hypostasis.

Plotinus' Theory of The One

EUGENE F. BALES

I

The purpose of this essay is to offer an interpretation of Plotinus' doctrine of The One or The Good, which is more adequate than the traditional interpretation and which, at the same time, indicates a fundamental difficulty with Plotinus' theory. For the purpose in mind, I have elected to concentrate only on the chronologically middle treatises of the *Enneads*. These treatises constitute not only the numerical bulk of that larger work, but also its most philosophically sophisticated part, if we can trust the judgment of Porphyry.[1]

Traditionally most commentators have distinguished a positive and a negative theology within Plotinus' doctrine of The One.[2] That is, Plotinus speaks on occasion as though The One radically transcends Being, is devoid of intelligible content, and so forth; and, on other occasions, as though The One is the highest Being, has an intelligible, if minimal, content, and so forth. The former is designated negative theology, the latter positive theology.

That this interpretation sheds light on Plotinus' theory is beyond question; but the contention here is that this interpretation is not entirely adequate. Specifically,

I wish to propose the existence of three modes of discourse that Plotinus uses in discussing The One or The Good: (1) The first mode of discourse is employed when he speaks of The One as though it transcends Being, Mind, Freedom, Will, Consciousness, and Form, and is thus void of all Act and intelligible content. This mode of discourse I shall refer to as *meontological* (from *mē ōn*, nonbeing). (2) The second mode of discourse is employed when Plotinus speaks of The Good as though it is within Being rather than beyond it, the essence of Act, containing all things potentially, as having some kind of Consciousness, Will, Mind, and as being the Transcendental Self. This mode of discourse I shall designate *ontological*. (3) The third mode of discourse is used to show the relationship between the first two modes of discourse. This occurs when The One is spoken of as a Formless Form, as everywhere and nowhere, as all things and nothing, as Being and Non-Being, and preeminently as Self-caused. This mode of discourse I will refer to as the *paradoxical*.

It is my contention, first of all, that this third mode of discourse is an essential addition to the first two, and that without the third, no sense can be made of the relation between the first two. But secondly, it is my belief that insuperable problems concerning the intelligibility of Plotinus' theory of The One arise precisely because of this third mode of discourse.

II

There are many passages in the middle treatises that assert The One's transcendent relation to Being. The following is typical:

> It follows that The First must be without form, and, if without form, then it is no Being; Being must have some definition and therefore be limited; but the First cannot be thought of as having definition and limit, for thus it would be not the Source but the particular item indicated by the definition assigned. . . . Not included among them, this can be described only as transcending them: but they are Being and the Beings; it therefore transcends Being.
>
> Note that the phrase "transcending Being" assigns no character, makes no assertion, allots no name, carries only the denial of particular being.[3]

This ultimate beyond Being in Plotinus' system is said to be beyond multiplicity, and thus to be Pure Unity, that is, a unity which, neither directly nor indirectly, has any parts:

> It was necessary that The First be utterly without multiplicity, for otherwise it must be again referred to a prior.[4]

A Pure Unity that has no duality in it, that is, no parts, has no content whatever either potentially or actually; thus one could say that it is a void:

> . . . containing, then, neither the good nor the not-good it contains nothing and, containing nothing, it is alone: it is void of all but itself.[5]

This characteristic vacuity of The One is further emphasized in that Activity cannot be predicated of it at all:

> That all-transcending cannot have had an activity by which to produce this
> activity—acting before act existed—or have had thought in order to produce
> thinking—applying thought before thought exists—all intellection, even of the Good,
> is beneath it.[6]

The lack of Activity in The One implies its lack of power or "metaphysical
abundance":

> Who has begotten such a child, this Intellectual-Principle, this lovely abundance so
> abundantly endowed?
>   The source of all this cannot be an Intellect; nor can it be an abundant power: it
> must have been before Intellect and abundance were; these are later and things of
> lack; abundance had to be made abundant and Intellection needed to know.[7]

The very perfection of The One is rooted in its lack of power, of act, of content.[8]

At one point this sheer vacuity of The One *seems* to have led Plotinus to the
extreme of ruling out its power to cause. If The One is pure Non-Being, of course,
it is quite unintelligible to propose that it *causes* Being. Any particular thing
would derive its finite being from Being, and not from Unity. This is, I believe,
the gist of the following rather odd passage:

> The single thing derives its unity by participation in Unity-Absolute; its being it
> derives from Being-Absolute, which in turn hold [sic] its Being from itself and its
> unity from Unity-Absolute.[9]

Although Plotinus usually asserts that Unity is the *source* of Being,[10] he seems here
to be saying that Being is its own source. The implication is that the One is the
cause of the unity in Being, but not of Being itself. There is no reason to think,
however, that this was Plotinus' ordinary view of the matter; indeed there are no
other passages in the *Enneads* that I know of that suggest such a theory.

If The One transcends Being, it transcends both subject and object:

> Anyone making the Good at once Thinker and Thought identifies it with Being
> and with the Intellection vested in Being so that it must stand as self-intellective: at
> once it becomes necessary to find another principle, one superior to that Good.[11]

The denial of Objectivity and Subjectivity within The One occupies much of
Plotinus' attention. There are any number of passages, for example, that deny that
The Good is, in fact, an Idea or Form:

> The Authentic Beauty, or rather the Beyond-Beauty, cannot be under measure and
> therefore cannot have admitted shape or be Idea: the primal Beauty, the First, must
> be without Form; the beauty of that higher realm must be, simply, the Nature of the
> Good.[12]

Thus it is the unshaped that gives shape; the formless that gives form. Further, if
the Good is not a Form, it is not a particular good, nor even the highest good,
since both of these are forms:

> . . . surely the First must be able to say "I possess Being"?
> But he does not possess Being.

Then, at least he must say "I am good"?

No: once more, that would be an affirmation of Being.

But surely he may affirm merely the goodness, adding nothing: the goodness would be taken without the being and all duality avoided?

No: such self-awareness as good must inevitably carry the affirmation "I am the Good."[13]

Thus, The Good is not good; rather as Non-Being it is beyond genera, and thus beyond the kinds or degrees of goodness. Goodness, even the highest goodness, is intrinsically intertwined with Being: to be good is to be something definite. Thus, metaphysically, The Good is not a Form of any kind.

While The Good is not an object of Thought, it is not a subject of some kind either. In the first place, Plotinus insists quite often that it has no intellection:

> There must have been something standing consummate independently of an intellectual act, something perfect in its own essence: thus that in which this comple tion is inherent must exist before intellection; in other words it has no need of intellection, having been always self-sufficing: this, then, will have no intellectual act.
>
> Thus we arrive at: a principle having no intellection, a principle having intellection primarily, a principle having it secondarily.[14]

Intellection, of course, demands a duality of some kind between knower and known; thus Pure Unity can never be a principle having intellection, since it stands apart from any duality.

In the same vein, Plotinus stipulates further that the One is beyond freedom, "higher than all will, will a thing beneath it.":[15]

> For This is principle of all, or, more strictly, unrelated to all and, in this consider ation, cannot be made to possess such laters as even freedom and self-disposal, which in fact indicate manifestation upon the extern.[16]

III

There are some very significant passages in which the *Being*, rather than the Non-Being, of The Good is stressed by Plotinus.

The first example is the most striking: it occurs in VI. 5 ("On the Integral Omnipresence of the Authentic Existent [II]"):

> Hence the Good is not to be sought outside; it could not have fallen outside of what is; it cannot possibly be found in non-Being; within Being the Good must lie, since it is never a non-Being.
>
> If that Good has Being and is within the realm of Being, then it is present, self-contained, in everything: we, therefore, are not separated from Being; we are in it; nor is Being separated from us: therefore all beings are one.[17]

Here the meontological character of the One is explicitly denied; the Good must lie "within Being." The very end of this quotation, I believe, throws some light on the meaning of this: Being is the ultimate because the final goal of the spiritual life—the unity of Being—is *in* Being and not *beyond* Being. The ontological character of this statement is unquestionable and directly conflicts with other accounts of The One as beyond Being.

A second example occurs in the treatise "On Free Will and the Will of The One" (VI. 8):

> Again; if He preeminently is because He holds firmly, so to speak, towards Himself, looking towards Himself, so that what we must call his being is this self-looking, He must again, since the word is inevitable, make Himself.[18]

Here The One is said to be preeminent, that is, to be the highest Being; and this Being (the infinitive *einai* is used here) is a kind of self-looking. What is significant here is the use of the verb "to be" in this description of The One, a verb that Plotinus is more often than not at pains to avoid using with reference to The One.

Even more indicative than the use of the verb "to be" in reference to The One is the assertion of its active character. The following passage is striking in this respect:

> Let no one suspect us of asserting that the first Activity is without Essence; on the contrary the Activity is the very reality. To suppose a reality without activity would be to make the Principle of all principles deficient; the supremely complete becomes incomplete. To make the Activity something superadded to the Essence is to shatter the unity. If then Activity is a more perfect thing than Essence and the First is all perfect, then the Activity is the First.[19]

The very essence of The One is said to be *energeia,* and this *energeia* is tied in with Being, as is evident in another passage from the same treatise as the preceding quote:

> The Being accompanies the Act in an eternal association: from the two (Being and Act) it forms itself into The Good, self-springing and unspringing.[20]

Besides the term "*energeia,*" the term "*dynamis*" is also used quite often in reference to The One:

> The Good is the older—not in time but by degree of reality—and it has the higher and earlier power, all power in fact, for the sequent holds only a power subordinate and delegated of which the prior remains sovereign.[21]

Power here, whether in the sense of *energeia* or *dynamis,* is to my mind a clear ontological characterization: it would be quite out of character to speak of Non-Being as having *dynamis* or *energeia.* Indeed there is a discussion of the ontological character of *dynamis* in VI.1, a treatise concerned with the categories within *Nous,* which confirms this. The passage in question occurs casually in the midst of a highly abstract discussion of Aristotle's category of Quality: Plotinus says that "power or a particular power may be regarded as Substance."[22] Now Plotinus is not talking about The One, and for that reason I would not want to press this passage too far; but if the *dynamis* in the realm of Being, whether general or particular (*tis*), is said to be Substance (*ousia*), would not the use of it in regard to The One have the same connotation as well? Does not the power of The One suggest the

Being of The One? Surely Plotinus does not want us to believe that *dynamis* predicated of The One has nothing in common with *dynamis* predicated of the lower Hypostases. For then how could *dynamis* in the former sense have any meaning at all?

In any case, The One, as the source of all, is thereby the potentiality of all:

> And what will such a Principle essentially be?
> The potentiality of the Universe: the potentiality whose non-existence would mean the non-existence of all the Universe and even of the Intellectual-Principle which is the primal Life and all Life.[23]

This potentiality is the power (*dynamis*) of Being of all things: without the Being of The One, nothing else could exist. Being itself is caused by the Being of The One. In this sense, The One is potentially all things, and thus is not a sheer void at all. This may account for Plotinus' unusual assertion in VI. 8 that The One has a content: "What then is there is of his content that is not Himself, what that is not his Act, what not his work?"[24] The word "content" does not occur in the Greek, but the repetition of *ti* ("what") suggests the same thing: The One can be characterized by various predicates, by *particular* kinds of notions, such as *energeia* or *ergon*.

If The One is understood by Plotinus as Being, it would not be surprising if it is also said to be like the Intellectual-Principle. Several passages in VI. 8 reflect this tendency to understand The One in the image of *Nous*:

> As self-dwelling Act and in some sense Intellectual-Principle, the most to be loved, He has given Himself existence.[25]
> What is present in Intellectual-Principle is present, though in a far transcendent mode, in the One . . . but Intellectual-Principle, the diffused and image light, is not different in kind from its prior.[26]

The close relationship established here between *Nous* and the One allows Plotinus to suggest other ways of talking about the One as well. Thus, the One can be said to be Form in some sense:

> We must admit in the case of Authentic and primary Intellectual-Principle that it is good; thus it becomes clear that every Idea is good and informed by the Good.[27]

The action of The Good upon the Ideas is that of forming them into good Ideas; or, to say the same thing, the Ideas participate in the Form of The Good. This, I believe, is also the point of the following passage:

> Unity is due to the presence of Unity; duality to that of Duality; it is precisely as things are white by Whiteness, just by Justice, beautiful by Beauty.[28]

The meaning of this is that beings participate in unity in the same way that white things participate in the form of Whiteness. Thus The One is by analogy a Form.

Similarly, The One is the Supreme Subject, or Self:

> It is the First, the Authentic, immune from chance, from blind effect and happening: God is cause of Himself; for Himself and of Himself He is what He is, the first self, transcendently The Self.[29]

Passages like this have given rise to speculation that Plotinus was under Oriental, specifically Hindu, influence. Whatever be the truth of that allegation, we have seen that it would not be unnatural for Plotinus to have arrived at this position anyway, given his ambivalence in characterizing The One as Being or Non-Being. For if the One is Being, it could be understood with equal justice as the Supreme Form or Object, or the Supreme Self or Subject.

This admission of the Selfhood of The One makes sense of some other characterizations. For example, The One as Self is said to have "knowledge" in some sense of the word: "it can have only an immediate intuition self-directed."[30] Indeed, its self-knowledge is real enough that Plotinus can refer to The One in VI. 8 as "intellect-in-Unity" as opposed to the duality of Intellectual-Principle itself (*Nous*):

> In the same way we are to take Intellectual-Principle and Being. This combined power springs from the Supreme, an outflow and as it were development from That and remaining dependent upon that Intellective nature, showing forth that, so to speak, Intellect-in-Unity which is not Intellectual-Principle since it is no duality.[31]

This is an extraordinary passage in the *Enneads*; at the very least it negates many other statements that The One is quite beyond intellection.

The Selfhood of The One also allows for the assertion of the Presence of Will within The One:

> If, then, we are to allow Activities in the Supreme and make them depend upon will—and certainly Act cannot There be will-less—and these Activities are to be the very essence, then will and essence in the Supreme must be identical. This admitted, as He willed to be so He is.[32]

Plotinus devotes the entirety of VI.8 to prove that Will can be meaningfully predicated of The One, indeed that it *must* be. There could be no more solid evidence that he was willing to make positive ontological characterizations of The One.

IV

The third mode of discourse is that which characterizes The One in terms of both Being and Non-Being. One notion in particular that stresses the paradoxical nature of this reality is that of self-causation. That which transcends Being participates in the character of Being inasmuch as it possesses the capacity to cause. This capacity to cause is most obviously relevant in explaining why there is Being or *Nous* at all: for The One is said to cause Being. But if Being needs to be explained, and if The One has certain features within it that are also clearly ontological, then why does not The One need to be explained itself? Strictly speaking, The One cannot be explained in terms of another more ultimate reality—since Plotinus does not admit such. But another kind of explanation did suggest itself to him: that of self-causation. In self-causation, two elements must be distinguished: that which causes and that which is caused. A dilemma arises about this theory, which Plotinus deals with explicitly in VI.8.20. The dilemma can be stated as follows: either that which causes exists or it does not, either it is Being or it is Non-Being. If it is Being, then it does not cause its own existence, since its existence is already presupposed. If it is Non-Being, it could not confer being on itself, since there would be no "it" to confer anything. Plotinus formulates the problem this way:

> The difficulty will be raised that God would seem to have existed before thus coming into existence; if He makes Himself, then in regard to the self which He makes, He is not yet in being and as maker He exists before this Himself thus made.[33]

Plotinus' solution is not entirely clear. At first he *seems* to take the position that actually in The One there is only that which causes, not that which is caused. Thus The One is sheer Activity, and

> there is no question of "existing before coming into existence"; then He acted He was not in some state that could be described as "before existing." He was already existent entirely.[34]

If this is the case, though, why speak of self-causation at all? Would it not be more appropriate to simply maintain that The One is, and that self-causation is meaningless in explaining the One, since The One cannot be explained? But this alternative would make The One a matter of chance or "happening-to-be"— a characterization that Plotinus rules out over and over again.

As a matter of fact, the above solution—of eliminating that which is caused in The One—is not Plotinus' final word. For he continues to speak of that which is caused by The One:

> Now assuredly an Activity not subjected to Essence is utterly free; God's self-hood, then, is of his own Act. If his being has to be ensured by something else, He is no longer the self-existent First: if it be true to say that He is his own container, then He inducts Himself, since from the beginning He caused the being of all that by nature He contains.[35]

Plotinus' *ultimate* solution, then, is not to deny the presence of that which is caused, but to insist on the strict identity of Cause and Caused: "his self-making is to be understood as simultaneous with Himself; the being is one and the same with the making."[36] Now if they *are* strictly identified, then one cannot speak of self-causation, since self-causation presupposes just such a distinction. The real solution, which Plotinus awkwardly sidesteps, is to admit the impossibility of the notion of self-causation. The attempt to combine Being and Non-Being into the unified concept of self-causation produces as a consequence an insoluble dilemma. Yet while self-causation is entirely self-contradictory and paradoxical, Plotinus does not feel obliged in the least to avoid such a conclusion.

The third mode of discourse, then, postulates that that which transcends Being is also the cause of its own Being. The notion of self-causation is the self-contradictory heart of the paradoxical unification of the Being and Non-Being of The One itself. But this whole problem arises once again, *mutatis mutandum*, in describing the causal relation that exists between The One and *Nous* or Being, the Second Hypostasis. The question of whether The One can cause itself is analogous, if not identical, with whether it can cause Being in its actuality, that is, specifically *Nous*. There are numerous passages that insist that The One is the cause of all beings, of which the following is typical:

> . . . philosophy must guard against attaching to the Supreme what is later and lower: moving above all that order, it is the cause and source of all these, and is none of them.
>
> For, once more, the nature of the Good is not such as to make it all things or a thing among all.[37]

Plotinus insists that we must not predicate of The One that which is properly predicated only of what is lower than The One. Yet he does just that when he adds that The One is the *cause* of all beings. For The Good is said to contain nothing in itself, and yet to be the cause of all; but to be the cause of all is certainly to be something as against nothing at all.

If The One is said to be the source or cause of Being, it is equally the source or cause of freedom,[38] and more especially of form:

> Life, then, as it looked towards That was undetermined; having looked it had determination though That had none. Life looks to unity and is determined by it, taking bound, limit, form. But this form is in the shaped, the shaper had none.[39]

Although Being derives its Form from The One, The One is quite formless: this leads to the paradox, occasionally expressed by Plotinus, that that Ultimate is a Formless Form.[40]

Another form of paradox is the admission that The One is both all things and none of them:

> It can be none of existing things; yet it is all: none, in that beings are later; all, as the wellspring from which they flow.[41]

Notice the way here in which The One is said to be all things—not in a strict pantheistic sense, but rather as the cause of all things. That latter phrase preserves the transcendence of The One under the cloak of the ontological predicate "cause." In any case, the point is clear: The One "partakes" of Being (in the sense of being the cause) as well as Non-Being (beyond Being).

There is another passage which, in a more literary and less technical way, suggests the paradoxical nature of The One:

> It is certainly thus that the Intellectual-Principle, hiding itself from all the outer, withdrawing to the inmost, seeing nothing, must have its vision—not of some other light in some other thing but of the light within itself, unmingled, pure, suddenly gleaming before it; so that we are left wondering whence it came, from within or without; and when it has gone, we say, "It was here. Yet no; it was beyond!"[42]

The above passage may tell more than Plotinus perhaps intended. The Good appears to Intellect, but when it does the Intellect is not sure whether it was here (in Being) or beyond (Non-Being). Perhaps this statement unconsciously and unintentionally records not the inadequacy of Intellect, but the self-contradictory nature of The One.

V

In the last analysis, what can be said about the validity of Plotinus' theory of The One? Plotinus employed two separate and distinct kinds of metaphysical languages to speak about the One, and unified these by means of a third kind of language that was originally designed as paradoxical. It should now be obvious that that term is not accurate; for a paradox is only a seeming contradiction, whereas it is most clear that the third mode of discourse is intrinsically self-contradictory. This point emerges clearly in Plotinus' attempt to explain the origin of Being through the notion of a Beyond-Being that causes itself and thus all other things. Self-causation is the logical and metaphysical miracle that is needed to ground ontological and meontological discourse in a more fundamental reality: the unification of Being and NonBeing, of all things and no thing. If then, Plotinus' theory concerns not merely the notion that The One can be described both ontologically and meontologically, but also *requires* that both descriptions merge into a higher paradox, then that theory must be accounted self-contradictory and impossible.

But this is not all. For the dilemma that arises from the superimposition of the first and second modes of discourse arises, *mutatis mutandum,* in describing the relation between *Nous* and The One. Consequently, any attempt to bridge the relation between the first two Hypostases by means of causality is bound to end in the same impossible self-contradiction.

Is the tradition of positive and negative theology brought to an end with these considerations? While this final question invites a lengthy response, I would like to offer just a few suggestions here.

The third or paradoxical mode of discourse is actually an altogether different and distinct kind of discourse from the first two. While it employs the first two as its "matter," so to speak, its form is intrinsically different. The impossibility of the third mode of discourse does not imply the impossibility of the first two modes if those modes are kept distinct and not combined into some kind of more ultimate language. There may be good reasons for speaking of Non-Being, and for speaking of Being; but there are no good reasons for believing they are the same or causally related. To use Plotinian terminology, both the First and the Second Hypostases, both The One and *Nous,* may be real; but neither can have the qualities of the other, and no causal language can be used to show their unity potentially or actually.

In short, positive and negative theology may have some justification if and only if they are not subsumed into a single, unified theology. Positive and negative theology have as their respective metaphysical concerns Being and Non-Being. The boundaries between them must be respected if contradictions are not to arise.

To suggest that positive and negative theology are not concerned about the same underlying reality is fatal to any monism, whether theistic or pantheistic, and thus to much of Western religious thought. Ironically, however, it was Plotinus and his progenitors who provided one of the few nonmonistic theologies of the West. Thus while Plotinus' final solution to the problem of the relation between positive and negative theology is unacceptable, it may be to Plotinus, and not to the Western religions, that we must look to find a satisfactory solution to this very problem.*

*I wish to express my gratitude to Dr. John Kultgen and Dr. Joseph Bien, both of the University of Missouri at Columbia, for their helpful advice and criticisms.

Vertical Causation in Plotinus

MICHAEL F. WAGNER

The core of Plotinus' philosophy is his theory of the progression (πρόοδος) with its three hypostases: the One, Intellect, and Soul. The theory states, roughly, that Intellect is a progression from the One, that Soul is a progression from Intellect and that this progression is the real metaphysical foundation of our universe. Accordingly, the bulk of contemporary scholarship on Plotinus has focused upon understanding the hypostases, their progression and their relation to our universe, and various related textual and philosophical issues.

In this essay, I shall focus upon Intellect—the Plotinian successor to Plato's Forms—and its relation to our universe. This second concern will require some discussion of Soul as well. I shall present an interpretation of Intellect and its progression that challenges some assumptions commonly made by Plotinian scholars. I shall also give serious treatment to Plotinus' criticisms of Aristotelian categorial theory and Aristotelian hylomorphism and to Plotinus' use of "Being," "Same," "Different," "Motion," and "Rest" in *Ennead* VI. Finally, I shall explain the primary philosophical role which the theory of progression plays in Plotinus' philosophy: What philosophical work does the theory of progression do for Plotinus?

As with any systematic interpretation of a philosopher, my interpretation of Plotinus may require some adjustments and qualifications as it is brought to bear on more and more actual texts. Moreover, I shall not commit myself on issues of Plotinus' consistency throughout the entire *Enneads* on all points of his philosophy. I shall, however, tie my interpretation to significant texts and I am convinced of the spirit, if not all the details, of my interpretation.

One assumption commonly made by Plotinian scholars is that Plotinus embraces a real *physical* world. John Rist, for example, seems to attribute a real physical universe to Plotinus throughout *Plotinus: The Road to Reality,* with the possible exception of his chapter "The Sensible Object."[1] A. H. Armstrong, similarly, discusses Plotinus' views about the *physical* universe throughout chapter 14 of *The Cambridge History,* although Armstrong also makes the puzzling and apparently inconsistent claim that "Plotinus is so concerned to stress the unreality of matter that he makes it very clear that anything observable *in the material universe* . . . is form, not matter" (p. 231; my emphasis).[2] Perhaps Plotinian scholars do not make this assumption and I have misconstrued their talk about the physical or material universe, but they are certainly confusing on the matter. I shall argue, in contrast, that Plotinus definitely does not embrace a real physical universe.

Accounts of Intellect and its progression commonly take what might be called Plotinus' noumenatic vocabulary as basic in the *Enneads.*[3] Contemplation, intellection, intelligibles, and the like are commonly taken as Plotinus' most perspicuous notions for explicating the nature of his Forms and of Intellect's progression. Thus, Armstrong maintains that for Plotinus

> our thought about intellect, if it [is] to have any content at all, must be a thought of something thinking about something, and thus involve a certain duality [of subject and object] (p. 237).

And Armstrong concludes that the Plotinian Forms, which compose Intellect, are to be construed as "a community of living minds" (p. 245).

I am less concerned with the Mentalistic twist which Armstrong gives to Intellect than I am with the exclusive emphasis upon Plotinus' noumenatics. In particular, I shall argue that Plotinus' noumenatics is not basic; it does not provide the philosophically most perspicuous way of construing Intellect and its progression. I shall not explicitly challenge any of the claims made within noumenatic interpretations of Plotinus. Rather, I shall examine the place of Plotinus' noumenatics in his complete philosophy and challenge the unquestioned importance placed upon it by Plotinian scholars. Without a doubt, Plotinus' noumenatics— which I shall also call his "vulgar" account, for reasons to be explained— dominates the *Enneads.* But this show of numbers does not prove that it is most basic to the philosophical theory presented in the *Enneads.* It might only show, for example, that Plotinus thought that it would be most perspicuous for (or perhaps acceptable to) the audiences at hand.

I

The only text I shall use in this section is *Ennead* VI.6, Plotinus' treatise "On Numbers." *Ennead* VI contains, on Porphyry's ordering of Plotinus' treatises, the most basic and philosophically precise presentations of Plotinus' philosophy. In *Ennead* VI, moreover, treatise 6 serves as a bridge between, on the one hand, Plotinus' discussions of categorial frameworks for doing metaphysics (treatises 1–3) and of the relationship between Intellect and the world we perceive (treatises 4 and 5) and, on the other hand, Plotinus' grand concluding treatises on the intelligible structure of Intellect and on the nature of the One and its relation to Intellect (treatises 7–9). I maintain that the contents of Plotinus' treatise on numbers more than justifies the place Porphyry accords it in *Ennead* VI.

Plotinus recognizes that, for most of us, reality is (or seems to be) composed of the things we perceive and which we ordinarily use our language to mention, namely, men, trees, colored things, eyes, and so on. A philosophical theory need not canonize these ordinary realities, but it must provide a basis for our talk and perceptions of them. Accordingly, the theory of progression need not be couched, when presented in its strictest and most proper form, in language obviously based upon our ordinary talk of men, trees, and so on, but it must admit of *some* characterization that grounds that talk—a characterization that renders our ordinary realities "well-founded" if not real *tout courte*. Throughout most of the *Enneads*, Plotinus does couch his theory in this latter form. *Ennead* VI.6 is unique and indispensable in its stress upon the derivative status of this characterization.[4]

In *Ennead* VI.6, Plotinus argues that an arithmetical characterization of the progression is basic. Plotinus argues that "the One and Number are primary" (VI.6.10.50), so that beings "come to be in accordance with Number" (VI.6. 15.24). Accordingly, we may talk about there being a Being (or Beings) for men—call it (or them) *man*—when basing our metaphysical account on the words of ordinary speech, but the Being(s) we are thereby referring to is really arithmetical in character: *man* is, at bottom, a principle or group of principles for ordering things in a certain way.

> Thus, Number, the First and the True, is the principle [ἀρχή] and underlying source of reality (VI.6.15.34).

Plotinus takes the initial progression from the One to be a breaking up of the One into a succession of numbers. As an initial progression from the One, the numbers are unities (see VI.6.10). Plotinus also calls these numbers "the First Numbers" (VI.6.15.34). And the first or pure numbers are to be distinguished from numbers as actually functioning to order or "number" things. The pure number Two, for example, is to be distinguished from "two" functioning to order dyads of trees, apples, parts of houses, and so on. The pure numbers that progress from the One function as arithmetical ordering principles by means of Soul. When Soul orders things in accordance with the order of pure numbers, the numbers are no longer just the resources of pure arithmetic but become principles of ordering. Plotinus calls the numbers functioning as principles of ordering "schemata," or "those which measure things in accordance with the Firsts" (VI.6.15.39).

In *Ennead* VI.6.6, Plotinus argues that the real nature of Being (or the Forms) is number functioning as schemata. Now Plotinus' claim that pure numbers progress from the One implies that they come to be in a successive and orderly manner. Plotinus does not himself spell out the theory of numbers or of arithmetical foundations which underlies his moves, and I shall not discuss Greek and Hellenistic arithmetic (and geometry) here. The point for now is that Soul's use of numbers as schemata is constrained by the ordered successiveness of the pure numbers as they progress from the One. Soul uses pure numbers so that the schemata are related to one another in a hierarchy, with more complex schemata coming from simpler schemata. In view of the general conflation in Greek and Hellenistic thought of geometry and arithmetic, moreover, the hierarchical relations of the schemata may be understood in terms of the derivation of geometrical theorems from one another and, ultimately, from the axioms and primitives of geometry.

Plotinus maintains that the extensional magnitudes of geometry result from applications of arithmetical principles of ordering to the phantasms of perception (VI.6.3.38). As we shall see, space (or extension) is a necessary feature of our using sensations to perceive things and does not exist apart from that use. Geometrical principles are thus derivative from arithmetical principles in that they are just arithmetical principles construed in terms that apply to the extended things of perception. Construed geometrically, however, the hierarchical relationship between schemata may be understood in terms of, say, the derivation of principles concerning triangles from the more basic principles concerning plane figures.

In sum, we may articulate the principles of ordering used by Soul by doing geometry, construing them as principles of geometrical objects. Ultimately, however, "enclosed" figures are measured by "discrete" figures (numbers) (VI.6.14.40). Plotinus maintains that things of magnitude do not come from real principles except insofar as their parts form a unity that is arithmetically measurable (VI.6.1.16), the extendedness of those parts again being a feature of the phantasms of sense. Two points will complete my initial sketch of Plotinus' doctrine of Intellect and its progression.

First, I have emphasized that the initial or "pure" unities function as schemata in a stepwise, orderly fashion, beginning with simpler principles from which more complex principles follow (also see VI.6.11). As the schemata become more and more complex, we get schemata which are complex enough to ground all of the structural distinctions we make concerning our ordinary realities. To show how the progression of schemata does this, we may take more complex schemata to be composed of arithmetical parts (subprinciples of ordering or subschemata) which are each further complications of the arithmetical parts of simpler schemata. In this way, we can break schemata down into the subschemata that make them up. The highly complex ordering principle(s) which is the arithmetical-cum-geometrical foundation for some man, for example, is composed of subprinciples for what we would call the man's organs (his eyes, arms, and so on).

We now have the following picture of the progression from the One. First, the One breaks up into a succession of unities, or pure numbers, which provide the foundation for Soul's orderings of things (also see VI.6.10.1–4). This provides an arithmetical-cum-geometrical foundation for structurally explaining the things we perceive and describe as men, trees, and so on. In using the numbers so that more complex schemata follow from simpler schemata, moreover, Soul introduces the means for talking about subschemata. In the words of our language, some of these subschemata are principles for ordering certain enclosed figures of sense into what we call "arms." Others are principles for ordering certain other things we perceive—or, from the point of view of each of ourselves, our visual sensations themselves—into what we call "eyes." And so on. My mention of "the words of our language" leads into the second point.

Earlier I noted that, while Plotinus' progression is at bottom arithmetical (-cum-geometrical) in character, Plotinus feels that it also provides a ground for our ordinary conceptions or talk of men and trees. This means that every distinction we perceive and have words to describe and conceptualize has a real counterpart distinction in the schemata of Intellect. We may talk about the principles and subprinciples used by Soul in words based upon our ordinary language and need not always be doing arithmetical sciences. In the last paragraph, for example, we talked about subschemata as being ordering principles for the things we call "arms," "eyes," and so forth. We might call these subschemata "the real arms," "the real eyes," and so on—or, more generally, "the real organs." And we might call the portion of hierarchy of principles-cum-subprinciples that we might appeal to in "measuring" an ordinary reality-man, "the real man." Plotinus maintains that the metaphysical principles of our ordinary realities—which he also calls "the bodylike things" (VI.6.17.25)—are schemata, but we can refer to them in terms of "what it is to be a certain living thing" or as "the First living things" (VI.6.17. 34–36); for example, as what it is to be a man or as the First man. *Ennead* VI.7, the treatise following "On Numbers," seems designed to present Intellect in this derivative way, as justified by *Ennead* VI.6.

The distinctions generated in Intellect's progression do not ground only the structural distinctions we commonly make in our ordinary realities. There are enough distinctions generated there to ground other distinctions as well. Plotinus at one point represents the initial progression from the One as providing the foundation for all the characterizing sorts of things we say about men, trees, etc., as well—that is, for our characterizing things as having qualities, as having quantities, and so forth (VI.2.21). Viewed in this way, the initial progression from the One might be thought of as a successive production of the basic predicates of a descriptively adequate language—perhaps, for example, the predicate *is six feet tall* or the predicate *is red*. The Soul's use of numbers that function as schemata becomes a use of predicates that cohere into batches of characterizings. When the Soul uses those batches to inform our perceptions, they are thereby applied to a subject. As a result, we apprehend a sortal thing by means of characterizing it (e.g., a man that is six feet tall and red). Accordingly, we might also call the batch (or batches) of predicates which ground our perceptions of men "humanity" or, in my convention, *man.*

My second point brings us to the topic of Plotinus' noumenatics. For, when the forms are construed in such an ordinary language-based way, the appeal to relations between arithmetical-cum-geometrical principles and their foundations in pure numbers and to the relations between a more primitive principle and a more derived principle in characterizing the progression of Intellect and Soul will not do. Other terms are needed. To characterize the progression of Beings (*man,* etc.), Plotinus uses the language of "intellection," "intelligibles," and, most importantly, "contemplation" (θεωρία). I have insisted in this section that this is a less perspicuous way of characterizing the progression for Plotinus; but it is also the more common way in the *Enneads,* as most of the *Enneads* seems addressed to various less sophisticated audiences which came to learn from Plotinus—the "vulgar," as it were.

In Section II, I shall supply more detail to the proper (arithmetical-cum-geometrical) way of viewing the progression. I shall also deliver on my introductory remarks concerning physical things. In Section III, I shall return to the terms of the "vulgar." Both sections, moreover, will center around the idea that Plotinus' theory of progression is primarily intended as providing a proper framework for understanding our universe—in a phrase, for real explanation of Plotinian science.

II

Plotinus maintains that the theory of progression is a theory about the real causes of our universe. In order to maintain this, Plotinus' conception of causation must be quite different from that of many modern and contemporary philosophers and, as well, from that of Aristotelians. I shall begin my discussion of some details of Plotinus' theory of progression with a discussion of causation, especially contrasting Plotinus' views with those of Aristotelians.

The notion of causation commonly has several associations not found in Plotinus, and one association which is the basis for Plotinus' denial of the others. One association is change. In preparation for my discussion of Aristotelian hylomorphism, we may distinguish two sorts of change: substantial change and change in the state of some substance. Thus, when a stone is thrown through the air and breaks a window, the change in place (motion) of the stone is a cause and the change in the window is an effect. Substantial change occurs when a substance comes into existence or ceases to exist, and may be reduced to changes in state if a person maintains that the passing away or coming to be of a substance is really a change in the state of some perduring matter. All causes and effects thus become changes in the state of some substance or matter. Substances that cause changes in state may be called "agents" and substances (or matter) that suffer effects may be called "patients." This general discussion of causation and change leads to some further associations.

First, states of substances are datable, and so changes take time or occur in time. More generally, causes and effects occur in time and agents and patients exist in time. As a result, atemporal items are commonly excluded from the causal order and references to time may be packed into analyses of causation—for example, as in the principle that a cause must precede or occur simultaneously with its effect.

Second, substances and pieces of matter are particulars. Hence, agents and patients are commonly taken to be particulars; causes and effects are particular states or changes in state. A person can (and we often do) make general causal claims (e.g., that smoking causes cancer), but actual causal connections occur only between particulars (e.g. between individual histories of smoking and individual cases of cancer). As a result, items that are not particulars (e.g., species or principles of geometry) are commonly taken to be outside of the causal order and therefore to be "abstract" rather than "concrete."

Third, regardless of a person's position on the existence of nonphysical particulars, physical bodies certainly seem to be clear instances of particulars which may be agents or patients, as in my example of the stone and the window. (But, again, even the Mentalist's nonphysical agents or nonphysical datable states are particulars—e.g., selves and volitions.) The physical universe is thus commonly taken to be a prime example of a causal order.

I shall call a theory which associates causation with change, temporality, particularity, or physicality a *theory of horizontal causation*. The problems with theories of horizontal causation are well known. One problem such theories have to face is how a relation between particular (hence, contingent) things or "states" (however loosely construed) could be a necessary relation. Another related problem is how, even assuming that horizontal causes may be necessary, we could ever be certain that we have a necessary connection in doing science (or anything else, for that matter). In view of such problems, causation (either as such or as knowable by us) often becomes nothing more than, for example, a conjunction of particulars or of particular states in a temporal sequence. Causal laws become inductive generalizations or expressions of probabilities, subjective expectations, or relations between the concepts by means of which particulars are apprehended.

Plotinus holds what I call a *theory of vertical causation*. On Plotinus' theory, the real causal order is atemporal (eternal) and unchanging; bodies are never causal agents and, indeed, bodies as founded on the real causal order are not particulars or physical at all. Only principles or Forms are real (vertical) agents and are, in this sense, concrete. Real "bodylike things"—men, trees, etc., as given a place in the real causal order—are "copies" of principles (or schemata). Using some Leibnizian jargon, real bodies are noumenal, where the contrast with noumenal bodies are not *physical* bodies but "things" apprehended by means of sensations—that is, *phenomenal* bodies.[5] A noumenal body is, in short, a schema as being the real foundation for (or, from here on, being the explanatory cause of) the perceptual objects we ordinarily take to be the real causes of our sensations. In Section I, I called noumenal bodies and their parts "the real organs," "the real man," or "the real tree." Our ordinary realities are really only phenomenal bodies for Plotinus.

A common association with causation that Plotinus does accept is that appeals to causes must yield explanations. But Plotinus sharply distinguishes perceptions of a world of phenomenal bodies from real explanation. Horizontal causes and effects are features of the world we discern (κρίνει) by means of the materials of sense.[6] But the discerning of phenomenal bodies is an activity which, as such, *explains* nothing about the things discerned. For an analogy to this discerning or perceptual making, a sculptor's sculpting of a statue provides a basis for explaining the statue only insofar as his motions and the resulting statue fall under principles of craftsmanship and they are considered as following in the order of principles, that is, being noumenal.

Intellect is the agent which, on Plotinus' theory, causes the noumenal universe to exist (and in a way the phenomenal universe as well). Soul is the activity by means of which the vertical progression and the end product of a universe is brought about. Body, construed as making a positive contribution to Soul's activity (namely, rendering its products phenomenal in the case of Soul's perceptual activities), is characterized by Plotinus as a "dumb" laborer (IV.3.26.7). And noumenal body, or body truly considered as following from principles of ordering, is not even a "dumb" *laborer*—it does not act at all—but is introduced in the progression as a result of introducing the notion of *Soul's* acting. Soul, on the other hand, is essentially active in that it is always the imparting of actuality to (or the making of) body, or "the other" (I.1.2.2–8). And Soul gets its principles of making from Intellect, so that Plotinus also characterizes Soul as the means by which (δία μέσου) Intellect acts (IV.3.11.18).

The idea that Soul is a progression from Intellect is implicit in the claim that Soul is that by means of which Intellect acts. Intellect acts only and always by means of Soul so that the function of Intellect is to render the universe ("the others") intelligible. Conversely, Soul is essentially active only in virtue of its being the acting of Intellect so that the universe which comes to be in Soul's activity is wholly intelligible. Intellect and Soul thus function together in Plotinus' system so that the universe is explanable and is neither physical nor wholly phenomenal.

In order fully to articulate Plotinus' framework for explanation, the progression, we must distinguish four kinds of soul: the hypostasis Soul, the World Soul, species souls, and individual souls. If these four kinds of soul are not distinguished for Plotinus, much of the *Enneads* become unintelligible. The mention of Soul in the context of discussing phenomenal bodies addresses individual souls. My use of "Soul" in Section I addresses the World Soul. And my claim that men, etc., are ultimately to be traced into the noumenal order only as "copies" of the Forms or schemata and not as items which add a positive nature of their own to the causal order (e.g., a physical nature) addresses Soul. What was said in Section I about organs, finally, has a bearing on species souls.

Intellect simply produces a universe by means of Soul (IV.3.11.18). But within this most basic role of being Intellect's acting, soul is said to be a one from which the "soul of the all" and all the "other souls" come (IV.3.4.14–16). The soul of the all is the World Soul. By means of the World Soul, the universe is led into a unison (συμθωνία) in accordance with reason (or ratio) (IV.3.12.15). This means that, on the one hand, the basic positive notion of the way Intellect acts is by arithmetically ordering things and that, on the other hand, the ordering activity of Intellect is most clearly seen in the regular and "symphonic" motions of the phenomenal heavens.

The "other souls" are individual souls, the means by which Intellect acts by means of the schematic copies of the World Soul so that we may ascribe activities to noumenal bodies themselves. The only sort of case here that Plotinus is interested in is conceptual activities of noumenal men—that is, our discernings of a phenomenal world and our reasoning. Whether the motions we ascribe to phenomenal animals and plants are to be seen as due to individual souls in the noumenal world or whether these are somehow due just to the World Soul alone is unclear in the *Enneads*.

Finally, in addition to the World Soul and individual souls, there are also souls that are "fastened in a succession to each of the Intellects [Forms], being the rationales and unfoldings of them" (IV.3.5.9–10). These are species souls and they are based upon the idea introduced in Section I that more complex schemata follow from simpler schemata in such a way that their increasing complexity comes from complications of the arithmetical components of simpler schemata. When this idea is articulated in terms of the systematic way in which the World Soul schematizes noumenal bodies, we have the idea of species souls—but much more on this later.

The fourfold distinction between kinds of soul may be directly expressed in terms of the distinction between noumenal and phenomenal bodies—the products of soul's activities. Three ways in which Plotinus talks about bodies are especially relevant. First, qua produced by Intellect: bodies are simply "copies of the Beings" (III.6.11.3). As seen in Section I, however, the most proper way of talking about the real nature of Being is arithmetically (and/or geometrically). Qua being produced according to principles of order when produced by means of Soul, secondly: bodies are "schematized things" (σχημάτιοσμα) (IV.4.33.34). As we shall see, Plotinus takes the initial products of schematization that all more-complex schematizations order to be air, earth, fire, and water (V.9.3.15–18). Third, qua being objects discerned by means of sensations: bodies are "perceptual objects" only—in my words, phenomenal bodies.

A crucial step in Plotinus' argument is the claim that in using sensations to discern a phenomenal world, we are not thereby discerning the real nature of bodies. Plotinus claims that his own conception of bodies is based upon the absence of reality (ὑποστάσεως) in phenomenal bodies as such (III.6.12.10).[7] We ordinarily suppose that bodies are colored, emit sounds, and so forth. But in reality, (noumenal) bodies "have nothing of the sorts usually supposed of them" (III.6.12.24). Plotinus does not even ascribe sensory shape (μορθή) to real bodies.

Color is likewise said to be an appearance (θαίνεσθαι) of what is not really colored (III.6.12.31).

At least part of Plotinus' reason for claiming that phenomenal bodies are "unreal" is that they are not causes or causal agents; they are always just products of individual souls' uses of sensations in perceiving. They are thus, in my words, not concrete. The men, trees, and so forth, that we perceive do not really cause even our sensations of them. The origins of our sensations or impressions (τύτοι) may be initially accounted for in terms of their having external, bodily causes. We might say that color sensations, for example, result from light activity in a medium initiated by an external luminous body (IV.5.7). Or we might say that sound sensations result from air vibrations, again initiated by some external body (IV.5.5). And analogous accounts can, presumably, be given for the other senses (except insofar as we would say that a medium is not required). In general, however, Plotinus says very little about the "horizontal" mechanics of sensations and perceptions.

Two important points need to be made here. First, Plotinus does clearly hold that a noumenal (ultimately, arithmetical-cum-geometrical) backing can be given to those horizontal accounts of causation that take bodies to be structural in nature. Plotinus seems quite satisfied with standard structural (perhaps Stoic) accounts of the horizontal mechanics of sensations and perceptions. Second, the reason why Plotinus himself shows a lack of concern for actually giving any detailed horizontal accounts is the theory of vertical causation and his overriding concern to emphasize the philosophical point of that theory. On the theory of vertical causation, real explanations are to be given in terms of Intellect's acting by means of soul, and any horizontal account must be cashed out in terms of its noumenal backing if it is to be shown to be of any real explanatory value. Plotinus hints at doing just this in *Ennead* IV.5.7, replacing the horizontal account in which light proceeds from a luminous body with an account in which something simply *is* (or has its being) in accordance with the form of luminous body (IV.5.7,36). Let us now look more closely at Plotinus' conception of bodies in order to clarify matters.

Plotinus' theory of vertical causation carries with it a doctrine on the real nature of bodies, as I have already hinted. In particular, real bodies are noumenal in nature; real bodies are men and the like considered solely as being the orderings prescribed by schemata, and they are not the phenomenal bodies we commonly identify with them. As a result, Plotinus' reply to a question like, "But what is being *ordered* by schemata?" must not introduce a material base or receptacle but must be couched in terms that can be unpacked in terms of the noumenal order alone. Accordingly, Plotinus holds what I call a noumenal hylomorphism, according to which noumenal bodies are complexes of matter and form but where "matter" and "form" is to be unpacked in terms of the stepwise way in which the World Soul acts.

Plotinus' noumenal universe may be thought of as having the most basic or simple orderings—call them air, earth, fire, and water—which the World Soul renders more and more complex as it mimics or copies the hierarchy of schemata.

Air, earth, fire, and water become "matter" for complex things by being associated with the four "first" or simplest schemata from which the World Soul works in its progressive activity. And if one asks Plotinus, "But what receives the first, most basic orderings?," his answer would have to be that nothing does; we must start somewhere, so let us start with something intelligible in nature rather than with any of the "bastard notions" (to adapt Plato's well-known phrase) of previous metaphysicians.

Plotinus takes Aristotle to be a prime example of a metaphysician who imports such "bastard notions" and who takes particulars to be real causal agents. An integral part of the Aristotelian conception of causation is the doctrine of hylomorphism, according to which particulars are informed matter. Plotinus rejects Aristotelian hylomorphism as a doctrine of the nature of real bodies. Plotinus' schematized things are indeed complex, but not in the Aristotelian manner. Moreover, the four elements which serve as "matter" for schematization are themselves not complex at all, just being the first and most basic acts of the World Soul. Being the firsts that all subsequent schematizations presuppose, the elements are called "simples" by Plotinus. Plotinus argues that elemental fire, for example, does not come to be by a substrate's receiving some sort of shape or by something's being set on fire (III.6.12.37). Plotinus rejects the notion of a substrate that receives shape (III.6.12.11), insisting that elemental fire is just a feature of the vertical order itself.

Plotinus' general explication of hylomorphism in *Ennead* V juxtaposes his own noumenal hylomorphism for complex bodies with an Aristotelian account of the elements or "simples."

> We see neither the things which are said to be wholly complex nor the simples as a one. . . . Thus, on the one hand, those naturally more complex things—the ones with substructures and which we call "compounded together"—divide first according to the Form which constrains the whole compound: a man, for example, first divides into a soul and a body, the body dividing in turn into the four elements. But, on the other hand, there are also those "compounds" [the simples] which result from matter having been shaped; for the matter of the elements is by itself shapeless. And, you will ask, from whence does the form come into matter? . . . But here too, the account [hylomorphism] has it, the substrate receives shape (V.9.3.8ff).

Plotinus shifts in this passage using "soul" and "body" when discussing complex things to using "shape" and "substrate" when discussing the elements. The reason for this shift in vocabulary is that hylomorphism is not wholly misguided in the case of complex bodies. Complex bodies are indeed complex, albeit not complex through being Aristotelian-informed matter. But no such concession is to be made for a hylomorphic construal of the elements. Phenomenal fire (the fire we see)—for example, the fire I discern in the fireplace—may be construed as complex, being a perceived subject which is hot or colored; but real elemental fire is not complex at all (IV.4.13.19–25).

As Plotinus sees it, the doctrine that real bodies are informed matter (or shaped substrate) misuses the fact that phenomenal bodies are always taken by us to be compounds (IV.4.13.19–25). Aristotelian hylomorphism takes our ordinary, perceptually based beliefs as serious metaphysical accounts of the real universe. We ordinarily take phenomenal bodies ("the things we see") as compounds (e.g., round balls, red barns) and Aristotelian hylomorphism turns this belief into a metaphysical doctrine about the real nature of bodies. Being a general metaphysical doctrine, moreover, the resulting hylomorphism is then applied even to the elements.

Plotinus maintains, in contrast, that the only sort of distinction that can be drawn in real bodies must be based upon something within the vertical order of the schemata. The only distinction there which would seem to do the job is the distinction between more complex schemata and simpler schemata; or, what comes to the same thing, the coming-to-be of a more complex schema from a simpler one in such a way that it is composed of subschemata or noumenal parts. In the case of the simplest schemata—those whose pure arithmetical foundations lie in the first numbers in the progression from the One—no such distinction can be drawn. The first schemata have no subschemata because there are no still simpler schemata for them to come from; they are therefore "simples," and may be taken as the real foundations for the elements of a physics.

After the simples, however, the activities of the World Soul may be taken as complications on the initial schemata (the elements). And at each stage in the World Soul's schematizing after the elemental stage, we can distinguish between the complications of the four elements (call it "body") and the fact that the resulting complex ordering is a structural unity in its own right, in virtue of its schema—the schema used by the World Soul owing its unity in turn to its being just a complication of a simpler schema, and so on up to the simplest schemata. Plotinus calls the structural unity of a complex ordering "the form constraining the whole" or just "soul," where the sort of soul being mentioned here is what I have called species soul. A species soul is a schema qua unifying an ordering activity of the World Soul. Plotinus also calls species souls "capacities" (δυναμεῖς) and their connection with schemata is as follows:

> Schemata have capacities, for the one is together with the other and vice versa. It is by means of capacities and schemata, then, that each [noumenal] thing is schematized and comes to be. . . . Thus, schemata are essentially such that they have capacities (IV.4.35.46–49).

Earlier I noted that a more complex schema may be thought of either (1) as a whole which is just more complex than a simpler schema, or (2) as a whole whose greater complexity may be broken down into subschemata. Accordingly, the noumenal (ultimately, arithmetical) items or "elements" that come to be in an ordering activity of the World Soul may be thought of either (1) as being just items in the ordering as a whole, or (2) as items in suborderings which, in turn, are ordered into the "measurable" whole. Taken in this latter way, Plotinus calls the capacities (species souls) that order noumenal items first and foremost into suborderings and only derivatively into the whole "capacities to undergo" (παθήτιχοι). Taken in the former and more direct way, Plotinus calls the capacities just "capacities"; he does not introduce a special term for them. I shall call them "capacities proper."

Expressed from the "vulgar" or phenomenal-body side, capacities to undergo are those capacities whose actualizations—the items they order—must occur in some one organ of the body. The capacity for vision, for example, is a capacity to undergo because whenever it is actualized, the eyes are the patients in which it is actualized (III.6.2.53).[8] In the noumenal body, actualizations of the capacity for vision are those noumenal items which are ordered into certain suborderings (the noumenal eyes), these suborderings providing the noumenal foundations for ordering visual sensations into phenomenal eyes.

Unlike actualizations of capacities to undergo (call them "undergoings", actualizations of capacities proper (call them "activities") are not essentially ordered into particular noumenal (and, derivatively, phenomenal) organs. Man's perceptions and reasonings are clear Plotinian examples of activities in this sense, so that conceptual activities differ from sensory or "bodily" undergoings (at least in part) in that their structural role is prescribed by the noumenal body as a whole rather than by noumenal organs.[9] Speaking with the vulgar, my *eyes* sense colors while *I* (as a whole, as a person, or whatever) perceive colored things.

Put in more schematic terms, Plotinus' idea seems to be that impressions (τύποι) are sensations to the extent that they are ordered by the subschemata of noumenal bodies, and impressions are, at the same time, used by the soul to discern things to the extent that their role in the noumenal body as a whole is such that they partially replicate the orderings that we call "other things"—for example, the noumenal body grounding the phenomenal tree I am discerning or the noumenal body grounding the phenomenal moon you and I are both discerning. In this way, certain orderings in my noumenal body play roles relative to my whole noumenal body that replicate the structural roles played by items ordered into other noumenal bodies relative to those whole noumenal bodies. As a result, we have a Plotinian "vertical" counterpart to the Aristotelian idea that sensation is the taking on of the ratio of another thing without its matter, which is subsequently used by the percipient's soul to perceive that other thing.

We might say for Plotinus that in perception my phenomenal body *represents* another phenomenal body (or some feature of it), with the caveat that my representing is grounded in a structural replication of some other noumenal ordering and not in there being some really existing phenomenal body which, say, causes my sensations. We may go along with the horizontal theorist a bit, as Plotinus is prepared to do, and talk about a sensation's being, say, a counterpart-redness to the redness of a phenomenal body I am perceiving. But the real, noumenal account must be kept in mind to unpack this.

I have thus far argued that Plotinus' real causes are not particulars or physical things. In addition, I have discussed Plotinus' rejection of Aristotelian hylomorphism, which is a principal source of the idea that causation involves change. In rejecting Aristotelian hylomorphism and maintaining that the basic model of causation is the coming-to-be of a more complex principle of ordering from a simpler one, Plotinus also rejects the idea that causation involves change. A related association which I have not explicitly addressed is temporality.

I shall close this section by emphasizing that Plotinus' progression does not occur through time and that his real (noumenal) universe does not exist in time as such, though it grounds those things (phenomenal bodies) that we discern as existing in time. Time and space are both relegated by Plotinus to the phantasms of sense, and they may be said to be "in" the noumenal order only to the extent that those phantasms are grounded in noumenal bodies (and, in turn, in schemata). I shall discuss time and space more as we proceed. I shall now return to the fourfold distinction between kinds of soul.

I have distinguished between Soul, the World Soul, species souls, and individual souls. At bottom, though, there is only one soul for Plotinus. Souls and what it is to be soul ($\psi\nu\chi\tilde{\eta}$ $\varepsilon\tilde{\iota}\nu\alpha\iota$—that is, the hypostasis Soul) are eternally one and the same, Plotinus maintains, where to be soul is to impart actuality to "the other" (I.1.2,2–8; IV.7.8.40–46). The imparting of actuality, in turn, is the same as the activity of Intellect. It is, as it were, Intellect progressing beyond itself, actually ordering "things" rather than being just principles of ordering. Strictly speaking, then, souls are identical with the activity of Intellect, and that activity is the only activity that really occurs in the universe. How, then, do the World Soul, species souls, and individual souls "come to be"?

Though Intellect's activity is the only real activity in the universe, that activity (i.e., Soul, or the production of the universe) can be analyzed by us in various partial ways in our attempt to articulate the vertical order and its relation to the ordinary realities we perceive. Since being is really principles of ordering, for example, Intellect's production may be thought of as orderings of schematized things, with the four elements of Greek and Hellenistic physics being grounded in the simplest or first stages of that schematizing. Soul is now being construed as the World Soul. Species souls come to be as by-products of the World Soul's activity, being expressions of the fact that the World Soul's activity reflects the systematic interrelationships between the schemata of Intellect and between the schemata and their arithmetically based (numerable) components. Individual souls are the most troublesome here. Roughly, they are certain whole orderings qua using sensory items, as discussed previously. Individual souls are also to be viewed for Plotinus as abstractions from what is really one, singular activity of Intellect.

The World Soul, species souls, and individual souls are not distinct from Soul but are notions derived by focusing upon (abstracting, in my sense of the word) certain features of Intellect's singular activity. The most difficult feature of Plotinus' views on the matters being discussed here is that Plotinus never gives us a clear account of precisely how we can move from noumena to phenomena and remain solely in the single vertical order (e.g., how phenomena can be mere abstractions from the noumenal order). Even if one maintains, as I am prepared to argue that Greek and Hellenistic philosophers do, that our sensations are not themselves objects, there still seems to be something about the phenomenal world that renders it *phenomenal* rather than noumenal, and Plotinus does not give an account of how that something comes to be in the vertical order. Thus, while Plotinus gets rid of the receptacle, substrates, and, in general, any basis for a real physical world, it is unclear how he gets rid of a positive foundation for there being a phenomenal world as such. It is one thing to say that men, trees, and the like, are really just noumenal orderings and quite another to say that Plotinus has thereby fully accounted in some manner for phenomenal men, phenomenal trees, and the like, as such and without remainder. I shall not pursue this issue here, but assume that I can get on with my explanation of Plotinus without settling the issue.

Plotinus summarizes the theme of the previous few paragraphs by maintaining that one and the same soul is identically present "everywhere" (IV.2.1; IV.3.2,3) but it can be considered as "becoming divided in regard to [first noumenal and then phenomenal] body" (IV.3.19.15). This last does not result in a real multiplicity of souls, however, because mention of various items called "bodies" is an abstraction from the single productive activity of Intellect. Similarly, Plotinus emphasizes my atemporality theme by claiming that in order to grasp bodies as they really are, we must consider the noumenal copy of Intellect in accordance with the eternal manner in which it comes to be as an entirety (IV.3.10.12). We must think of real body as coming from Intellect "all at once" (V.8.7.17) and not serially or by a succession of acts.[10] Intellect's production of the universe is not just the only *kind* of real activity there is in the universe; there is only one such act—*the* production of the noumenal universe as an eternal whole. In short, Plotinus maintains, the *universe* is a copy of True Substance (Intellect) only when taken as a timeless whole (VI.3.3.31). No abstractable part of it is a copy, those abstractable parts themselves being in time only when apprehended by means of sensations, as particulars discerned by individual souls.

III

Section II focused on Plotinus' conception of causation, emphasizing more what it is not than what it is and relying on the discussion of Section I for filling in the latter. In its most basic formulation, Intellect's progression is strictly analogous to the derivation of more derived theorems of arithmetic (and/or geometry) from more basic theorems, and these in turn from the basic axioms and primitive resources of arithmetic. Soul enters the theory of progression as the notion of principles of ordering actually yielding orderings. The progression stops with the soul's activity, however, and the question, *"What* is thereby ordered by Soul?" is a bad question in Plotinus' view. As a result, however, I have noted the difficulties which Plotinus is left with concerning sensations and the discerning (or from the vertical order's point of view, abstracting) of a *phenomenal* world.

This section will develop the account Plotinus gives of the progression in terms that more directly ground our talk of men, trees, etc.—what in my introduction I called Plotinus noumenatics. But in so doing, I shall also emphasize certain features of the proper account, for example, that each lower level in Intellect is an arithmetical-cum-geometrical complication of a higher level which is "derived" from it rather than adding something to it. Important details will be added to the proper account as well.

Plotinus maintains that the best way for us to understand in a more ordinary or "vulgar" way how the progression of Intellect occurs is in terms of the notion of contemplation (θεωρία). Plotinus argues that "natural production" is not a matter of "pushing and levering" (III.8.2.5).[11] It is not a matter, for example, of arranging or rearranging material atoms or of pushing on and impressing a material substrate. In *Ennead* III.8, Plotinus argues that natural production is a matter of contemplation. By natural production, Plotinus has in mind the production of the real universe; but, as we shall see, the notion of contemplation is also used by Plotinus for the progression of Intellect itself.

I shall focus on the more basic progression, that of Intellect itself, and discuss how Plotinus' contemplation account supplements the proper account outlined in Section I. My discussion will have three parts. First, I shall discuss Plotinus' view that Aristotelian metaphysics does not provide an adequate framework for real explanation. Second, I shall discuss why an Aristotelian framework is inadequate. Third, these two discussions will provide a basis for explaining Plotinus' framework and the sort of ground Plotinus feels his framework provides for more "ordinary" Platonic explanations of men, trees, etc. in terms of contemplation.

Plotinus discusses Aristotelian categories in *Ennead* VI. 3, and he argues that they provide a means for categorizing the phenomenal world which, like Aristotelian hylomorphism, will not do for a serious metaphysical account of the real universe. Plotinus' own Aristotelian-type categorial framework for the phenomenal world begins with two basic categories: substances and things concerning substances. A substance is that which is "neither in a subject nor concerns another subject" (VI. 3.5.14–15). Socrates or a man is a subtance, for example, because in discerning something as Socrates or as a man, we are discerning the subject of the perception itself rather than a subject as relative to something else. A man is not a man *of* some subject; rather, a subject of perception just *is a* man.

Plotinus then divides things concerning substances into what he calls "categories" and accidents. Plotinus "categories" are the obvious relative-to's (πρὸς τι) of Aristotle's *Categories*—for example, a slave, which is relative to a master, or a cause, which is relative to an effect. To call them relative-to's means, roughly, that a slave is not a slave unless there is some other subject that is a master. In short, there are slaves in the world if and only if there are masters which the slaves are the slaves *of* (VI.3.3.31).

Unlike "categories," an accident is not relative to some *other subject,* but it is still a relative-to. A color, for example, is always a color *of* something (in particular, *of* some substance—a man, a tree, etc.). In general, a quality, for example, "is a capacity to impute by means of itself the 'what a quality is' to substances" (VI.1.10.19). That is, qualities are such that we impute the "what they are" (e.g., white) to substances. A similar remark holds for all accidents, which include quantity, quality, and *space* and *time* as well (VI.3.3). As a result, things concerning substances collapse into relative-to's; they always presuppose something else for their existence in the world, and so this something else is always needed in any explanation of them. Substances help explain things concerning substances but not vice versa.

The next, and most important, step Plotinus makes is to reduce substances to relative-to's as well. Substances are not relative to other substances (or subjects of perceptions) but they are still relative-to's. In particular, the substances of the phenomenal world are relative to our perceptions (or discernments) of them. The substances of the phenomenal world depend for their existence upon our perceptions rather than helping explain the phenomenal world. Phenomenal bodies are items that individual souls make by means of sensations, and their substance is a result of that making.[12] Accordingly, Plotinus defends his reduction of substances to relative-to's by cautioning that

> what has been said is not absurd since the account concerns the substance of a perceptual object . . . [and a perceptual object is always] relative to a perception (VI.3.10.12–14).

Plotinus' basic criticism of Aristotelian-type categories is that they apply to things only relative to our discernments of them. The phenomenal world is to be explained by means of what explains our perceptions, and it does not exist independent of our discerning it. In order to see why this result renders Aristotelian-type categories inadequate as a framework for real explanation, a few more explicit words about the nature of relative-to's are needed. As we shall see, it is not just being a relative-to that disqualifies a category from serious metaphysical usage; it is being a relative-to that is relative only to our conceptual activities (e.g., perceptions), which disqualifies a category in this way. Plotinus maintains that a categorial framework for real explanation must explain or constrain our own conceptual activities as well as the ordinary realities we initially wanted explained. This brings us to the second part of this section.

As Plotinus sees it, real explanation must consist in giving reasons (λόγοι); and reasons—I shall also call them "rationales" to clearly distinguish them from the activity of reasoning (διανοία)—are tied up with relative-to's in two ways: first, in their internal structure and, second, in their relations to what they are reasons *of*. The first is based on the fact that rationales are always more complex than what they are rationales *of*. "Everything comes out as compounded," Plotinus claims, "when analyzed by means of rationales and reasoning" (IV.3.9.19–20).

Using the Aristotelian doctrine that bodies are informed matter as an example, we can say that "informed matter" is a rationale of "bodies" and that the items in the rationale are each relative to the other. The sense of the term "form" and the sense of the term "matter" each depend upon the sense of the rationale informed matter, so that nothing is informed but matter and matter must always be informed. The first sense in which rationales generally are tied up with relative-to's is analogous to this Aristotelian example, that is, a rationale is always a complex whose parts are essentially relative to one another. The significance of this point for explanatory rationales and for distinguishing them from nonexplanatory rationales can be brought out by using Plotinus' own example of the relative-to's *double* and *half*.

Double and half are relative to one another (for short, they are correlatives) because they

> occur relative to one another . . . and such that the former is not prior to the latter and vice versa, but they occur simultaneously (VI.1.7.34–38).

The import of this passage is that nothing is a double or a half by itself but only relative to something else. Four, for example, is a double only relative to two, and two is a half only relative to four. Moreover, four is not a double in virtue of two's being a number, being less than four, or whatever, but only insofar as two is simultaneously taken as a half. In short, correlative terms perspicuously apply only together and not separately.

A further and more important point, however, is that four may also be a half (viz., when considered relative to eight when eight is simultaneously taken as a double). A similar point can be made about two's being a double relative to one taken as a half. Thus, this pair of correlatives, double and half, are variable in their applications to numbers and to things.

I have just noted two features of correlatives. First, correlatives are mutually dependent upon one another; they apply only together and not separately. Second, at least some correlatives are variable or "mutable." Something might be a double when considered relative to one number, for example, and a half when considered relative to another number. It is this second feature of certain correlatives that renders them inadequate for use in a rationale that really explains something. Plotinus feels that a real explanation must employ rationales which apply immutably. This brings us to the second way in which rationales are tied up with relative-to's; namely, in the relation between a rationale and what it is a rational *of*.

The second way in which rationales are tied up with relative-to's may be introduced by saying that the correlatives internal to a rationale do not apply to something(s) *in vaccuo* but only from what I shall call "a point of view." Four is the double of two and two is half of four, for example, only from the point of view of their numerical ratio. More importantly, Plotinus maintains, on the basis of what was said in Section II about Aristotelian hylomorphism and what has been said in this section about Aristotelian categories, that body is informed matter (or a substance-thing concerning substance compound) only from the point of view of human percipients. Real explanatory rationales, in contrast, must apply from a point of view which humans *may* occupy but which does not depend essentially upon their doing so. This second restriction on explanatory rationales is related to the first in that one test for whether or not a rationale depends essentially upon humans occupying the point of view from which it applies is whether or not there is any variability in how we use it.

Plotinus argues in *Ennead* VI.2 that a categorial framework which makes real explanation possible is provided by "Being, Same, Different, Motion, and Rest."[13] I shall call these five the *Platonic genera*. To what extent Plotinus' use of these five is the same as Plato's (e.g., in *Timeaus* or *Sophist*) will not be discussed here. Plotinus' motivation for adopting the Platonic genera, presented in *Ennead* VI.2. 7,8, uses the notion of relative-to's (or correlatives). That motivation may be understood in terms of the doctrine that explanatory rationales must not be variable in their application or depend essentially upon human perceivers (or, more generally, conceivers).

In particular, Plotinus maintains: (1) The items in a Platonic rationale are always differents; thus, a Platonic rationale always applies to something only as a different; and (2) the point of view from which rationales of differents apply is just Sameness itself. Anyone who begins with Plotinus' principles of being (the Platonic genera) taken as primitive must, in principle at least, always arrive at the same explanation or set of rationales. In sum, Plotinus takes the Platonic genera to prescribe a methodology (generally called "dialectic") for systematically and non-arbitrarily arriving at a set of rationales and which, therefore, determines how we reason rather than our reasoning determining the rationales.

The foregoing introduction of the Platonic genera indicates that Same and Different are the most important of the five. In *Ennead* VI.2.7.8, Plotinus explicates the function of the Platonic genera as follows. Motion accounts for the basic progression of Intellect. But Rest applies simultaneously with Motion, so that the "motion" of Intellect is eternal. The nature of Intellect's motion is unpacked in terms of Same and Different. More precisely, Intellect's motion is unpacked in terms of differentiation, and differentiation is based upon Different; for "everything after a differentiation stands dual [or as a dyad], destroying the One" (VI.2. 9.16). Moreover, differentiation presupposes that there is something that is differentiated—something that the resulting differents are different *of*. Accordingly, Same enters as the point of view from which differents *are*. Rationales which articulate Intellect are, in short, dyads of differents which each apply in virtue of a same.

Thus far in this section, I have discussed what is inadequate about Aristotelian-type frameworks for doing metaphysics and why the Platonic genera will do the job. This last can be seen more clearly by relating my discussion of the Platonic genera to the account outlined in Section I. Recall that in its initial progression from the One, Intellect is a succession of the resources of pure arithmetic (-cum-geometry). Similarly, we have just seen that the "motion" of Intellect is a successive differentiation into dyads. From the One, taken as Same rather than as the *tout courte,* Different yields a dyad. From each different in that dyad, we get another dyad, and so on.[4] Taken as the pure progression of a first dyad from the One and then of successive dyads from the pure differents of the first and of each subsequent dyad, Intellect is the resource for pure arithmetic. Taken as the ground for the basic resources of our language, these differents are forms called after the predicates of our language; they are no longer "pure" but now have "conceptual content." Taken in this latter way, moreover, the progression of Intellect from the One is a genus-species hierarchy.

Plotinus summarizes the dual way in which the progression of Intellect may be construed, and in a manner which preserves the point made in Section I that the latter ("vulgar") way is secondary to the former (arithmetical), as follows:

> All intellectual objects are structured into one nature, such that Intellect is composed of all of them. This we call Being, and it is a system. If this is the case, then not only are they [i.e., the Platonic genera] genera but they are at the same time the principles holding for Being. They are genera because from them come other lesser genera and after those come species and finally the uncutables [or atoms]. And they are also principles because Being is thus from a many and the entire thing [i.e., Intellect] comes from them (VI.2.2,8–14).

In this passage, which expresses the view Plotinus proceeds to adopt later in the treatise, Plotinus argues (1) that the Platonic genera generates Intellect as a genera-species hierarchy, but (2) this hierarchical construal of Intellect is secondary to the Platonic genera's being principles—principles (ἀρχαί) which, according to *Ennead* VI.6, generate the successive unities-cum-schemata of the proper account. The most proper sort of rationales to be given in real explanation are schematic; they are nonarbitrary and they determine human arithmetical-cum-geometrical reasoning for Plotinus, as truths of arithmetic and/or geometry do for many other philosophers as well. Moreover, this same sort of necessity is shared by genera-species hierarchies articulated by using our language and conceptual abilities as the material for dialectic, the counterpart in the genera-species case to arithmetical deduction being contemplation, to which I shall now turn.

Plotinus is sensitive to what his metaphysics does and does not allow us to say about the real universe. Two related things that Plotinus' metaphysics does *not* warrant us in saying are: (1) that principles and real bodies differ from one another spatially or temporally, and (2) that principles differ from one another in some more "ontologically grounded" sense than just that one is expressible by a more or by a less complex rationale (or level of rationales) than another one is—whether these rationales be expressed in the words we use doing arithmetic or geometry or in the more ordinary words we use in articulating genera-species hierarchies.

Contemplation is an especially useful notion in emphasizing these two points because, as Plotinus understands it, contemplation is an activity in which one understands something by producing or exfoliating what is implicit in it—as when a geometer seeks to understand geometry by tracing the entailments of its basic axioms and primitives.[15] Applies to Intellect, the idea becomes that Intellect progresses by means of contemplation in that every lower level of differents is an articulation of (rather than an addition to) what is implicit in a higher level, in view of the "primitives" and "axioms" of being—that is, the Platonic genera and how they function.

The essential feature of contemplation is that it is the articulation of something implicit in the resources used by the contemplater. Spatiality and temporality are not essential features of contemplation as they are with "pushing" and "levering"—and as temporality at least might be in the special case of a *human* contemplater. Plotinus emphasizes the atemporality of contemplation as such in saying that producing has been revealed by us to [in reality] be contemplation. For it is the perfection of a contemplation to remain contemplation and not to be *doing* any particular thing. With respect to what it is, we might say that contemplation is a "having had produced" (III.8.3.21).

Plotinus expresses the second point above, that "ontological difference" in Intellect is solely a matter of differing complexities in the rationales (or levels of rationales) used to articulate its implicit structure, in terms of contemplation as well, claiming that a rationale is really *both* a contemplation and the object of the contemplation (III.8.4).

A rationale is an object of contemplation in virtue of its complexity and it is also a contemplation in virtue of its unity.[16] As in the case of species souls, the distinction between the unifying measure (or unity) of a particular level in Intellect and the simpler level from which it comes is a distinction that collapses; the distinction collapses because, throughout his account, Plotinus has in mind that everything in Intellect is already implicit in the Platonic genera. It really does not matter except for certain limited exegetical purposes where we draw the line between what is in one level of Intellect and what is in another level. All that matters here is that Intellect does provide the ground for our articulating systems of explanatory rationales that do represent Intellect as a derivational system. Plotinus expresses this basic point in terms of contemplation as follows:

> The One is both in itself and relative to the many others. And the One is also Being, making itself into many by means of a kind of motion [i.e., differentiation]. But the resulting whole is still a one, just as contemplation is a one which works in various ways. Thus, the Being-One does not remain in itself but is the capacity for all things. And contemplation is the cause of its appearing many, such that there is intellection. For if only the One appeared, there would be no intellection but only the One. (VI.2.6.13–20).

In sum, when we move from the proper account of the progression to the "vulgar" account, Plotinus takes contemplation as the model for how the progression proceeds and what it "does," as contemplation is the articulating of what is implicit in being or, more anthropomorphically, becoming conscious of what is in one's own mind. As a result, there is a clear sense in which contemplation (or the resources of contemplation) controls the contemplater rather than vice versa. This last, of course, brings Plotinus' use of the notion of contemplation in line with the two demands for explanatory rationales discussed earlier.

Plotinus' noumenatics are indeed to be taken seriously—I do not deny that. Plotinus' noumenatic account is, however, derivative from his account in terms of pure differentiation—the successive generation of the resources for arithmetically based sciences. The connection between these two accounts lies in that the resources for our language or conceptual abilities admit of genus-species articulation. The structure of our conceptual abilities is like that of Intellect, and it provides the means for our endowing the pure sames and differents of Intellect with content. More precisely, I would argue, at another time, that Plotinus takes the conceptual content of our language to be due to its having a structure—its items playing structurally describable roles, so that Plotinus can say that the structure of Intellect causes the conceptual content of our language rather than, strictly speaking, our language endowing Intellect with content. But the subtleties of this point need not detain us here.

The Ontological Basis of Plotinus' Criticism of Aristotle's Theory of Categories

CHRISTOS EVANGELIOU

Aristotle uses or refers to the theory of categories in all his major works. The small treatise which is known to us by the conventional title *Categories*[1] is devoted exclusively to the exposition and elucidation of this theory. Traditionally, the treatise is included in the collection of the Aristotelian logical treatises and is considered a part of the *Organon*.[2] Ever since the first edition of the Aristotelian corpus prepared by Andronicus of Rhodes in the first century B.C., *Categories* has been the subject of numerous commentaries and debates among Platonists, Peripatetics, Stoics, and Neoplatonists alike.[3] The debates were considered philosophically important for the reasons that Dexippus has summarized and explained.[4] Plotinus was a later participant in those debates. Although he did not prepare a technical commentary on the *Categories*, Plotinus wrote a long treatise, an ἀντιλογία,[5] against Aristotle's theory of categories. In a long series of Platonists who found Aristotle's categories unacceptable, Plotinus was the last to criticize them.[6] Porphyry, Plotinus' most distinguished disciple, editor, commentator, and successor as head of the Neoplatonic school in Rome, was to put an end to the debates about Aristotle's categorial doctrine. In his two commentaries on the *Categories*,

Porphyry proposed an ingenious interpretation of Aristotle's categories designed to show its defensibility in theory and its usefulness.[7] As a result of Porphyry's work, after the third century A.D. and for many centuries to come the *Categories* was incorporated in the Neoplatonic logical tradition and Plotinus' ἀντιλογία was forgotten. Yet, for the student who is interested in the history of the categorial doctrine and its transformations, Plotinus' criticism of the Aristotelian categories is important for at least two reasons: first, because Plotinus is both the last and only critic whose arguments and critical remarks have been preserved in a complete form; and secondly, because his criticism is directed not against the logic but against the ontology that underlies Aristotle's categorial doctrine, so that it is devastating in its intentions, to say the least.

This essay does not offer by any means a detailed exposition and assessment of Plotinus' many and at times complicated arguments against each of the ten Aristotelian categories. Its limited scope is to explore critically the underlying principles of Plotinus' criticism of the Aristotelian categories. It is an attempt to establish the thesis that both Plotinus' rejection and his reduction of Aristotle's categories are based on grounds and considerations that are not logical but ontological in essence. It will show that, regarding the problem presented to Neoplatonism by Aristotle's categorial doctrine, Plotinus' position was determined by two basic factors: (1) the Neoplatonic ontological distinction between the intelligible realm of real being (κόσμος νοητός), and the sensible realm of mere becoming (κόσμος αἰσθήτος) related to each other as archetype (ἀρχέτυπον) to its image (εἰκὼν); and (2) the strictly ontological interpretation of Aristotle's categories which Plotinus follows. By considering the categories as "genera of being," this interpretation juxtaposed Aristotle and Plato and had to be abandoned by Porphyry, who sought the reconciliation of the two philosophers. It will become clear, I hope, that Plotinus was neither an Aristotelian in his theory of categories nor in the sense in which his disciple, Porphyry, may be called an Aristotelian.[8]

II

Plotinus' criticism of Aristotle's categories is to be found in his treatise περὶ τῶν γενῶν τοῦ ὄντος (*On the Genera of Being*). This treatise is divided into three books or parts which, according to Porphyry's thematic arrangement of the Plotinian treatises, constitute the first one-third of the sixth *Ennead* (VI.1, VI.2, VI.3). Part 1 deals with the Aristotelian tenfold (VI.1. 1–24) and the Stoic fourfold (VI.1. 25–30) theories of categories. Plotinus finds both these sets of categories unacceptable for the reason that they are irrelevant and inapplicable to the realm of real being (κόσμυς νοητός).[9] Part 2 is entirely devoted to an elaborate exposition of Plato's five *summa genera* which Plotinus considers to be both the only genera applicable to the realm of real being and the "highest genera" (πρῶτα γένη) of that realm. Part 3 deals with the realm of mere becoming (γιγνόμενον), considered as ontologically other than the realm of real being. Here Plotinus proposes a set of five categories that may be called "genera" with some allowance, but never "genera of being." Plotinus' set of categories is a radically reduced and modified list of the Aristotelian ten categories insofar as the number and the names are concerned. With the "genera of being," Plotinus' categories of becoming share in the same number, five, and some of them share the same name, which opens the door to homonymy and its dangers (VI.3.1.19–21).

From the title of Plotinus' treatise (as well as from its opening paragraph), it is clear that his purpose is to discuss the question of being (περὶ τῶν ὄντων) and to determine both the right number and the real nature of the "genera of being," in case there is a plurality of *onta*. It is precisely because he takes Aristotle's categories to be competitors of Plato's genera for the high position of the "genera of being" that Plotinus thinks it necessary to criticize and reject the former as incompatible with the latter. The only merit of the Aristotelian tenfold division of ὄντα, according to Plotinus, is that it avoids the fallacies of both the uncritical ontological monism, which reduces all kinds of being to one genus, and its contrary view which holds that *onta* are infinite in kind, thus making scientific knowledge (ἐπισεήμη) impossible (VI.1.1.8–9).[10] Plotinus thinks that Aristotle was right in proposing a definite number of genera, but he was wrong in proposing ten instead of five, as Plato had done. It is Plotinus' opinion that on this matter he is in complete agreement with Plato. In VI. 2, he defends Plato and restores his five γένη to the high position of "genera of being." Having done so, he opens VI.3 in the following way: "We have now explained our conception of Reality (True Being) and considered how far it agrees with the teaching of Plato."

However, it would be mistaken to assume that the only fault with Aristotle's categories is their number. Even if they were less than ten, the Aristotelian categories would have to be rejected for their ontological claims. The reason for this is given by Plotinus as follows: "These thinkers [the Peripatetics] are however not considering the Intellectual realm [νοητὰ] in their division; the Supreme [τὰ μάλιστα ὄντα] they overlooked" (VI.1.1.28–30). Accordingly, the Peripatetics erred in that their categorial net was intended to capture only the phenomenal world of becoming which they mistook as the real world of being which, in turn, they overlooked. It was precisely this Aristotelian mistake—to distinguish between the two levels of reality—that provided Plotinus with a basis for attacking Aristotle's categories and their ontological claims. It may be well, then, to consider in some detail the historical ontological distinction between real being and mere becoming.

III

The doctrine of the existence of two ontologically distinct realms of being, the authentic and its image, goes back to Plato's cosmology and the "likely story" told in the *Timaeus,* as is well known. It seems that the epistemological distinction between true opinion (δόξα ἀληθὴς) and knowledge (ἐπιστήτη) provided the grounds on which Plato based the ontological distinction between the sensible and the intelligible worlds.[11] In Plato's figurative language, we are told that the two realms are related as original or pattern (παράδειγμοι) to its imitation or image (εἰκών).[12] However, neither in the *Timaeus* nor in any other dialogue did Plato explain precisely (1) how the sensibles relate to the intelligibles, or (2) how the intelligibles are related to each other, or (3) what is the first unifying principle (or principles) (ἀρχαὶ) of all things. On the contrary, in a characteristic passage Timaeus remarks that no one should imagine that he has the right or the power to undertake so great and difficult a task.[13]

Now, it is true that in the *Sophist,* where the discussion is about the possibility of combination of Forms (συμβλοκὴ εἰδῶν), Plato uses five γένη (genera; kinds or Forms) in order to prove his thesis that some forms can combine and some cannot, with the corollary doctrine that each Form is both being and non-being at the same time without violating the law of contradiction. Plato's five γένη are: Being (το ὄν), rest (στάσις), motion (κίνησις), sameness (ταύτον), and difference (ἔρερον).[14] They are called "μέγιστα γένη," an expression that may mean either the "most general genera" or "the most important Forms." In Plotinus these five all-pervasive Platonic Forms are identified as "genera of being" which, in turn, are said to constitute the realm of the authentic being as its principles (ἀρχαί) and its elements (στοιχεῖα): "We have here not merely genera, but genera which are at the same time principles of Being. They are genera because they have subordinates—other genera, and successively species and individuals; they are also principles since from this plurality Being takes its rise, constituted in its entirety from these its elements" (VI.2.2.10–14).

Let it be noted here that the expression "genera of being" (γένη τοῦ ὄντος) is Plotinus' coinage. Neither Plato nor Aristotle ever used it. However, given (1) the fact that Plato's εἴδη or γένη ("forms") are ὄντους ὄντα ("really real entities") and ἀεὶ ὄντα ("unchangeable") in contrast to the sensible things that are always in the process of becoming and never actually are, and (2) the possible meaning of the expression "μέγιστα γένη" construed as "the most general and pervasive forms," it may seem permissible to use the combination "genera of beings" (in plural). This would mean that the Platonic five γένη are real beings qua Forms, and that they are genera of the other forms, by virtue of their capability to be predicated of all forms. From this possible Platonic position to that of Plotinus, who considers the five genera as both predicable and generative principles of being (in singular), there is a considerable distance. Is it possible to cover this distance without overstepping the limits set by the Platonic *Timaeus?* Plotinus thinks it is.

Be it as it may, the important point is that throughout the *Enneads,* and especially in the treatise *On the Genera of Being,* the fundamental ontological distinction between the two realms is taken for granted. Unless it is taken seriously under consideration, and stressed, a great part of Plotinus' philosophy and particularly his criticism of Aristotle cannot be properly understood and appreciated. Passages like the one that follows must be read with this ontological distinction in mind in order to make sense:

> But a graver problem confronts us at the outset: Are the ten found alike in the Intellectual and in the Sensible realms? Or are all found in the Sensible and some only in the Intellectual? All in the Intellectual and some in the Sensible is manifestly impossible.
>
> At this point it would be natural to investigate which of the ten belong to both

spheres, and whether the Existents of the Intellectual are to be ranged under one and the same genus with the Existents in the Sensible, or whether the term "Existence" (or Substance) is equivocal as applied to both realms (VI.1.1.19–24).

If we compare the respective sets of genera of the sensible and the intelligible realms, it will be easier to understand Plotinus' answer to the questions raised above:[15]

REALM OF REAL BEING		REALM OF MERE BECOMING	
1. Οὐσία	Substance	οὐσία	so-called substance
(ὄν νοῦς)		(λεγομένη)	
2. Κίνησις	Motion	ποιόν	quality
(ζωὴ ἐνέργεια)		(ποιότης)	
3. Στάσις	Rest	ποσόν	quantity
(ἀεί εἶναι)		(ποσότης)	
4. Ἕτερον	Difference	κίνησις	motion
(ἑτεροτης)		(ζωή)	
5. Ταὐτόν	Sameness	πρός τι	relation
(ταυτότης)		(σχέσις)	

Now, Plotinus' answers to the questions raised in the preceding quoted passage are as follows: (1) the number of the "genera" of becoming is the same as the number of the "genera of being," that is, five; (2) some genera of the sensible realm, such as quality and quantity, are found in the intelligible realm as well, but they are not primary (πρῶτα) in the sense that the five authentic "genera of being" are primary (VI.2.13–14); (3) it is impossible to have more genera in the intelligible realm than in the sensible realm, for the reason that the one, as simple, displays a greater unity than the other, the compound;[16] (4) to range under one and the same genus the authentic ὄντα of the intelligible and the so-called "ὄντα" of the sensible would be as absurd as to make "one genus of Socrates and his portrait" (VI.2.1.24–25); (5) even if some genera of the sensible realm (e.g., οὐσία) share the same name with one of the real genera of being, no one should be misled by the equivocation.

Given this ontological distinction between being and becoming, Plotinus has no difficulty in drawing the conclusion that Aristotle's categories, which were not intended for the realm of being but for that of becoming, cannot be "genera of being," let alone the "highest" (πρῶτα) genera for which he was searching. If his premises are granted, Plotinus' conclusion seems to follow. But Plotinus does not stop here. He is prepared to go so far as to question whether Aristotle's categories can be called even simple "genera" in the Aristotelian logical sense of this term. In this respect, Plotinus' criticism appears more realistic and more challenging. Since the term "genus" is instrumental to his strategy of attacking Aristotle's categories, it will be well to take a look at the various meanings of the term and Plotinus' use of them.

To use an Aristotelian expression, the Greek word "γένος" is a πολλαχῶς λεγόμενον, that is, it has more than one meaning and can be used in more than one sense. Basically, two usages of this term may be distinguished: the common or nontechnical usage, and the technical or philosophical usage. The first relates to generation, while the second usage relates to predication. Since generation involves both generators and generated, the meaning of the term "genus" is split. So for the parents, "genus" refers to their offspring collectively, whereas the parents themselves are said to be the source (ἀρχή) or genus (γένος) of the offspring, and more so the father as the more active of the two generators. In this sense, the genus of all Hellenes is Hellen who was their first generator.[17] With regard to predication, "genus" is a predicable. In a proposition, it usually occupies the position of the predicate, but every generic term with the exception of the highest genus (γένος γενικώτατον) can also be the subject of the proposition. As Aristotle puts it, "genus" is also the "first constituent element" of definition and stands to differentiae as matter stands to form.[18] Also, things are said to be "other in genus" if they cannot be analyzed into one another or into some other thing. It is in this sense that the categories are said to be "other in genus."[19] As a technical, logical term, "genus" is defined as follows: "A 'genue' is what is predicated of things exhibiting differences in kind."[20]

To return to Plotinus now and the "genera of being," for which he is searching and from which he excludes Aristotle's categories, it may be useful for our understanding to keep in mind the following: (1) the Plotinian genera must be the "highest" (πρῶτα) genera, that is, not subject to predication which would reduce then to species; (2) they must be able to be predicated equally (ἐπίσης) of what is subordinated to them; (3) above all they must be endowed with generative power implied in the nontechnical sense of the word "genus," so they may function as principles (ἀρχαί) of being and as "genera of being." According to Plotinus, Aristotle's categories (a) do not meet evidently the criterion of (3); (b) they do not meet (2) because *ousia*, for example, is not equally predicated of matter and form (VI.1.2.9–10); (c) they do seem to meet the criterion of (1) since they are not subject to predication, but to call them πρῶτα would be false since it would be misleading to call them "genera of being" given the ontological distinction between being and becoming and their restriction to the latter; (d) they are not "other in genus" because they are analyzable or, to say the least, half of them are (VI.1. 13–14. 23–24).

Thus far, Plotinus has tried to approach Aristotle's categories negatively. In other words, he has tried to determine not what the categories are but what they are not. In his view, they are not "genera of being." Moreover, they are neither the "highest genera" nor even "genera," strictly speaking. In drawing these conclusions, Plotinus follows simply the premises (1) that reality is ontologically divided into two realms, and (2) that Aristotle's categories do not apply to the higher level of reality. Also, his broad conception of "γένος" as a predicable term of which nothing can be predicated and as powerful generative principle or source, has some bearing in the exclusion of the categories from the realm of real being. Even so, one may wonder what the Aristotelian categories are, in Plotinus' understanding, and how they function. Plotinus's answer to questions like these is that the categories—which Aristotle calls falsely genera and genera of being[21]—are simply categories of becoming. He means by this that the categories lack the unity that the genera possess. In his opinion, they are loose classifications based on some common characteristics shared by groups of sensible objects of the phenomenal realm. Thus, the referential efficacy of the categories is restricted to the lower level of reality and their unifying power is lesser compared with that of the genera, in the Plotinian sense of the term.

Consequently, Plotinus' lengthy discussions of the four basic Aristotelian categories (namely, substance, quantity, quality, relation) lead to the same conclusion that none of them is a genus. A simple comparison of the following relevant passages may help to clarify this point:

> The properties adduced may indeed be allowed to distinguish Substance from the other Existents. They afford a means of grouping substances together and calling them by a common name. They do not however establish the unity of a genus, and they do not bring to light the concept and the nature of Substance (VI.1.3.19–23).

· · ·

> Equality and inequality must be regarded as properties of Quantity-Absolute, not of the participants, or of them not essentially but only accidentally: such participants as "three yards' length" which becomes a quantity, not as belonging to a single genus of Quantity, but by being subsumed under the one head, the one category (VI.1.5. 22–26).

· · ·

> If however the Reason-Principles (governing the correlatives) stand oppose and have the differences to which we have referred, they may perhaps not be a single genus, but this will not prevent all relatives being expressed in terms of a certain likeness, and falling under a single category (VI.1.9.27–30).

· · ·

> Again, not all qualities can be regarded as Reason-Principles: chronic disease cannot be a Reason-Principle. Perhaps, however, we must speak in such cases of privations, restricting the term "Qualities" to Ideal-Forms and powers. Thus we shall have, not a single genus, but reference only to the unity of a category (VI.1.10.40–42).

Let it be noted here that these four Aristotelian categories, together with κίνησις ("motion")—evidently a new Plotinian category of Platonic roots— constitute the set of five "genera" which are "different" (ἕτερα) from the "genera of being" and are proposed by Plotinus for the realm of *becoming*. As to the other six Aristotelian categories, Plotinus thinks that they can be reduced to the above five basic categories. Thus two Aristotelian categories, to wit, action and passion, can be subsumed under the category of motion, which is a genus of becoming analogous but different from the homonymous genus of being (VI.3.21–27). For the categories of ποῦ ("where" in place) and ποτὲ ("when" in time), Plotinus proposes that they may be reduced to space and time, respectively, which in their turn may be reduced to the category of quantity (VI.1.13–14). As for the two last categories in the Aristotelian list, possession and situation (ἔχειν, κεῖσθαι), in Plotinus' view, they are combinations of two or more categories, so that they cannot be simple and without combination (VI.1.23–24).[22]

Plotinus' position that most of Aristotle's categories are reducible and unnecessary is a strong position and amounts to a serious criticism because it challenges the doctrine of categories in the very domain of the sensible world that it was intended to render intelligible and knowable. If Plotinus' criticism is well-founded, then the implication will be that Aristotle did not know what he was doing when he postulated more categories than he needed. Starting with Porphyry, the later Neoplatonist commentators had a difficult task in their efforts to defend the irreducibility of Aristotle's categories.[23] However, the fact that they were able to defend successfully Aristotle and rescue him from Plotinus' severe attack indicates that the Plotinian method of criticism was somewhat objectionable.

To defend Aristotle against the charge that his categories do not apply adequately to the intelligible realm and, consequently, that they do not qualify for the position of "genera of being" was certainly not that difficult. For after all, one may not see the reason why Aristotle's categories (which were not intended for the intelligible realm, as Plotinus admits) should be criticized for their being inapplicable to that realm. Following this line of argument, Dexippus attempted to give an answer to Plotinus' questions regarding Aristotle's categories and their relations to the real being.[24] Yet, the question still remains: What was the reason for which Plotinus first considered Aristotle's categories as "genera of being," and then made this very consideration the basis for his criticism of the Aristotelian categorial doctrine? This question should be discussed in the light of the historical fact that in the third century A.D, there were various competing interpretations of this doctrine.

IV

It is known that, according to an established tradition, the commentator of a classical treatise was supposed to discuss and settle a few preliminary questions before proceeding to make his comments on the text. In the later commentaries, these questions are to be found codified as follows: (1) Who is the author of the treatise? (2) What is its correct title (ἐπιγραφή)? (3) What is its purpose or subject (σκοπός, πρόθεσις)? (4) What is its order? (5) What is its utility? and (6) What is its division into chapters? With regard to Aristotle's *Categories*, the most debatable of the above questions were (2) and especially (3).

It is understandable that the late commentators had to debate the issue of the correct title of the treatise, given the fact that more than one title had been preserved. Thus they had to choose among the following alternatives: *Ten Categories, Categories, On the Ten Genera, On the Genera of Being,* and *Pretopics.*[25] A commentator was expected not simply to choose, but also to defend his choice. To take an example, Porphyry thought, as we today think, that the correct title of the treatise was Κατηγορίαι and provided reasons to support his position and to reject the other proposals.[26] He particularly argued that the treatise should not be titled περι τῶν γενῶν τοῦ ὄντος, contrary to Plotinus.[27]

It is not difficult to see that closely related to the question of the correct title of the treatise was the more important question of its purpose. The title of a treatise is usually indicative of its content and the purpose it serves. It is no accident that the choice of the title of the treatise on categories, which a commentator or critic prefers, reflects in a way his position and interpretation of its purpose. This brings us to the central and difficult question of the purpose of Aristotle's *Categories*. What are the categories? Are they classifications of words, things, concepts, or what? On this question neither the ancient commentators nor the modern scholars seem to have reached an agreement. These are four possible answers to this question and all of them had been tried by the time of Porphyry. Since then they have been repeated with more or less fidelity. By way of labeling these interpretations, the following scheme is obtained:[28] (1) the grammatical or phonetic interpretation, (2) the ontological or pragmatic interpretation, (3) the psychological or noetic interpretation, and (4) the logical or synthetic interpretation.

It falls outside the limited scope of this paper to analyze the arguments and counterarguments by which the supporters of each of the above interpretations of the Aristotelian categorial doctrine tried to support their respective positions. To comment briefly on each of them, it may be said that interpretation number (1) claims that the categories are word or sounds (φωναί) and about words. The opponents of this view contend that to deal with φωναί qua φωναί is the task not of the philosopher but of the grammarian, and Aristotle was not a grammarian. The supporters of (2) think that the categories are about beings or things (ὄντα, πράγματα). The main objection to this view is that it takes the treatise out of the *Organon* and makes it a part of *Metaphysics*, where the discussion is of ὄντα qua ὄντα. According to (3), the purpose of the treatise is to deal neither with φωναί nor with *onta*, but with the intermediary νοήματα ("concepts"). But to deal with concepts qua mental entities and processes is the task of the psychologist, not of the philosopher. The fourth (4) and evidently more enlightened view considers the other three as one-sided and attempts to synthesize them by claiming that the categories are about significant sounds (φωναὶ σημαντικαὶ) which signify things (πράγματα) by way of signifying concepts (νοήματα).[29] After Porphyry, who gave a definite formulation to this interpretation by emphasizing the role of φωναὶ σημαντικαὶ, every commentator of Aristotle's *Categories* took pains to make it clear that he followed the synthetic or logical interpretation.

To return to Plotinus, it may be useful to know that he was a follower of the strictly ontological interpretation (2) of the categorial doctrine. On this we have Simplicius' testimony.[30] Being consistent with this interpretation, Plotinus (a) titles Aristotle's treatise not *Categories* but *On the Genera of Being*, as we have seen; (b) considers the categories in their claims as "genera of being"; (c) views the categories as competitors of Plato's μέγιστι γένη for the position of "genera of being"; (d) thinks that he has to choose between Plato and Aristotle on this matter, and (e) criticizes and rejects Aristotle's categories as irrelevant and inapplicable to the realm of real being, but he thinks that with some modifications they can serve the realm of becoming.

However, Plotinus' successors, who found it difficult to choose between Plato and Aristotle, had to abandon the ontological interpretation of the categorial theory in their efforts to reconcile the two philosophers. Thus Porphyry proposes a new interpretation that placed the emphasis on the logical aspects of the categorial doctrine. The categories are interpreted now not as "genera of being," that is, not as ὄντα but as φῶναι which signify ὄντα. What sort of ὄντα they signify, Porphyry did not specify. The ontological status of the *significata* was left an open question.[31] It could mean that Porphyry's ὄντα referred back to Aristotle's πρώτη οὐσία ("first substance"), in which case species and genera (the universals) would seem to be simple abstractions and empty names. But this line of thought would have to make Porphyry seem more an Aristotelian and less a Neoplatonist pupil of Plotinus. On the other hand, it could be that Porphyry's ὄντα pointed towards Plotinus' πρῶτα γένη τοῦ ὄντος ("highest genera of being"), in which case the species and genera of which we speak as "universals" would again be almost empty names compared with the universals of universals (πρῶτα γένη) of the Plotinian κόσμος νοητός. The point is that the Neoplatonic split of the universal makes even Plato's ontological realism of the εἴδη seem like nominalism when compared to Plotinus' ontological realism of the πρῶτα γένη. This somewhat strange nominalism may be called the Neoplatonic version of nominalism.

V

By way of summarizing the thesis of this essay, it can be stated that the reasons for which Plotinus criticized so severely and rejected Aristotle's categories were strictly ontological and due to two facts: first, Plotinus had accepted the ontological interpretation of the Aristotelian categorial theory and drew from that the conclusions to which it leads logically; and secondly, Aristotle's ontology with its emphasis on the concrete individual (τόδε τι) and its restriction to the realm of phenomena, was in sharp contrast with reinforced Platonism of the Plotinian type that (1) places the emphasis not simply on the universal (Plato's εἶδος), but especially on the universal of universals (Plotinus' γένος), and (2) tends to go not only beyond the sensible realm (Aristotle), but also beyond the intelligible (Plato) towards the Absolute and Ineffable One.

The implications of Plotinus' ontological presuppositions are grave for the Aristotelian categorial doctrine and the Aristotelian logic in general. They certainly cannot be of great value to one who, like Plotinus, is concerned with the ἐπέκεινα ("beyond") and the really real conceived as ἕτερον ("other") than the sensible. For such a journey, neither the senses and the common sense nor logic in its syllogistic (Aristotelian) form or in its propositional (Stoic) form can be of much help. Another method is needed by which the ἀναγωγή ("lifting up") of the soul and its ἐπιστροφή ("return") to the Primordial Source can be accomplished. This method may be called "The Dialectic of Eros." But this is another story.

Plotinus and
Self-Predication

JOHN FIELDER

Although there are problems of predication associated with the rather ordinary statement that Socrates is just, Platonists are faced with even more serious problems in the assertion that Justice (the Form) is just. This latter type of predication is a consequence of the relationship of forms and sensibles. Since Socrates is just by virtue of his participation in Justice, and Justice functions as a standard for judging whether one is just or not, it is natural to assert that Justice, too, is just. It would be rather odd to deny that Justice itself lacked justice.

However, since Justice and Socrates are radically different kinds of things, it seems equally odd to say that Justice is just in the same sense that Socrates is just. How can something incorporeal be just? or hot? or large? As R. E. Allen put it, no one can scratch Doghood behind the Ears or take a nap in the intelligible Bed.[1]

The assumption that "is just" means the same when applied to Socrates and to justice leads to immediately obvious absurdities. For a Platonist to hold such a theory of predication would require that he overlook or not recognize the absurd consequences of the theory. Since we can hardly credit Plato or Plotinus or any other major philosopher with a mistake of this magnitude, we must assume that those men held some other more philosophically plausible theory concerning the meaning of "Justice is just."

A current proposal for a philosophically plausible theory of "Justice is just" is Pauline predication.[2] The idea is taken from Paul's discussion of charity in Corinthians. There he states that "charity suffers long and is kind . . ., rejoices with the truth and bears all things." Paul is not making an assertion about the abstract entity, charity. In that sense it would be absurd to speak of charity enduring anything. The grammar of Paul's statement suggests that he is speaking about charity, the abstract entity, but a moment's reflection shows that he is actually speaking about those individuals who have charity. It is they who endure all, not charity itself. Hence, what looks like a statement about an abstract entity is really a statement about a class of objects related to that entity, namely individuals sharing that characteristic.

If we apply this idea to "Justice is just," it becomes a way of saying that the individuals who participate in Justice are just. Instead of being an assertion about the Form, Justice, it is an assertion about the class of individuals who participate in Justice. Thus "Justice is just" regarded as an instance of Pauline predication means "Justice is such that whatever participates in Justice is just." Pauline predications thus avoid the difficulties attendant upon speaking of Forms and sensibles as being just in the same sense.

II

The argument I have sketched above is a philosophical one, appealing not to texts but the philosophical intelligibility of theories of predication as it applies to Forms and sensibles. As such it applies to Plato and Neoplatonist alike insofar as they share the basic features of the theory of Forms. Further, this argument has two important methodological implications that bear on the textual inquiry necessary to determine whether Plato or Plotinus actually held either of these theories. First, the claim that Plotinus or any other major philosopher used the same sense of "is just" for Forms and sensibles will require much stronger evidence if this view is considered to be philosophically mistaken in an obvious way. One would have to submit overwhelming textual proof to back up the claim that a thinker of Plotinus' stature made such an obvious and fundamental mistake.

Second, the argument entails that any other philosophical doctrine that is based on applying the same predicate in the same sense to Forms and sensibles would also be philosophically incoherent and would require much more evidence to establish that Plotinus held it. This means that the copy theory, in order to be philosophically acceptable, could not be based on a view of likeness that involved the sharing of properties by forms and their corporeal images. Consequently, it is necessary to assess the soundness of this argument asserting the philosophical absurdity of one account of predication before examining our texts.

III

The best statement of the view that an obvious absurdity results from applying the same predicates to forms and sensibles is in a recent article by Gregory Vlastos.[3] He is writing about Plato, but the argument, as I have shown, is a philosophical one and applies equally to Plotinus. Accordingly, I have taken the liberty of replacing references to Plato with references to Plotinus. Here is Vlastos's argument, which is the major consideration in favor of Pauline predication.

The most common use of the copula in Greek and English is "to indicate that the individual name by the subject-term is a member of the class of those possessing the attribute expressed by the predicate-term."[4] Thus "Socrates is wise" asserts that Socrates belongs to the class of wise individuals. Vlastos indicates this reading of "is" by the use of the letter epsilon: "Socrates ε wise."[5] Many true assertions about Forms have this character, for example, "Justice ε incorporeal" or "Justice ε intelligible." But if we treat the statements like "Justice is just," as epsilon predications we must attribute what Vlastos thinks is a stupendous philosophical error to Plotinus. For to assert that "Fire ε hot" is to admit that Plotinus is guilty of

> a piece of egregious nonsense: Heat is a property which only corporeal things could have. . . . We would be supposing that he wants to say in all seriousness that one of his incorporeal Forms has a corporeal property.[6]

In a similar fashion "Justice ε just" would make the mistake of treating an abstract Form as if it had "a property which only concrete individuals—persons—and by legitimate extension, their actions, dispositions, institutions, laws, etc., could possibly have."[7] In both cases epsilon predication commits the categorial mistake of applying properties to the Form that could only be possessed by the Form's corporeal instances. Asserting that an incorporeal Form has a corporeal property is such an obvious absurdity we can hardly believe that Plotinus would allow it. Hence we cannot read statements like "Justice is just" as epsilon predications.

Vlastos appears to be making the following argument:

1. There are at least two types of properties, corporeal and incorporeal.
2. Corporeal subjects may only have corporeal properties.
3. Incorporeal subjects may have only incorporeal properties.
4. The assertion that an incorporeal subject may have a corporeal property or vice versa is philosophically absurd.
5. Justice is an incorporeal subject, a form.
6. To be "just" is a corporeal property.
7. "Justice is just" asserts that an incorporeal subject has a corporeal property.
8. Therefore, "Justice is just" is philosophically absurd.

I take this argument to be the substance of Vlastos's claims that "heat is a property which only corporeal things could have" and that it would be a philosophical mistake to hold that "one of his incorporeal Forms has a corporeal property." Thus premises 1 and 2 embody Vlastos's distinction between corporeal and incorporeal subjects and properties; premise 3 states the requirement that statements must have the same type of subject and property; and premise 4 holds that violation of the requirement of premise 3 results in a philosophical mistake. In the remaining premises, these general principles are applied to the case of "Justice is just." It is clear that the argument can be applied to other similar assertions about Forms.

Premise 4 needs some further explanation as to why it is absurd to join subject and property of different types (i.e., corporeal and incorporeal). Again, Vlastos's argument is not explicit, but the idea seems to be that if an *in*corporeal subject (a Form) can have a *corporeal* property, then it is no longer possible to speak of it as an incorporeal subject. A corporeal subject must be made up of corporeal properties, otherwise the distinction between corporeal and incorporeal reality is undermined.

Vlastos concludes that epsilon predication contains an obvious philosophical mistake, one that a major philosopher could hardly be expected to make. Hence we have strong reasons for supposing that statements like "Justice is just" are Pauline predications.

Vlastos is certainly correct in pointing out that epsilon predication, as he has presented it, leads to clear absurdities. But this only proves that *his version* of Pauline predication involves an obvious philosophical mistake. Vlastos seems to assume that there is only one way to develop a theory of epsilon predication and that, therefore, it can be eliminated as a serious philosophical theory by his argument. But this is hardly plausible: there are a number of different versions of Pauline predication, and one would certainly think that there may be more than one conception of epsilon predication as well.

I suspect that if Vlastos and Allen were more familiar with Neoplatonic thought, they would not be so hasty in rejecting epsilon predication. Plotinus approaches a number of philosophical problems of the Theory of Forms from a different direction and provides philosophical solutions not found in Plato. It is not surprising, therefore, that Plotinus' view of "justice is just" and similar statements about forms utilizes a version of epsilon predication that is not subject to the difficulties inherent in Vlastos's account.

IV

The best way to approach Plotinus' understanding of statements about Forms is to begin with "Socrates is just" and see how it is related to "Justice is just." As Vlastos suggests, the former type of assertion is regarded by Plotinus as an instance of epsilon predication. That is, the subject is said to possess the property expressed by the predicate. Thus "white and black are predicated of an object having one or other of these qualities . . ., knowledge is predicated of the subject in whom knowledge exists" (VI. 3. 4). And, in fact, the sensible subject is regarded by Plotinus as a collection of these properties in matter.[8] In VI. 3. 8., at the end of a discussion of sensible substance, he concludes that sensible substance is a "coagulation of qualities and Matter; all the qualities taken together as coagulating in a uniform matter constitute [sensible] substance." Accidental properties are part of the collection but they "take independent rank and are not submerged in the mixture."

It might be supposed that it is necessary to distinguish the particular, individual property as found in a subject from the universal characteristic it shares with other subjects. Thus we would distinguish the particular "white" of this portion of milk from the whiteness it shares with other white things. But Plotinus does not make such a distinction, at least not in a way that results in two different entities, the universal and the particular individual features of a subject. Rather, for Plotinus, the particular property functions as a universal.[9] The particular white of this portion of milk is one and the same white that is found in a different portion of milk.

> The whiteness in a portion of milk is not a part of the whiteness of milk in general: we have the whiteness of a portion, not a portion of whiteness; for whiteness is utterly without magnitude; has nothing whatever to do with quantity (IV.3.2).

And similarly for grammar:

> Grammar is not posterior to the particular grammar: on the contrary, the grammar as in you depends upon the prior existence of grammar as such: the grammar as in you becomes particular by being in you; it is otherwise identical to grammar the universal (VI.3.9).

It is a philosophical error, Plotinus holds, to separate the particular white of a subject from whiteness, the universal. We make such an error because we treat the particular property like a sensible object. The portion of milk clearly cannot be in many places at once without being divided, but its white color can, because it is "utterly without magnitude." The bundle of properties that comprise the portion of milk are without matter, for they "coagulate in a uniform Matter." It (the property) is not a corporeal individual and, therefore, is capable of being completely present throughout a number of sensible objects.

Hence when we predicate "is white" of a member of sensible subjects, the predicate picks out a single property that is identically and wholly present in those subjects. This capacity to be wholly present throughout a number of different individuals is characteristic of intelligible reality. The properties that make up sensible objects are intelligible existents and sensibles acquire them through participation.

> It is not Socrates who bestows manhood upon what was previously not Man, but Man upon Socrates; the individual man exists by participation in the universal (VI.3.9).

Participation is simply the act by which intelligible existents enter matter and provide some characteristic to the sensible subject.

The intelligible existent that enters matter is Soul. After speaking of the capacity to be present in many without partition, Plotinus remarks that:

> To have penetrated this idea is to know the greatness of Soul and its power, the
> divinity and wonder of its being, as a nature transcending the sphere of things
> (VI.2.1).

And in the two treatises devoted to the integral omnipresence of authentic existence, Plotinus begins with the question, "How are we to explain the omnipresence of Soul?" (VI. 4. 1).

We appear, then, to have three levels of reality and two intelligible existents.
The three levels are sensible, Soul, and Form (in Nous). There are only two
intelligibles, since Soul is in Sensibles. But this appearance is somewhat misleading. As a number of Plotinian scholars have pointed out, the distinction between
Nous and Soul tends to disappear.[10] Soul, for example, possesses no material
principle to differentiate it from *Nous*. Both *Nous* and the sensible world are made
distinct from their previous hypostases by principles of matter. John Deck points
out that Plotinus argues for the direct participation of sensibles in *Nous*, making
Soul an unnecessary hypostasis.[11] Deck concludes that "the sensible world, as
being, is *Nous*."[12] R. T. Wallis has developed a similar view of the relation of *Nous*
and Soul.[13] My own view is that Soul should be regarded as *Nous* in its function of
generating a sensible world. It is its role that may be distinguished rather than
viewing Soul as a separate hypostasis. Just as Plotinus found reason to collapse
the distinction between the particular property and the universal, so also he was
driven to assimilate Soul to *Nous*.

It is reasonable to believe that instead of three levels and two intelligible
existents, the true Plotinian view of the relationship of Form and sensibles is that
there are two levels, *Nous* and the sensible world, and only one intelligible reality,
Nous. Soul is simply the *Nous* in its role of permeating matter, generating the
sensible world. Instead of an additional hypostasis, Soul is simply one aspect of
Nous.

The result of this for the problem of predication is profound. For it entails
that the properties that make up sensible existents are the Forms themselves. They
are the intelligible existents that are present in Matter, and in which sensibles
participate.

V

When we say that Socrates is just, we are claiming that the Form of Justice is
immanent in Socrates, according to Plotinus. The justice in Socrates is Justice
itself, present in Matter. As a consequence, predicating "is just" of Socrates is not
so greatly different from predicating "is just" of the Form itself. In both cases the
predicate asserts the presence of Justice in the subject. In the case of Socrates,
Justice is immanent in the Matter that constitutes the subject, Socrates. In the case
of justice itself, what the predicate signifies *is* the entire subject, not just part of
the subject, as in the case of Socrates. Although there are important differences in
the two propositions that "justice is just" and "Socrates is just," the predicate has
the same meaning.

Regardless of the philosophical merit of Plotinus' theory of predication, two points are clear. First, it is a theory based on epsilon predication rather than Pauline predication. Second, whatever the difficulties this theory generates, it is not obviously absurd. It cannot be disqualified as unworthy of a major thinker or as so incoherent that significantly more evidence is needed to establish it as Plotinus' view. Rather than being a philosophical liability, as Vlastos and others think, epsilon predication provides a coherent account of how predicates are applied to Forms and Sensibles. And it does so in a way that reinforces a number of central Platonic themes (the copy theory, participation, and the role of Forms as Epistemological standards), all of which present serious problems for Pauline predication.

Omnipresence, Participation, and Eidetic Causation in Plotinus

JONATHAN SCOTT LEE

Émile Bréhier has written that "fourth and fifth treatises of the sixth *Ennead* . . . can easily be read without any reference to Greek philosophy."[1] In this paper I shall argue, to the contrary, that the philosophical import of these treatises on "The Integral Omnipresence of Being" can only be determined in the context of the Greek metaphysical tradition. In particular, I want to argue that in these treatises, Plotinus' central concern is the notoriously elusive concept at the heart of metaphysical Platonism, the concept of participation. This can be shown by reference to two major problems with which Plotinus deals in VI.4–5. 22–23.[2]

I

The first problem (and this is the problem that, in effect, sets the entire argument of the treatises into motion) derives from *Parmenides* 130e4–131c11. Here, Plato (in the persona of the pre-Socratic philosopher Parmenides) raises a pair of objections against the notion of participation. These objections center around a conception of participation as the relation between my given *eidos* and the multiplicity of sensible particulars that participate in that *eidos*. Because of the importance of this Platonic text to the argument of VI.4–5, it will be useful to cite Parmenides' objections more fully:

> "Then, is it the case that each thing participating participates in either the whole of the *eidos* or in a part of it? Or might there be some other mode of participation besides these?"
>
> "How could there be?" he said.
>
> "Does it seem to you, then, that the *eidos* as a whole, being one, is in each of the many, or how?
>
> "What hinders this, Parmenides?" said Socrates.
>
> "Then, a thing that is one and the same would be at the same time, as a whole, in many things which are separate, and hence it would be separate from itself" (131a4–b2).

Parmenides leads the young Socrates on to consider the second alternative presented at 131a4–5: that each thing participating participates only in a part of the *eidos*. The argument then resumes:

> "Then, Socrates," he said, "the *eide* themselves would be divisible, and the things participating in them would participate in a part. No longer would an *eidos* be in each as a whole; rather, a part of each *eidos* would be in each."
>
> "So it seems."
>
> "Then, would you be willing, Socrates, to say to us that in truth the one *eidos* is divided and yet that it is one?"
>
> "Certainly not," he said (131c–11).

These objections take the form of a dilemma: either the *eidos* as a whole is in each of the many sensible particulars that participate in it, in which case the *eidos* will be separate from itself, or else only a part of the *eidos* is in each of the sensible particulars, in which case the *eidos* will be divided and, hence, not one.

Now, in the *Parmenides* Socrates suggests a way in which this dilemma can be avoided and the many sensible particulars can be said to participate in an *eidos* as a whole. This suggestion is put in terms of a metaphor at 131b3–6:

> [The *eidos* would not be separate from itself] if it were like one and the same day [ἡμέρα], which is in many places at the same time and yet is in no way separate from itself, if each of the *eide* is in all [the things participating in it] at the same time as one and the same thing in this way.

Socrates' suggestion is not pursued in the *Parmenides*; rather, Parmenides distorts it into the clearly materialistic analogy of a sail spread over a number of people, an analogy that sets up Parmenides' presentation of the second half of the dilemma (quoted above). However, the analogy of the day accomplishes two quite important things even within the context of Plato's dialogue. In the first place, Socrates' suggestion opens up the possibility of an escape from the Parmenidean dilemma, an escape involving the acceptance of the first horn of the dilemma together with a denial of the apparent consequence that each *eidos* will be separate from itself. In the second place, the fact that the analogy of the day appears to offer an escape from the dilemma casts doubt on Parmenides' assumption that the relation between *eide* and sensible particulars is like the ordinary relation between a whole and its parts. Such a conception of the whole/part relation seems to be quite appropriate in the context of material objects, that is, the sensible particulars that occupy space. However, it appears to lose its usefulness in the context of nonmaterial things such as the Platonic *eide*. This latter point is made doubly apparent by Parmenides' inability to deal in any effective way with the analogy of the day (compare 131b7–c4) and by his grotesque illustration of the dilemma discussed above in terms of a crude, materialistic analysis of the *eide* of largeness, equality, and smallness at 131c12–e7. The analogy of the day, thus, provides a means by which the relation between nonmaterial entities like the *eide* and material or sensible particulars can be conceived. In successfully accomplishing this, the analogy, in effect, challenges the propriety of an ordinary conception of the relation between wholes and parts in the context of a treatment of participation.

As will soon become apparent, Plotinus' response to the objections of *Parmenides* 130e4–131c11 is very much in the spirit of Socrates' analogy of the day: the Plotinian escape from the dilemma involves the acceptance of its first horn together with a denial of the apparent consequence that each *eidos* will be separate from itself. Of course, Plato's discussion concerns the relation between individual *eide* and their participants in the sensible world, while Plotinus' discussion concerns the relation between the intelligible world as a whole (τὸ ὄν) and the sensible world. However, this difference is merely one of emphasis, since the characterization of the participation relation with respect to one *eidos* ought to be applicable to that relation with respect to all *eide* (i.e., to the intelligible world as a whole).

Plotinus offers three separate, but fundamentally similar, direct responses to the dilemma posed in the *Parmenides*; these occur at VI.4.8.2–45, VI.4.13.6–26, and VI.5.3.1–21. For the purposes of this discussion, I shall concentrate on the last of these because it is here that Plotinus' argument is most fully elaborated.

The argument of VI.5.3 rests on a rather Aristotelian preliminary discussion of philosophical methodology in VI.5.2. Plotinus here claims that the materialists (like the Parmenides of Plato's dialogue) fail to be persuaded of the truth of the nonmaterialistic metaphysics of Platonism "because they have not made a start of their inquiry from appropriate principles" (VI.5.2.5–6).[3] In discussing the intelligible world and its relation to the sensible world, Plotinis insists that ". . . it is necessary for us to take principles appropriate for proof to the account of the One which exists everywhere; and, since this account is of intelligibles, it is necessary for us to take principles of the intelligibles closely linked with true Being" (VI.5. 2.7–9). This advice already contains the kernel of Plotinus' response to Parmenides: the intelligible world must be regarded as "the One which exists everywhere," that is, as the One which is omnipresent to the sensible world. The omnipresence of the intelligible world, however, will be proved (after a fashion) by Plotinus in VI.5.3, on the basis of an accurate description of the basic features of the intelligible world and the sensible world. Hence, the intelligible world's omnipresence is not just a matter of definition; rather, it is a logical consequence of the nature of being.

Plotinus goes on to outline the basic features of the sensible and the intelligible worlds, obviously taking this general description to provide the relevant "appropriate principles" for metaphysical inquiry:

> Now, on the one hand, there is that which is in motion, which undergoes every sort of change, and which is distributed in every place; this, indeed, might best be named Becoming, rather than Being. On the other hand, there is that which always is, existing always in the same way, which neither comes into being nor perishes, which occupies no region of space, neither a place nor some base [τινα ἕδραν], which neither goes out from some place nor again enters into another, but which remains in itself (VI.5.2.9–16).[4]

Armed with this general description of the sensible world and the intelligible world, which description he takes to be an adequate account of the "essences" of the two worlds (compare VI.5.2.19–28), Plotinus is prepared to tackle the Parmenidean dilemma.

He begins, in effect, by considering the second half of the dilemma—that only a part of an *eidos* is in each of the sensible particulars participating in that *eidos*—and argues that this possibility is ruled out by the essential nature of the intelligible world. He writes:

> If, then, our subject is true Being, which (as was said) exists always in the same way, which does not go forth from itself, which is not in any relation of coming-to-be, and which is not in place, it is obviously necessary that it, being thus, always be with itself, that it be not divided from itself, that it be not part here and part there, and that it not give up anything from itself. For, otherwise, it would be in one thing and another thing (things different from itself), and in general it would be in something else, rather than being in itself and impassible (for if it were in something other than itself, it would be affected). But, if it is in an impassible condition [as was said], then it is not in anything other than itself (VI.5.3.1–8).

In other words, Plotinus argues that the division of a Platonic intelligible world (or of a single *eidos*) into parts is inconsistent with the essential character of Being, as described in VI.5.2. In the context of the Parmenidean dilemma, Plotinus is in effect arguing that the participation of sensible particulars in *eide* cannot be understood as participation in parts of *eide*, since such an analysis requires that the *eide* be divided into parts and, thus, modified by their relation to the sensible world, which view is in conflict with the impassible or immutable nature of the intelligible world. Hence, participation cannot be explained in terms of the apportionment of parts of the intelligible world to sensible particulars. It follows that participation involves the relation between sensible particulars and each *eidos* as an integral whole or, more generally, that the sensible world is related to the intelligible world as an integral whole. This, of course, forces Plotinus into the consideration of the first half of the Parmenidean dilemma—that an *eidos* as a whole is in each of the sensible particulars that participate in that *eidos* and is, thus, separate from itself.

Plotinus' response to the first half of Parmenides' dilemma is somewhat more obscure than the argument quoted above and will require some effort to reconstruct. At VI.5.3.8–14, immediately following the preceding passage, Plotinus writes:

> Therefore, if Being does not separate from itself, if it has not been divided into parts, and if it changes itself in no way whatever, and, furthermore, if it is to be in many things at the same time as a single whole while remaining in itself, its being in many things must involve the existence of the same thing everywhere; that is, it is both in itself and yet not in itself. Hence, all that can be said is that, on the one hand, Being is in nothing at all, and, on the other hand, the things other than Being participate in it. . . .

In the light of this Plotinus concludes:

> Hence, either it is necessary to reject our hypotheses and principles, saying that there exists no nature such as that described, or else, if such a rejection is impossible, then such a nature—Being—must necessarily exist, and we must admit the position maintained at the beginning [cf., VI. 4. 1–3]: Being is one and the same in number, not having been divided into parts but, rather, existing as a whole and being remote from no one of the things other than it (VI.5.3.15–21).

Now, the argument embedded in these passages can be reconstructed as follows:[5] Given the nature of the Platonic intelligible world previously sketched, this world cannot be divided into parts in order to account for participation. Such a division would be inconsistent with this world's essential character. Hence, the intelligible world must remain an integral whole. Given this Plotinian account of the intelligible world, *Parmenides* 131a4–b2 appears to draw the absurd consequence that the intelligible world, if it is participated in by sensible particulars, becomes separate from itself because it then exists as an integral whole "in many things which are separate." Such a consequence appears to entail the impossibility of participation and, thus, the untenability of metaphysical Platonism. Plotinus' response to this objection is simply to deny the derivation of the Parmenidean consequence: if the intelligible world has the essential nature attributed to it in VI.5.2, then it must always remain an integral whole (VI.5.3.1–8); if participation is to be possible (as it must be, given the observed fact of the existence of sensible particulars), then the intelligible world must (somehow) "be in many things at the same time as a single whole while remaining in itself" (line 10); since this involves "the existence of the same thing [namely, Being or the intelligible world] everywhere" (lines 10–11), participation requires the omnipresence of Being as an integral whole, that is, the integral omnipresence of Being. In effect, Plotinus is arguing that the objection at *Parmenides* 131a4–b2 stems from Parmenides' failure to understand the essential nature of Being, his failure to understand that Being is such as to be integrally omnipresent to the sensible world if it is present to it at all.

It is not perhaps entirely clear how VI.5.3 serves as an *argued* response to Parmenides. *Parmenides* 131a4–b2 purports to offer an argument to the effect that the claim that the intelligible world as a whole is involved in the participation of diverse sensible particulars in Being entails the absurdity that the intelligible world is separate from itself. Plotinus clearly denies the propriety of deriving this absurd consequence from the Platonic theory (i.e., from his formulation of this theory); however, he appears to provide no argument for this denial. Now, as I suggested above, the main point of Plotinus' response to Parmenides seems to be that the Parmenidean objection draws its force from a failure to understand the essential nature of the intelligible world. Plotinus is arguing, in effect, that once one understands the essence of the intelligible world as an integral whole, one is forced to the conclusion that participation requires the integral omnipresence of this whole to the sensible world, even though this omnipresence cannot be adequately formulated in terms of our ordinary conception of the relation between wholes and parts. I am suggesting, then, that Plotinus is here acting on "the principle that the best defense is attack"[6] and that this is a reasonable procedure for dealing with the Parmenidean dilemma (assuming, of course, that some sense can be made of the Plotinian conception of the intelligible world as integrally omnipresent to the sensible world). In his article, "Universals and Metaphysical Realism," Alan Donagan (in defense of a form of realism) advocates this very response to a slight variant of *Parmenides* 130e4–131c11. He writes:

> To say that [a universal] is "entire and yet divided from itself" is objectionable, because it presupposes that to be exemplified in two different places at once implies being divided. It is true that a *particular* can only be in two places at once if one part of it is at one place, and another part at the other; but, by their very nature, universals are not divisible into parts.[7]

The moral of Plotinus' argument is obvious: Parmenides' analysis of the intelligible world in its relation to the sensible world—an analysis centrally involving our ordinary conception of the whole/part relation—must be supplanted by a new analysis, an analysis that embodies the fact that Being is indivisible and, thus, must remain an integral whole in its relation to the sensible world. In effect, Plotinus is arguing that the consequences derived from Parmenides' analysis of the intelligible world are at odds with brute metaphysical fact, namely, the essential nature of the intelligible world as an integral whole omnipresent to the sensible world. Hence, Parmenides' understanding of the intelligible world is simply in error, and his method of dealing with problems concerning the intelligible in its relation to the sensible is inappropriate. In the light of this fact, Plotinus argues, the objections of *Parmenides* 130e4–131c11 lose their force.

Regardless of the ultimate success of his response to Parmenides, it is surely clear that Plotinus is, in VI. 4–5, offering his own essentially Platonic solution to these objections drawn from the text of Plato; he is attempting to develop a technical account of the relation between the intelligible and the sensible that is immune to the objections posed in the *Parmenides*.

II

A second major problem that Plotinus faces in VI.4–5 again arises quite simply from the metaphysical tradition of Platonism. At *Phaedo* 100c4–d8, the relation between the *eide* and things in the sensible world is described in an account of causality (αἰτία), and by implication the *eide* are described as the (possibly unique) *causes* (τὰ αἴτια) of particulars in the sensible world. In other words, Plato here suggests that the problem of participation is to be resolved by the elaboration of a theory of what I shall call "eidetic causation," that is, a theory of the way in which the *eide* that make up the intelligible world of Being are the causes of sensible particulars.

This suggestion that a theory of eidetic causation is central to Platonic metaphysics leads to one of Aristotle's most telling objections against metaphysical Platonism. At *Metaphysics* A. 9. 991a8–11 (compare M. 5. 1079b12–15), he writes:

> Above all one might discuss the question, what on earth the *eide* contribute to sensible things, either to those that are eternal or to those that come into being and cease to be. For they cause neither movement nor any change in them.[8]

This charge that the *eide* cannot be the causes of change in the sensible world is repeated and elaborated at *De generatione et corruptione* B. 9. 335b18–21, where Aristotle attacks the theory adumbrated in the *Phaedo* that the *eide* are the causes of the particulars that make up the sensible world. Here, he writes:

> If the *eide* are causes [αἴτια], why do they not always generate continually but only intermittently, since the *eide* and the things participating in them are always there?[9]

In other words, Aristotle's argument is designed to show that a Platonic account of the sensible world in terms of eidetic causation alone cannot adequately explain the ubiquitous phenomenon of change in the sensible world.

In Section I of this paper I argued that Plotinus in *Ennead* VI.4–5 is attempting to develop a solution to the problem of participation and that this solution involves the doctrine of the integral omnipresence of the intelligible world to the sensible world. This doctrine is, in effect, the fundamental feature of Plotinus' theory of eidetic causation. However, the claim that eidetic causation is to be elucidated along Plotinian lines in terms of the integral omnipresence of Being rasies an obvious question, a question very much in the spirit of the Aristotelian objection to Platonism introduced above: how is it that not all *eide* are manifested at all points in sensible space (or matter) at all times? In other words, how is it that, say, the *eidos* of man, though integrally omnipresent to the sensible world, is only seen to be present in certain regions of space (where people exist) and not in others (e.g., where rocks exist)? There appears to be a serious tension between the integral omnipresence of the intelligible world and its intermittent causal efficacy. In this section, I shall (1) elaborate a key strand of Plotinus' account of eidetic causation and (2) use this account to sketch a Plotinian answer to Aristotle's objection concerning the intermittent causal efficacy of the *eide*.

1. Plotinus devotes much of VI.5 to an explanation of the dynamic of eidetic causation, that is, to an explanation of *how* the intelligible is omnipresent to the sensible in such a way that the sensible world appears as it does. The heart of this explanation (see, in particular, VI.5.7.passim; 9.1–31; and 12.1–31) lies in the doctrine that *psyche* is an intermediary between the intelligible world and the

sensible world (a doctrine derived from *Timaeus* 35a1–8). It is *psyche,* present to the sensible world "as one life" (VI.5.12.1), that is the productive cause (τὸ αἴτιον, τὸ ποιοῦν) of the sensible world (VI.5.9.1–13).

The key to understanding the role of *psyche* in Plotinus' conception of eidetic causation is the doctrine of productive contemplation, a doctrine that is developed at some length in *Ennead* III.8[30], "On Nature and Contemplation and the One," a treatise written shortly after VI.4–5. The doctrine is simply that contemplation (θεωρία) is in some way to be understood as productive, that is, that contemplation involves production or making (ποίησις). The Plotinian claim that I will try to elucidate is that *psyche,* and in particular the *psyche* that Plotinus calls "Nature," exercises a form of contemplation that produces (i.e., causally brings into existence) the sensible particulars that make up the sensible world. In passing, I might mention that this doctrine of productive contemplation seems to mark one of Plotinus' most original achievements, since it appears to run counter to the traditional Greek conception of contemplation as something opposed to both production and action (πρᾶξις).[10] This traditional conception is, of course, that of Aristotle, who contrasts contemplation with action at *Nichomachean Ethics* X.7, by maintaining that "nothing comes from contemplation except the contemplating, but from practical activities we acquire more or less apart from the action" (1177b 2–4). If Plotinus is right, what we gain from (a kind of) contemplation is nothing less that the whole of the sensible world.

What, then, is involved in Plotinus' doctrine of productive contemplation? There appear to be basically two interrelated theses here. In the first is the claim that contemplation is productive or, as Plotinus prefers to put it, that production *is* contemplation. This comes out at III.8.3.20–23, where he writes:

> So Nature's making has been revealed to us as contemplation, for it is a result of contemplation, and the contemplation stays unchanged and does not do anything else but makes by being contemplation.[11]

The second thesis involved in Plotinus' account of productive contemplation is that the whole of the sensible world "comes from" the contemplation exercised by the particular *psyche* which is Nature and, thus, that *psyche* (i.e., Nature) is the cause of the sensible world, by virtue of its act of contemplation. This aspect of the doctrine of productive contemplation is brought out at III.8.7.1–4:

> That all things come from contemplation and are contemplation [at least in the sense of "being contemplated"], both the things which truly exist [i.e., the *eide* and the *psychai*] and the things which come from them when they contemplate and are themselves objects of contemplation, some by sense perception and some by knowledge or opinion [is clear].

Thus, what the *psyche*'s (i.e., Nature's) productive contemplation is productive of is, for Plotinus, the whole of the sensible world.

In chapter 4 of III.8, Plotinus asks Nature to explain her contemplative production of the sensible world, which she does by means of an analogy:

My act of contemplation makes an object of contemplation, as the geometers draw their figures while they contemplate. But I do not draw; rather, as I contemplate, the lines which bound bodies come to be as if they fell from my contemplation (III.8.4.7–10).

Although the apparent allusion to Plato's account of the construction of the regular solids at *Timaeus* 53c4–55c6 here is intriguing,[12] Nature's words leave me quite mystified: the production of the sensible world (in this case, of "the lines which bound bodies") just seems to happen as a result of Nature's contemplation. The details of the account are lacking, and the result is quite unsatisfactory from a philosophical point of view. What is clear here is that Nature's act of contemplation produces an object of contemplation, a θεώρημα, which *theorem* is the sensible world.

Plotinus follows up this statement from Nature with the following difficult, but illuminating, analysis:

What does this mean? That what is called Nature is a *pysche*, the offspring of a prior *psyche* with a stronger life; that it quietly holds contemplation in itself, not directed upwards or even downwards, but at rest in what it is, in its own repose and a kind of self-perception [or "self-consciousness," συναισθήσει], and in this consciousness and self-perception it sees what comes after it, as far as it can, and seeks no longer, but has accomplished a vision [θεώρημα] of splendour and delight (III.8.4.15–22).

This passage introduces the notion of self-consciousness (συναίσθησις) into the account of productive contemplation: the contemplation that is productive of the sensible world is a contemplation involving a *psyche*'s consciousness of itself. Nevertheless, the central question remains: How is this contemplative self-consciousness productive of the sensible world?

As a step towards the understanding and reconstruction of the doctrine of productive contemplation, it will prove useful to consider Plotinus' conception of the *psyche* in the light of the distinctively Neoplatonic interpretation of Plato's *Parmenides*. According to the Neoplatonic reading of the second half of the *Parmenides*, each of the first five (affirmative) hypotheses corresponds to and is descriptive of a particular level of reality. The third hypothesis, *Parmenides* 155e4–157b5, which is described as a "corollary on becoming in time" rather than as an independent hypothesis by F. M. Cornford,[13] deals with the metaphysical level of *psyche*, according to the Neoplatonic interpretation of Plato. While dealing with *psyche*, the third hypothesis serves as a sort of synthesis of the negative conclusions of the first hypothesis and the parallel positive conclusions of the second hypothesis. Thus, the *psyche* is conceived as an entity that somehow, in its nature, reconciles the negations of the first hypothesis with the affirmations of the second.[14]

However, since the psyche cannot be, for example, both at rest and in motion at the same time, the psyche's reconciliation of such opposites must be spread out over time, from which comes the derivation of time at the level of psyche for the Neoplatonists (compare *Ennead* III.7[45].11, discussed later in this section). Moreover, the actual passage in the psyche from rest to motion cannot take place at a particular time, since the psyche cannot be in both of two such contrary states at the same time; rather, this passage or change takes place in what Plato calls "the instant [τὸ ἐξαίφνης]," an "absurd thing" that occupies no time at all (see the *Parmenides* 156d1–e3). Thus, the *psyche*'s essential activity—which, in effect, amounts to the reconciliation of the opposite conclusions of the first two hypotheses of the *Parmenides*—occupies no time at all, though the possibility of this reconciliation presupposes the continued existence of the psyche over time. Moreover, the psyche is in a sense pure negativity since (at least in the course of its essential mediating activity) it is neither, for example, at rest nor in motion (nor is it any one of any pair of such contraries). Rather, the *psyche* makes the transition from rest to motion possible (and from any other state to its opposite), by providing a neutral point, the instant, at which this transition can take place. Hence, the Neoplatonic interpretation of the third hypothesis of the *Parmenides* reveals the *psyche* to be in itself a locus of pure negativity.[15]

Given this analysis of the *psyche* as pure negativity, I think that the doctrine of productive contemplation may begin to make some sense. We must begin by considering what it is that Nature contemplates when it contemplatively produces the sensible world. The previous quotation cited from III.8.4 suggests that Nature's object here is simply Nature itself as a *psyche,* since Nature is said to be "at rest in what it is, in its own repose and a kind of self-consciousness" (lines 18–19); however, we must not be led to think that Nature's object is itself pure negativity. Rather, its object is itself reflecting the intelligible world of *eide* in *logoi* (or psychical representations) because Nature "stays unmoved as it makes, and stays in itself, and is a *logos*" (III.8.3.2–3). In short, the object of Nature's (*psyche*'s) self-consciousness is really the intelligible world as reflected in Nature (psyche) (compare VI.5.9.23–48).

The question now arises: Where does the negativity of *psyche* come in? I suggest that the negativity of *psyche,* for Plotinus, consists in the negativity of self-consciousness, which sets itself over against the *eide* as something separate and distinct. As something distinct from Being, of course, self-consciousness must set itself up as (quite literally) nonbeing. Prior to the exercise of self-conscious contemplation, the *psyche* was in noetic identity with the intelligible world; however, once the *self* is added to the objects of *psyche*'s contemplation, the *psyche* itself becomes more of a nonentity. This is made quite clear at VI.5.12.19–22, where Plotinus writes:

> Formerly, you were the All [i.e., the intelligible world]. But, because you added something different to the All, you made yourself a lesser thing by this addition. For the addition was not from the All—you can add nothing to that—but from nonbeing.

(Note the use of the second person in this passage, which helps to emphasize the fact that the issue at hand here is *self*-conscious contemplation.) In passing, it is worthy of note that the psyche's interest in itself, its contemplative self-consciousness, is the source of the *psyche*'s moral evil according to Plotinus. This interest in self makes the *psyche* "a lesser thing," that is, a morally deficient being. The moral quality of self-consciousness is made strikingly clear at the beginning of the treatise "On the Three Primary Hypostases," V.1[10].1.3–5, where Plotinus writes:

> Thus, the beginning of evil for individual *psychai* is their audacity [τόλμα], their generation, their first difference, and their desire to be self-centered.

But, now, how does this doctrine of self-consciousness explain the contemplative production of the sensible world? I suggest that this is accomplished in the following way. When a *psyche* self-consciously contemplates (or, as in the present case, when Nature self-consciously contemplates) an eidos (for example, that of oak tree), what it is actually contemplating is that eidos as reflected in some logos or psychical representation. In other words, the *psyche* (i.e., Nature) is contemplating a *logos,* which is at once both a reflection of the *eidos* of oak tree and an aspect of the psyche itself, since each *psyche* is a "sum of *logoi*" (VI. 2[43].5.12). The self-consciousness of the *psyche*—by virtue of its desire to be self-centered, its desire to emphasize itself as a locus of pure negativity—sets its *logos* of oak tree over against the *eidos* of oak tree, attempting to set this *logos* up as something separate and distinct from the *eidos.* It is this *logos* of oak tree, made to seem separate and distinct from its *eidos* by the power of *psyche*'s (i.e., Nature's) negativity, that we call an oak tree in the sensible world. It is Nature's similar treatment of its *logoi* of other *eide* that leads to the production of the whole of the sensible world, with all of that world's complexity, all of its "splendour and delight."[16]

2. On the basis of the preceding analysis of psyche's central role in Plotinus' theory of eidetic causation, we are now in a position to sketch a Plotinian solution to Aristotle's objection concerning the intermittent causal efficacy of the *eide.* That psyche which Plotinus calls "Nature" effects the (omni-)presence of the intelligible world to the sensible world through its exercise of productive contemplation. One of the salient features of this contemplative activity is that it is discursive; that is, it involves a successive sort of understanding that can take place only in time. The essentially temporal character of *psyche*'s discursive contemplation is brought out in the Neoplatonic interpretation of the third hypothesis of the *Parmenides* as description of the metaphysical level occupied by psyche. If the *psyche* is (in its essential nature) the locus of the reconciliation of such opposites as motion and rest, and if such a reconciliation can occur only over a period of time, then it seems clear that the psyche must exist and act in time, at least to the extent that it is involved in some form of nonnoetic (and distinctively psychical) contemplation.[17] Indeed, as Plotinus makes clear in his important treatise "On Eternity and Time" (III.7[45]), time owes its derivation to the discursive character of psyche's essential activity (its "life"). At III.7.11.27–45, Plotinus develops his theory of the psychical nature of time (a theory designed to incorporate the view of *Timaeus* 37d5–7 that time is "an everlasting image moving according to number" of eternity) as follows:

> . . . *psyche,* making the sensible world in imitation of that other world, moving with a motion which is not that which exists there, but like it, and intending to be an image of it, first of all put itself into time, which it made instead of eternity, and then handed over that which came into being as a slave to time, by making

the whole of it exist in time and encompassing all its ways with time. . . . For as *psyche* presents one activity after another, and then again another in ordered succession, it produces the succession along with activity. . . . So the spreading out of life involves time; life's continual progress involves continuity of time, and life which is past involves past time. So would it be sense to say that time is the life of *psyche* in a movement of passage from one way of life to another? [Yes].[18]

When it is recalled that, at VI.5.12.1, Plotinus answers the question, "How is Being present to the sensible world [πάρεστιν οὖν πῶς]?, with the three words, "As one life ['Ως ζωὴ μία]," it becomes clear that the temporal character of the *psyche*'s (Nature's) nonnoetic discursive contemplation (which is productive of the sensible world) must play some role in the Plotinian theory of eidetic causation. This role is indicated by Plotinus at VI.5.11.15–16, where time is described as "being dispersed always toward separation [τοῦ μὲν σκιδναμένου ἀεὶ πρὸς διάστασιν]."[19] Hence, we may expect the temporal character of the *psyche*'s productive contemplation to figure in the Plotinian explanation (by eidetic causation) of the separation and disjointedness that are characteristic of the sensible world.

In fact, the discursive and, thus, temporal character of productive contemplation provides a solution to Aristotle's problem of the intermittent causal efficacy of the *eide*. If the *psyche* engaged in self-conscious, nonnoetic, discursive contemplation is continually redirecting its contemplative attention towards different *eide*, then the *logoi* derived from this contemplation and the particulars constituting the sensible world (which simply *are* these *logoi* set up as separate and distinct by the *psyche*'s self-consciousness) will be continually coming into being and passing away. This has the effect that only certain *eide* can be said to be fully present to the sensible world at any given time since only certain *eide* are the objects of Nature's productive contemplation at that time. Thus, each *eidos*'s causal efficacy vis-à-vis the sensible world is not continuous but intermittent because the *psyche*'s productive contemplation is the central link in the chain of eidetic causation.

In the preceding account, I have ignored an alternative theory accounting for the intermittent character of eidetic causation which appears to play a major role in VI.4–5 (e.g., VI.4.3.11–23; 11.3–14; VI.5.8.1–39). This alternative theory seems to attribute to matter a role in the causation of the sensible world, and the intermittent character of eidetic causation is explained by reference to the doctrine of "reception according to the capacity of the recipient." Since this theory appears to be in blatant contradiction to the thesis of the impassibility of matter (argued at great length at III.6[26].6–19), I think the theory sketched in this paper must be regarded as more representative of Plotinus, as well as being more satisfactory from a philosophical point of view.[20]

III

At the beginning of this paper, I quoted Émile Bréhier as saying that the "fourth and fifth treatises of the sixth *Ennead* . . . can easily be read without any reference to Greek philosophy."[21] I have argued, to the contrary, that these treatises on "The

Integral Omnipresence of Being" provide Plotinus' carefully developed elucidation of the concept of eidetic causation or participation, a concept that lies at the heart of metaphysical Platonism. This generates an obvious question: On what basis does Bréhier divorce VI.4–5 from the Greek metaphysical tradition?

Bréhier apparently regards the main task of VI.4–5 to be the elucidation of Plotinus' doctrine concerning "the relations of the individual soul to the universal Soul."[22] He goes on to argue that Plotinus' treatment of the relation between the individual *psyche* and the hypostasis *Psyche* is strikingly similar to the account of the relation between the Atman and Brahman to be found in the Upanishads[23] and strikingly different from anything to be found in the Greek metaphysical tradition.[24] It is on this basis that Bréhier separates VI.4–5 from the mainstream of the history of Platonism.

To be sure, there can be no doubt that Plotinus' monopsychism plays a significant role in the argument of the treatises on omnipresence (e.g., VI.4.14–15 are devoted to answering standard objections to the monopsychistic theory affirmed in VI.4.6). However, if the general argument of this paper is sound, then one of Plotinus' main concerns in VI.4–5 is to develop a philosophically adequate account of eidetic causation or participation; the doctrine of monopsychism comes up in the course of his analysis of eidetic causation, but it never assumes the status of the central problem of the treatises. Thus, I think we may conclude that Bréhier's divorce of VI.4–5 from the Greek metaphysical tradition rests on a certain misdirection of emphasis in his interpretation of the treatises, a misdirection of emphasis towards the problems of monopsychism and away from the problems of eidetic causation and participation.

I have claimed that the doctrine of monopsychism comes up in the course of Plotinus' analysis of eidetic causation, and this raises a final question: Why does Plotinus introduce a theory of monopsychism into his account of eidetic causation? I think this question can be answered along the following lines. In Section II of this paper, Plotinus' account of the *psyche*'s causal relation to the sensible world was discussed as a central aspect of this theory of eidetic causation, and I think it is fair to describe this theory of the sensible world as a form of metaphysical idealism. This theory, in common with all idealistic accounts of the sensible world (e.g., phenomenalism), faces the difficult problem of reconciling the intersubjective accessibility of the sensible world with the idealistic account of its existence. I suggest that Plotinus, in common with many other idealistic metaphysicians, offers a theory of monopsychism in order to explain (on idealistic principles) how there can be one sensible world, equally accessible to all experiencing subjects (or *psychai*).[25]

This explanation of Plotinus' adoption of monopsychism in the theory of eidetic causation may seem rather speculative; however, I think it derives some support from an obscure passage in VI.5. At VI.5.9.1–13, Plotinus offers the following argument in defense of monopsychism:

> Now, if someone were to maintain that the totality of the elements already having come into being are [brought together] in a single spherical figure, then it

would be clear that the sphere is not produced by many [causes] working with regard to parts, one part being separated from another which itself works toward the production of a part. Rather, the cause of the production must be one, producing as a whole in itself and not producing different parts of the sphere by different parts of itself. Otherwise, there would be many again, unless you refer the production to a unity without parts, or, better, unless the thing producing the sphere is a unity without parts which is not itself spread throughout the sphere by the producing; rather, the whole sphere is dependent upon the thing producing it. Thus, one and the same life possesses the sphere, the sphere itself having been placed in one life; moreover, all the things in the sphere [i.e., the totality of the elements] are in one life. Therefore, all *psychai* are one.

At first glance, this argument may seem rather peculiar since the argument itself (lines 1–10) appears to establish only that there must be a single cause of the totality of the elements (i.e., of the sensible world). The monopsychistic conclusion (indeed, the "psychistic" conclusion) is derived from the identification of this single cause of the sensible with a single life, and in the light of Section II, such an identification is not at all unexpected. What remains somewhat unclear is the reasoning that Plotinus uses to support the claim that the productive cause of the sensible world must be a unity. At one level, we might see in this an application of the traditional Platonic principle that "like causes like," the unity of the sensible thus being caused by the unity of the *psyche* responsible for it. However, at a deeper level, I think that the obscure words of VI.5.9 can be seen to mark Plotinus' recognition of the important fact that the sensible world is a public world. To explain the sensible world in terms of a multiplicity of psychical causes (particularly if this multiplicity were to include all individual *psychai*) would appear to leave the intersubjective accessibility and, indeed, the "objectivity" of this world a mystery. Thus, I suggest that Plotinus introduces monopsychism into his account of eidetic causation in order to solve a general problem that faces any idealistic account of the sensible world.

My consideration of several major problems dealt with by Plotinus in VI.4–5 clearly shows that the treatises on "The Integral Omnipresence of Being" fall squarely within the tradition of Greek metaphysics. In these treatises, Plotinus deals at length with a number of philosophical problems that stem from the fundamental problem of metaphysical Platonism—the problem of characterizing the relation between the intelligible world and the sensible world. In coming to grips with these difficulties, Plotinus offers us a subtle and carefully developed explication of the Platonic concept of eidetic causation or participation.

Cantor's Sets and Proclus' Wholes

ROBERT S. BRUMBAUGH

I

This paper is rather an agenda for discussion than a finished argument. I started out with the intention of translating Stamatis's 1958 article on Cantor and Proclus, as the basis for a reevaluation of Proclus as a mathematician. (The article, which has received some attention in Scandinavia, but not in England or the United States, is Evangelos Stamatis, "Peri tēs theōrias tōn Synolōn para Platōni," *Praktika tēs Akademias Athenōn,* 1958, pp. 298–303.) Rather soon, however, it occurred to me that Proclus' philosophical position exactly fits the needs of contemporary mathematicians committed to *logicism* as a philosophic context for their mathematics. The crucial point here, for the mathematician, is that certain axioms which are needed, but which seem somehow extramathematical, appear in Neoplatonism as *philosophic* truths.

It next occurred to me that the similarities between Proclus' logic of parts and wholes and Cantor's operations with sets justified identifying set theory with the formal development of that science studying the kinship of all mathematical art which Plato projected in *Republic* VII, but which was not formally developed in the classical period. This, if correct, offers a welcome addition to our Platonic formal logic and dialetic.

But the most interesting aspect of the paper was one that I recognized last, namely, that it is a case study of the way in which Neoplatonism can clarify and discuss twentieth-century technical philosophic problems. It is not only in foundations of mathematics that this can happen. The whole theory of democracy, whether called "participatory" or not, depends on a proper analysis of participation. The question of authority involves decisions as to the status and effectiveness of the principles of hierarchy in viable organizational structures. Other contemporary issues, ranging from psychology to religion, invite exploration of the implications of Neoplatonism.

II

Over the past twelve months, American mathematicians have opened a lively discussion of the foundations of mathematics. The most popular position is one called *logicism*. This view is "realistic" (i.e., Platonic) in its view of the subject matter of the discipline; and it *defines* "mathematics" as the theorems that can be deduced from Cantor's set theory as formalized in eight axioms by Zermelo and Fraenkel (the Z-F axioms).[1]

One difficulty with the logicist project is that two of the needed axioms seem extramathematical in their stipulations of existence and constructibility. But these conditions, as well as the presupposed metaphysical "realism," would be satisfied if our colleagues would take Neoplatonism as their contextual philosophy. At least, this is one thesis my paper will explore.

The current discussion suggests a converse relation, as well. In 1958, in an original but highly technical paper, Professor Stamatis suggested that one section of Proclus' *Elements* (sec. H) anticipated the key definitions (if not the formalization) of Cantor's general theory of sets.[2] If this is true, it suggests that we must reevaluate Proclus' ability as a mathematician. Beyond that, it suggests to me that Cantor may finally have found the formal structure of a general mathematical science that studies "how the [other] mathematical sciences are akin." Plato projected this as the final study prior to "dialectic" in *Republic* VII; Iamblichus put together an anthology on the topic; Proclus, if Stamatis is right, almost hit upon it; but its full development may have had to wait until A.D. 1883. If so, we may be able to incorporate a new and powerful formal tool as part of our contemporary Neoplatonic philosophy.

III

The Neoplatonists, Iamblichus and Proclus, thought that there should be a discipline of universal mathematics mediating between the world of ordinary language and mystical silence. But because the mathematics of their time was dominated by geometry, a suitable formal system was not at hand. Proclus, indeed, in pursuit of the needed study wrote a *Commentary on Book I of Euclid's Elements*.[3] The result was a creditable venture in the history of geometry, but later scholars have found the talent revealed was moderately mathematical, if at all.[4] In quite another context, his *Elements of Theology,* Proclus started along another line by setting up—verbally, however, not algebraically—some theorems about parts, wholes, and elements that were more general than Aristotelian logic or Euclidean geometry.[5] The scheme vaguely outlined there was filled out in tight formal detail in 1883, by Georg Cantor, under the name of *general set theory.*[6]

The recognition of the similarities of Proclus and Cantor was first presented, as I mentioned, in the paper by E. Stamatis in the *Praktika tēs Akademias Athenōn* in 1958.[7] This article, in modern Greek and in a journal philosophers do not ordinarily read, has attracted some attention in Scandinavia, but has gone unnoticed in England and America. Meanwhile, Neoplatonists today have not claimed that their philosophic position is a viable one for precise work in the contemporary philosophy of mathematics, formal logic, or philosophy of science. By and large, its studies have been restricted to natural language and have tended, within that restriction, to focus on *eikasia* where emanation reaches the level of semblance, or on *noesis* where discipline attains mystical culmination. That concentration clearly does not contribute very much to current logic, physics, ethics, or politics; and even might lead a skeptic to wonder whether Neoplatonism can, by our century, represent more than antiquarian studies of magic, literary footnotes, and an invitation to mystical theology.

IV

One very modest intention of my present discussion is to return to Proclus and to argue that we should revise the generally accepted notion that he was not a very talented mathematician or logician. This appraisal, which rests mainly on his Euclid commentary (plus his rather wooden work with Aristotelian syllogistic), suggests that his contributions do not fall in the history of formal science proper. In turn, since Proclus was, of all the Neoplatonists, the one most enthusiastic about formalization, this suggests in turn that precision and Neoplatonic formalism may be incompatible; that our philosophy cannot be formalized; and even that, given any question of contemporary interest, we are likely, at best, to express a misty grievance over the fall of the Soul from Mind to Time.

As a ground for this reappraisal of Proclus, consider the following argument. Sir Thomas Heath, whose heroes were the great geometers, says in his chapter on Eudoxus that the talent of Eudoxus is evident from the fact that his definition of "number" is an exact anticipation of Dedekind's epoch-making definition of a "cut."[8] If the thesis of Stamatis's article is correct, his claim that Proclus anticipated the definitions of Cantor's general set theory would lead to the parallel conclusion that Proclus' talent—for mathematics of this algebraic type, even if not for plane geometry—must have been somewhat comparable to Cantor's.

What that order of talent is can be indicated by a brief note on the contemporary importance of set theory. We have already seen that contemporary proponents of the position of logicism as the foundation of mathematics simply define mathematics as the theorems formally deducible from the axioms of set theory.[9] And as we look at the special cases this includes, the inventory is impressive. This approach provides a new basis for the foundations of mathematics; it gives an entire new precision to the treatment of "infinite" amounts and numbers; it sharpens the definitions of "relative frequency" which ground the study of probability; it includes mathematical logic as a special case (hence it also includes Aristotelian logic, which is, as seen by a modern mathematician, simply a cumbersome and degenerate case of mathematical logic). In short, Cantor's achievement certainly ranks with Dedekind's, and so by an extension of Heath's argument, we should conclude that Proclus and Eudoxus are somewhere close together.

V

Turning now to modern mathematics, I want to suggest that the current logicist program for developing the science is possible if, but perhaps only if, Neoplatonic metaphysics is a correct description of reality. Recall that the logicist program calls for the deduction of mathematics from the eight Z-F axioms that Zermelo and Fraenkel formulated as the basis of set theory.[10] Now, a recent appraisal of this enterprise in the *American Mathematical Monthly,* by an author who favors it, concedes that the program "is only 75% successful" because "two of the Z-F axioms have empirical content and so are not properly 'logical.'" These are the so-called Axiom of Infinity and the Axiom of Choice.[11]

The *Axiom of Infinity* asserts that there exist a transfinite number of entities on each level of set "elements." The *Axiom of Choice* asserts that a mathematician can construct special subsets by appropriate selection of elements from given sets. (But this "construction" is a definition by selective attention, not a creation *ex nihilo.*)

In effect, the comment that these axioms are not purely logical, on the level of *dianoia,* seems correct. The reason is, I think, that the axioms in question are rather philosophical descriptions or specifications of the universe in which mathematical logicism is possible. Thus the Axiom of Infinity describes the world of nature, with its separate individuals—its divisible material objects and successive generations of plants and animals. Given the Neoplatonic principle of limitation, which makes natural individuals *definite,* and the principle of plenitude which makes their generations *successive,* this condition of infinity will be satisfied. The Axiom of Choice describes the way of knowing of a human soul, which after its descent to time must recover ideas discursively and progressively. The ideas are together in a timeless system of relations, but we must learn this piece by piece, by acts of selective attention. Thus the first philosophical axiom stipulates that the world, being presupposed, is one that has definite individuality and succession on the relevant levels, and the second that the world also has freedom for selective attention and inquiry on the level of soul.

As a basis for discussion, let me define in more detail what I mean by "a Neoplatonic universe." In the first place, such a universe is stratified: there are in it abstract entities, concrete individual instances, and collections of like individuals. These differ in their properties, but they are related. The abstract entities define—and in some sense cause—the extensional classes that *exemplify* them, and they are *instantiated* by the individual members of those classes. Things are arranged in hierarchies, with the more abstract and general entities serving as explanations and unifying causes for less general orders. One fundamental characteristic, then, is that there are at least these three levels, which are distinct but which are causally connected. There is also a background limitation of hierarchical structure and a foreground plenitude of contrast differentiation. Any two different forms are included in some hierarchy that has a third single form as its vertex. And any one form can be pluralized, on a more specific level, by division through cross-classification, adding contrary specifying attributes. Forms retain their self-identity; thus, from the standpoint of F, FA and FA' are equally F; and, similarly, FA is self-identical in FAB and FAB'. This algebraic symbolism avoids muddled puzzlements of "late learners" trapped in ordinary language, or limited to the visual constructions of plane geometry.[12]

Notice that where some Platonic universes may be tolerant of continuity and borderline cases, Neoplatonic ones are more definite and restrictive, and have quantum jumps. Thus the levels of being, though internally related, are discontinuous; participation of individual instances in form is subject to the law of contradiction; the membership of an extensional class is exactly determined. This may mean that the universe we have defined is more abstract and tidier than the one we actually inhabit. But since the two are isomorphic, we can use universal mathematics as the key to the world's structure with logic, ethics, aesthetics, and so on, as special cases.

VI

In the present context, however, it is the other direction of the relation between the mathematical logician and the Neoplatonic philosopher that is of more interest to us. We may or we may not persuade a majority of the members of the American Mathematical Society to join us because we are Neoplatonists. But should *we* join *them* because they have formalized fundamental logical rules for our world of Neoplatonism? I think that we should, and that the alliance may give some new ideas to our philosophy. Let me turn now to that formal logic, via a more detailed consideration of set theory.[13]

In *Republic* VII, Plato recognized the need to develop two new mathematical sciences. The first of these was to be "solid geometry," a systematic deductive study of geometry in three dimensions.[14] The second, coming at the end of the mathematics courses and at the beginning of the study of dialectic, was to be a study of "how all the mathematical sciences are akin," "what they have in common."[15] No special name is given this in the *Republic,* but Aristotle's "universal mathematics"—a discipline he defined but did not develop—sounds rather like the same thing.[16] In any case, what the mathematical sciences do have in common is an abstract formal structure and a clear deductive proof procedure. It is interesting that the first of these desired discoveries was made within Plato's own lifetime, by Theaetetus and Eudoxus in the Academy; whereas the second had to await the nineteenth century, and the work of Georg Cantor, for its full formal realization.[17] In the interim, the idea was not wholly forgotten: Iamblichus, for example, wrote a treatise (or anthology) on *The Community of the Mathematical Sciences,* and Proclus, as we have mentioned, had some very general formalization—particularly of the relations of forms, classes extensionally defined, and parts—in his *Elements of Theology.*[18]

But what is set theory? It has been described, half seriously, as a general formal system of which everything else in mathematics is a special case. The key to the enterprise is given by two of Cantor's characterizations of "set."

He writes: "A set is a bringing together of determinate clearly differentiable objects (*Objekte*), whether of our intuition or our thought—which [objects] will be called the elements of the set—into a whole."

In another, more illuminating, passage we find the following:

> I view as collections, or sets, all multiplicities which are such as to be thought of as one, that is, all determinate collections of elements of such a kind that it is possible to find a single criterion capable of bringing them together, and I believe that in this way I define something which is akin to that which Plato, in his dialogue *Philebus,* calls "the mixed."

These definitions are clear enough, though very general. They suggest that wherever there is a Platonic form, it can serve as a criterion for class membership; the extensional definition of such a form will be the total collection of its instances, regarded as a whole; and, as we have seen, each "element" will be such that it determinately does possess the attribute which serves as membership criterion for the extensional set.

To see how this theory develops, I will follow the presentation of a modern mathematics text that has become a classic, Courant and Robbins, *What Is Mathematics?,* in their summary of "the algebra of sets" (pp. 108–117).[19]

At the outset, sets are defined in terms very like Cantor's.

> A set is defined by any property or attribute A (Italic A) which each object considered must either possess or not possess; those objects which possess the property form a corresponding set A (Roman A). Thus, if we consider the integers and the property Italic A is that of being a prime, the corresponding set Roman A() is the set of all primes 2, 3, 5, 7 · · ·.[20]

An important additional notion is next introduced.

> *I* will denote a fixed set of objects of any nature, called the universal set or universe of discourse, and Roman A, B, C, will denote arbitrary subsets of *I*.[21]

This addition has the effect, desirable for our purposes, of adding a principle of hierarchy to the full generality of the first definition. For every convergent hierarchy (converging at a single topmost form) constitutes a universe of discourse within which subdivisions can be made by what Plato called "the great method of division"; but the top term (Courant and Robbins's *I*) cannot be defined within its hierarchy; it can be treated only if it can be included in a more general universe of discourse.

We will now turn briefly to the defined relations and algebraic operations of sets. *Definition of subset*: A is a subset of B if there is no object in A that is not also in B (written A ⊂ B or B ⊃ A). *Definition of* equality: If both A ⊂ B and B ⊂ A, we say A equals B (A = B). Two operations are next defined: Set union (or logical sum) and set intersection (or logical product). *Definition of logical sum*: The sum of A and B (A + B, or A v B) is the set of all the objects that are in either A or B, including those in both. Thus, if A = /1,2,3/ and B = /2,3,4/, A + B = /1,2,3,4/. *Definition of logical product*: The logical product of A and B (written A.B, or AB) is the set consisting of only those elements that are in *both* A and B. Thus, if A = /1,2,3/ and B = /2,3,5/, A·B = /2,3/.

This system is more general than arithmetic. Taking a notion from Boethius's *de trinitate* (where it is introduced to defend Christianity against the charge of tritheism), we can say that this is an algebra for operation in the category of substance, whereas our ordinary arithmetic operates in the category of *quantity*. Thus "A and A" equals A, since A is not changed by being twice referred to. All the rules of the ordinary algebra of numbers are also valid in the theory of sets. Three laws, however, which have no numerical counterparts, "give this algebra of sets a simpler structure than the algebra of numbers."[22] These laws (10, 11, and 13 in the Courant and Robbins list) are: A + A = A; AA = A; A + (BC) = (A + B) · (A + C). In addition, there is the notion of "complement": the complement of A, A′, is the set of all the objects in *I* that are not in A. Thus, A + A′ = *I*, and AA′ = O.

The power of this basic formal system becomes clear when we look at some of its special applications and cases.

We can look now at some special applications and cases. The School mathematics Study Group has devised texts that show how ordinary algebra and arithmetic can be developed as one set of special cases of set theory. Mathematical logic can also be treated as an interpretation, both as class calculus and propositional calculus. The theory is thus general enough to include, or to be isomorphic with, a formal scheme that represents valid deductive reasoning in a symbolic form. The development of the computer rests on an extension of propositional calculus, originating in the recognition that "truth values," 0 and 1, can also represent open and closed values for two-position electric switches.[23] Thus, in handling information, A + B = 1 if A = 1 or B = 1, and A·B = 1 if A = 1 and B = 1. Calculation in this system involves only very high-speed repetitions of the operation of "logical addition." In effect, this is a dialectical scheme remembering and comparing patterns of relations of being, same, and other. The superiority of mathematical logic and computer programs to the Aristotelian syllogistic system will be evident to anyone who has ever tried to design switches and circuitry for the automatic checking of the validity of Aritotelian syllogism and sorites.

In addition, as was mentioned before, set theory leads naturally to a new way of defining probability—an interesting bonus but perhaps one not immediately relevant to our present philosophical interests. However, it also leads to remarkable results when it considers "infinity": transfinite sets with transfinite cardinal and ordinal numbers. Precise definitions of orders of infinity, and of "greater than" among transfinite numbers, clears up a good many of the confusions hidden behind the *word* "infinite." Further, it was shown by Robert Hartman that this extended set theory offers a model for formal value theory that avoids the counter-intuitive results of value theories that use only finite numbers for value comparison. This last point is philosophically very interesting since a good Platonic formalism ought to have applications to the theory of value as well as to more formal, abstract ontology.[24]

VII

Let me now turn to Stamatis's suggested equivalence of Cantor's sets and Proclus' wholes, in his article "Peri tēs Theōrias tōn Synolōn para Platōni," *Praktika tēs Akademias Athenōn* 33 (1958), pp. 298–303.

The article opens with a quotation of Cantor's definition of set with its reference to Plato's *Philebus* at the end, which I quoted above. Stamatis next cites two passages from Plato's *Parmenides* (137C, 157D–E), which suggest that there could be a formalized treatment of parts and wholes. And he finds exactly such a treatment carried out in section VIII of Proclus' *Elements of Theology,* more specifically in propositions 66–69.[25] These are the following:

Proclus, *Prop. 66*:
All beings are related to one another either as wholes or parts, either as same or different.

Proclus, *Prop. 67*:
All wholeness is either prior to the parts, or arises from the parts collectively, or is in the parts singly. For we see that the form is the cause of each whole, and we call this the whole prior to the parts, which exists in the cause. Or the form is [considered] as participated in by the parts. And this is in one of two ways. For either the parts all share it, [as a collection] and it is this whole made of the [totality of] the parts, which will be destroyed if any part is removed; or each single part is a participant in it, so that each part is generated by its participation in the whole. And this makes the part a partial (*merikōs*) whole. Thus the whole as it exists [extensionally] is constituted from its parts; but as cause, it is prior to its parts; and as participated in, it is in each single part. And this holds even to the limiting whole [i.e., a least part] which is like the whole composed from parts, at least when it is not a part just by chance, but able to be included in a whole the parts of which are also wholes.

Proclus, *Prop. 68*:
Every whole which is in a part, is a part of the whole of the parts. For if it is a part, it is a part of some whole, and either of the whole in it itself—so that the whole is spoken of as the whole in the part; and in that way it is a part of itself, and the part will be equal to the whole, and in that case they are the same—or [it is part] of some other whole. And if of another, either it is the only part of this—and thus, again, it differs from the whole in nothing—because one existent part (*element*) partakes of one; or it is able to be included in another set, of which the parts are wholes.

Proclus, *Prop. 69*:
Everything which is a whole of parts participates in the wholeness which is prior to the parts.

Stamatis suggests that the three part-to-whole relations Proclus distinguishes match Cantor's basic definitions of his set theory.[26] Thus, what Cantor calls the criterion or defining attribute (Italic *A*, etc.) is what Proclus calls a "*holon*" in the sense of an *eidos*, the "whole prior to its parts." (Proclus goes beyond Cantor here in assigning these *eidē* a causal role.) The whole "as existing," that is, as the extensional set of all the elements that have the defining attribute, is Cantor's set Roman A, exactly matching Proclus' "whole as coming to be from the together-ness of its component parts." Proclus' notion of a "part" and a "least part," however, does not exactly match Cantor's "element." Cantor's elements must have definite identities, so that they are unambiguously self-identical or other; Proclus' parts seem to satisfy that condition. The elements must be related to the Italic *A*, and so on, defining attributes by a definite either-or relation in Cantor's system. Proclus seems to leave room for "parts" that "are parts just by chance," and so do not imitate unity or wholeness in the way more proper parts do. In Cantor's scheme, it seems that the "objects" we perceive or think about are also "elements," and that for any attribute, every "object" either falls in the set Roman A defined by that attribute or in the complement of that set, Roman A'. But Proclus is less restrictive in his ontology. In the twentieth century, there have been theories of "fuzzy sets" where the notions of part or element are closer to Proclus than to Cantor.[27]

Cantor's scheme is clearer and easier to handle than Proclus' would be even if it were formalized. But it is clear that Stamatis's thesis is correct, and that Proclus' "wholes" are defined by the same three conditions used later to define his "sets" by Cantor.

In the context I have sketched, this not only commits us to a reappraisal of the role of Proclus and Iamblichus in the history of mathematics, and of their mathematical-logical abilities, but it also commits us to taking sides in the current controversy over the foundations of mathematics. We are not only committed to the *logicist* position, with its "realism" and set theoretical formalization, but we come prepared to explain and defend the "philosophic" axioms necessary for the logicist enterprise axioms that fall in the field of metaphysics and epistemology rather than being formal logical axioms proper.

VIII

Set theory exactly matches the worldview of a Neoplatonic modification of Plato's metaphysics—perhaps influenced by Aristotle—in which forms ingress in all-or-nothing way, and beings are located definitely and determinately on one or another level of emanation. This modification seems to me to correct, or at least to offer an alternative to, Plato's reliance on continuity and geometry, and to give more formal precision to the definition of the basic structure of participation.[28]

When Plato offered his project for the new science to explore the kinship of mathematical sciences, it was evidently something like formal logic that he had in mind. But for a thousand years, as the record of the Platonic scholia shows, his followers tried to realize this goal either by a "logic" of geometrical symbolism, or by an analysis of natural language ordered in Aristotelian syllogism.[29] What was needed to carry out the project was—as Proclus saw—something more like Aristotle's "universal mathematics," a nonverbal formalism like algebra rather than like geometry. And the success of Cantor's system suggests that, in fact, a philosophy of formalism should consider his *Mengenlehre* as a leading candidate for the desired science of the formal structure of reality.

The materials are ready at hand for assembling a new systematic treatise on Neoplatonic philosophy, as an expansion of Proclus' system. Chapters could begin with metaphysics and general set theory; they could proceed to formal logic; then general arithmetic and algebra can be derived; and a theory of probability follows. The study of transfinite number is an elegant and useful extension. (For the moment, I will bypass the way in which we will introduce geometry.) And as a final section, there is already a good formal beginning toward extending the transfinite numbers and using them as models for a formal axiology, a mathematics of value.[30] This could bring together Cantor and Proclus: the pure mathematical formalism of the one, in the philosophic context of Platonism (and attendant mysticism) of the other.

The Mathematics of Mysticism: Plotinus and Proclus

CARL R. KORDIG

One of the two great Neoplatonists is Plotinus. Dominus, Syrianus, Aedesius, and Iamblichus followed. Much more important, however, than any of these men is the celebrated Proclus of Athens. I wish to deal with Plotinus' views here. I also wish to deal with the later Scholarch Proclus Diodachus. I will focus on the question of self-reference and some related, logical-mathematical issues.

Proclus possessed a wide knowledge concerning the philosophies of Plato, Aristotle, and his predecessors. He combined with this knowledge a great interest in and enthusiasm for religion, both theory and practice. For example, he seems to have seriously believed he received, in some sense, revelations and was, in some sense of the word, the reincarnation of the Neo-Pythagorean Nicomachus. And at one time he toyed with the idea of solving the participation problem—the problem of the one and the many—by locating the participation relation itself in various occult "symbols" that reside in certain stones, herbs, and animals. Some say that Proclus was superstitious, that he believed in mermaids and goat-footed Pans and that his arguments from analogy were not always perfect as they might have been; for example, "from the fact that the Man in the Moon has eyes and ears but no nose or mouth he can argue seriously that [all the] astral gods possess only the two higher senses" (Proclus *The Elements of Theology*, E. R. Dodds, trans., 2nd ed. Oxford: Oxford University Press, 1963, p. xxv). This is one picture that has been painted of Proclus. There are others and surprisingly sometimes by the same people. He had a universal wealth of information and learning at his disposal, such as his knowledge of the Pre-Socratics, Plato, Aristotle, and the earlier Neoplatonists. In this he had a serious and good influence on medieval thought; for example, I think, on Saint Thomas Aquinas. Proclus, at any rate, attempted to combine these elements in one carefully articulated system—a task his dialectical ability made possible. He was perhaps "a lively and living work of art," a human torch. Other pictures painted of Proclus go still further. Thomas Taylor stresses that "of that golden chain of philosophers, who, having themselves happily penetrated, luminously unfolded to others the profundities of the philosophy of Plato, Proclus is indisputably the largest and most refulgent link. . . . Born . . . a genius, . . . he exhibited in his own person a union of the rarest kind [and that his] *Commentaries* [of Plato] were written by him . . . in the flower of his age." Some go still further. The late Dr. Charles Burney, on being asked by Thomas Taylor whether he had ever read Proclus' *Commentaries*, replied that they were too much for him, at the same time exclaiming, "What a giant was Proclus compared to Longinus!" And Marinus says—I think rightly—"that he was a man laborious to a miracle." And the eulogium of Ammonius Hermeas "that Proclus possessed the power of unfolding the opinions of the ancients and a scientific judgement of the nature of things, in the highest perfection possible to humanity," does go too far; yet some think it should, as Thomas Taylor has it, "be immediately assented to by everyone who is an adept in the writings of this incomparable man" (for sources compare Thomas Taylor's introduction to Proclus' *Commentary on the Timaeus*).

The importance of Proclus perhaps seems to have been underestimated somewhat in the twentieth century. Fortunately, however, this situation is beginning to be rectified—especially since the clandestine founding some twelve years ago at Yale, under Professor Robert S. Brumbaugh's auspices, of the Clusion Society, and of the subject Clusion Network Theory, a founding *so clandestine* that it was clandestine even to its founders. "Objective links" have indeed recently been discovered between Proclus and medieval thought.

Saint Albertus Magnus, according to Dodds, and the Byzantine Neoplatonist Michael Psellus (1018–1078) were "steeped in Proclus."

Copelston, Sambursky, and others have indeed recognized the brilliance, of Proclus. Paul Schaich has assured me that there is, in *The Elements of Theology* of Proclus, a deep anticipation of Bradley's argument against relations.

Proclus' entire system proceeds as follows: from the One emanate the Henads—a finite number; from the Henads emanates the sphere of *Nous* which subdivides as Being, Life, and Thought; from the sphere of *Nous* emanates the sphere of the Soul which subdivides into divine souls, demonic souls—angels, demons, and heroes—and human souls, for example, myself. There is a strong mystical strain running through his framework and the Neoplatonic tradition generally. It arises from the claim that the One is absolutely transcendent, beyond all thought and all being, ineffable and incomprehensible. This claim readily appears in the doctrines of Plotinus,[1] Iamblichus,[2] and Damascius.[3] It is, however, most carefully dealt with and receives its most systematic espousal from the celebrated Proclus of Athens. Proclus' *Commentary On The Parmenides*[4] is a polished espousal of the first hypothesis of Plato's *Parmenides*. It is there that he expresses his own view of the One and shows his acute sensitivity to logical problems arising from it. I will attempt, among other things, to examine the tenability of Proclus' view of the One. In the course of this examination, I will evaluate some of his solutions to the logical difficulties resulting from his position as to the One. I wish to argue that the letter of his position, strictly speaking, is beset with insurmountable difficulties and that his solutions to them are unsatisfactory. It needs emendation.

Proclus does not merely interpret Plato's *Parmenides*. He also uses it dialectically to develop systematically what he feels are truths of theology and metaphysics. Viewing the eight hypotheses as metaphysical options, Proclus takes the first to be the correct one. As a correct interpretation of Plato's *intention* in the *Parmenides,* this is certainly suspect.[5] But Proclus is not merely an interpreter; he is also a metaphysician. He is concerned with the nature of things and with the development of truths of speculative metaphysics, and this must be evaluated independently of whether or not his interpretation of Plato is correct.

Proclus saw the point of the hypothesis as constituting a proof that there is an absolutely transcendent One. For Proclus and Plotinus, the One exceeds all qualification whatsoever. It transcends all properties and relations, all predicates, and all statements on our part. It transcends the predicates "Unity," "Cause," and "Good," just as it transcends "Being": "That which transcends all cannot, as has been shown, be susceptible of even a hint of a relationship to anything else."[6] It is beyond existence, "nothing at all . . . belongs to it" (p. 45 [7]; compare also p. 67 [22–24]). It "is before every power and before assertions" (p. 75[3–4]); even negations are not true of it and are removed from it (pp. 71 [35–37], 77[4–5]). The "most glorious One is neither expressible nor knowable" (p. 71[30]). It is impossible for any property to apply to it, being "inexpressible" and "unutterable" (pp. 41[25], 67[3,35]). No name or description applies to it; there is no perception or knowledge of it; there is no opinion that fits it (pp. 45 [6–14], 47 [21]–49 [12], 51 [25–30]). This is, of course, not because it is less than any of these things but because it is more; for example, "it is superior to being and existence and better than intelligible objects" (p. 45[32–33])—so superior that it is "the object of desire to all things" (p. 57[37]). It is essentially unintelligible, yet so important that all being, practice, and knowledge presuppose it. Proclus later (in *The Elements of Theology*) incorporates this conception into a comprehensive metaphysical system. And by so doing he arrives at what is perhaps the most systematic and thoroughgoing negative mysticism known to man.

I now wish to argue that Proclus' and Plotinus' position as to the One is beset with insurmountable logical difficulties. Proclus and Plotinus claim that no descriptive predicate whatsoever applies to the One. Let us assume this. Now let us introduce a new term "Proclusian" in the following way: for any x, x is Proclusian if and only if x is such that no descriptive predicate applies to it. The phrase "such that no descriptive predicate applies to it" is, if meaningful, obviously a descriptive predicate; therefore, so is the term "Proclusian," which is merely an abbreviation for the latter phrase. The One of Plotinus and Proclus is such that no descriptive predicate applies to it; therefore, from the definition of the descriptive predicate "Proclusian," the One is Proclusian. But since "Proclusian" itself is a descriptive predicate, it also follows that the One is not Proclusian. But strictly speaking this is contradictory, which is absurd. Proclus'—and Plotinus'—claim that no descriptive predicate whatsoever applies to the One leads to contradiction and must therefore be abandoned. If the One is "Proclusian," it follows that it is not the case that the One is such that no descriptive predicate applies to it, and hence not Proclusian. The claim that the One is such that no descriptive predicate applies to it implies its own negation. Hence it is untenable; if we asserted it, we would also be forced to asset its negation, and we cannot intelligently assert both it and its negation. Claiming that no descriptive predicate applies to the One *ipso facto* forces us to also make the contradictory claim that some descriptive predicates apply to the One. This claim of Plotinus and Proclus, is, therefore, strictly speaking, logically untenable. I have argued in detail elsewhere[7] that Proclus' own and quite sophisticated replies to this objection fail. His replies, although more detailed and in many ways more sophisticated, are just like Quine's advocation of ontological relativity and of the revisability of logical laws, and they fail for the same reason: namely, they are self-refuting.[8] I find it reasonable to conclude, therefore, that Proclus' main thesis in his *Commentary On The Parmenides*—that the One is not expressible—is untenable.

Proclus ends his *Commentary* with two sentences that succinctly express the principal theme and outlook of the Neoplatonic tradition: "For by means of a negation Parmenides has removed all negations. With silence he concludes the contemplation of the One." Now a silence justified by irrational means (i.e., by untenable claims and bad arguments) is not really justified. It is an irrational silence. And I have argued that there are insurmountable logical difficulties with the "means" by which Proclus "has removed all negations." By a demonstrably untenable negation, Proclus has removed all negations. Therefore, I feel that such a mystical "silence," for Proclus, would be unjustified.[9] For these reasons, then, I think that an espousal and development of the first hypothesis in Plato's *Parmenides* will not result in a viable metaphysics, as Robert S. Brumbaugh has argued in his book, *Plato On The One* (New Haven: Yale University Press, 1961).

This conclusion, of course, need not hold with respect to more positive mystical characterizations of the One. If we are inclined to sketch the One in a more satisfactory manner, then we should also be prepared to deal with its mystical features in a more positive way.[10] Any degree of ineffability that remains might then be recognized as arising because most categories that we apply to ordinary, finite objects are not applicable to the One, and not because no categories whatsoever are applicable to it. If we feel that the concept of the One may be a viable concept, then indeed we must be prepared to recognize that it is something that has properties, although admittedly quite special properties. If we feel this way, however, then we must also be prepared to construct an adequate logic governing the rules and guiding principles of such a notion in which all absurdity will be carefully circumvented. This Professor Brumbaugh has also begun to do by stressing the analogies between Proclus' work and Cantor's set theory (see his "Cantor's Sets and Proclus' Wholes," pp. 104–113 of this volume).

Robert S. Brumbaugh suggests that set theory is "a leading candidate for the desired science of the formal structure of reality." Indeed, I think that the Plotinian or Proclusian One could be used to define Kurt Gödel's set theory, for example, U, the universal class which is not a member of any class but which contains every set (sets are members; classes that are not sets are not). Let the logical notion of membership and the metaphysical notion of participation correspond to each other, which seems natural. Then to say that the universal class U is not a member of any class is to say that it is unparticipated. Hence we could say that the One that defines the universal class U is also unparticipated because what it defines—the universal class—is unparticipated.

A further point suggested to me by Brumbaugh for exploration is the possibility of asymetrical relations between the One and other entities in the Neoplatonic system. All beings since they are one are like the One, but the One is by nature like no being other than itself. Or put simply, we are like the One, but the One is not like us. Participated being, however, does resemble the One in this: they have existence in common, and things receiving existence from the One resemble the One, which is the primary and universal source of all existence.

The objection, however, is that resemblance is a symetrical relation. Hence, if some participated beings were like the One, the One would be like a participated being which is false; as Isaiah puts it: "to whom will you liken, God?" (Isaiah 40:18). The reply is that resemblance between cause and effect is not a symetrical relation: for example, we would call a photograph a likeness of a woman but not vice versa. Saint Thomas Aquinas makes the same point in his answer to the question, "Can creatures be said to resemble God?" (*Summa Theologica,* The First Part IA, question 4, article 3, objection 4).

The set-theoretical axiom of infinity postulates an infinite number of objects. Dodd's, however, interprets Plotinus as assuming a finite number of forms. And Proclus, in proposition 94 with respect to a numerical infinity, adopts an Aristotelian concept of the potentially infinite. The upshot is that Robert S. Brumbaugh's suggestion that Proclus is committed to contemporary logicist-realist ontology may not be entirely accurate. Plotinus and Proclus may not be committed to the logicist-realist position with its axiom of infinity since, if Dodds is right, Plotinus and Proclus believed in a finite number of forms. Logicism-Realism with its set-theoretical Axiom of Infinity is, therefore, even more Neoplatonic than Plotinus and Proclus! And this conclusion will elate the hearts of Neoplatonists of the Robert S. Brumbaugh variety.

One attempt at reconciling logicism-realism and Neoplatonism would be to simply rely on the notion of the potentially infinite in interpreting the Axiom of Infinity. Yet, this would be less realist than logicist-realist ontology, such as the early Russell's and, I believe, Kurt Gödel's; yet, it would be more in accord with

Plotinus and Proclus who surprisingly are usually cited as illustrations of the excessive proliferation of entities. Interestingly, it also would be compatible with Aristotle's idea of the potentially infinite.

Nevertheless, in spite of all this I, like Brumbaugh, agree with much of the spirit of Plotinus and Proclus. I do think that much of what is true and valuable in their systems can be preserved intact. Therefore, I now wish to defend the plausibility of the existence of one "highest" form—whether it be the One of the *Parmenides,* the Good of the *Republic,* or the Beautiful of the *Symposium.* I will deal with three principal objections to such a highest form. Each objection will try to deny the possibility of a superform that is the cause of the unity, beauty, or goodness of everything else.

The first objection could be stated as follows: Either such a One (Good, Beauty, etc.) is itself part of some system or not. If it is, then we have an element of a system causing the unity of that same system, which is absurd. If it is not, and the One is outside the rest of the universe, it then could not "get together" with the rest of the universe. I would reply to this objection by maintaining that neither horn of the dilemma is absurd. Considering the first horn of the dilemma, I see nothing wrong with an element of a system causing the unity of that same system; the center element or component of a picture (system of related components) is itself an element of the picture yet this need not prevent it from causing that same picture's (system's) unity or beauty. For other reasons, however, this is perhaps not true of the One. The later horn of the dilemma—that if the One is outside the rest of the universe, it could not get together with it—presupposes that an explanation be required of the notion of participation; otherwise, it is not problematic. Participation is, however, a primitive notion (as Robert S. Brumbaugh has argued in his book *Plato on the One*). Hence, no explanation is required since participation would have to be based on either a physical model whose ordered pairs would be composed *entirely* of concrete physical entries or on an abstract formula or equation (e.g., $y = 4x$) whose ordered pairs would be composed *entirely* of abstract entries. Participation, however, *also* relates the concrete to the nonconcrete. Poetry might suggest such participation, but it could scarcely (or simply *would not*) be regarded by most as an explanation.

The second objection to the plausibility of there existing one single highest form—be it the One of the *Parmenides,* the Good of the *Republic,* or the Beautiful of the *Symposium*—could be stated as follows: Whatever we call this highest form, by its very definition it must be *all*-inclusive. But then the participation relation, too, must presuppose this highest form. This is absurd, however, since I have just argued that the participation relation is a primitive notion (i.e., simple and unexplainable in terms of other primitives, one of which is this highest form). That is, the participation relation is not explained by the "overform," since, if it were, participation would no longer be primitive. I would answer this objection as follows: One could only state that the participation relation derives its being ultimately from this highest form by saying that participation *participates* in the Overform. But this is equivalent to saying that participation *is* primitive in a logical or epistemological sense (although admittedly not in an ontological sense) since it flows from the all-inclusive overform. Here, it would seem, is an example where an ontology is not exactly reflected by its epistemology.

The third and last objection to the existence of a highest form that I will consider might go as follows: That which particulars share, or that which particulars have in common, is a form. Hence, since all the forms are, in fact, forms or have the properties of form in common, one could assert that there must also exist a form called Formness. That is to say, the very same reason for positing the existence of each individual form (namely, that it could be "seen" to be common to a group of individuals)—as, for example, the form Number upon observing odd and even numbers—would exist for positing the form Formness, since each form is, in fact, a form. Thus we now have a form that would definitely seem to be an instance of itself. This is because Formness is a form. But now since the phrase "is an instance of itself" is meaningful, the phrase "is not an instance of itself" also would seem to be meaningful. Thus, one could conceive of the form of all-and-only those forms that are not instances of itself. But this form leads to Russell's Paradox by substituting "Form" for "set," and "is an instance of" for "is a member of." If this form were of the same logical type as those of which it is the form, then the contradiction would follow if one asked of it if it, itself, were an instance of itself. Since if it was, it would not be, and if was was not, it would be. Thus one should deny that the form of all those and only those that are not instances of themselves exists in the same way that one should deny that the paradoxical Russell set exists, namely, by the introduction of a set theory designed to avoid such paradoxes. Professor Brumbaugh's suggestion that set theory is the apt formalism for ontology, therefore, is again vindicated. Indeed, as the late Bar-Hillel puts it, in his book on set theory, the Russell paradox arises only if the paradoxical Russell set of all sets that are not members of themselves exists, not if it does not exist. And set theory is designed to bar the existence of such sets.

One might still object to the notion of an "Overform" by saying that on the copy theory view,[11] since all the other forms are copies of this one, there must exist still another, even higher form, namely the form of resemblance by which the Overform and its "copiers" are similar. I agree with this objection and would meet it by simply denying the validity of the copy theory. A degree of participation theory would not, I think, yield the same contradiction regarding the Overform because one could claim that, although each other form partook of the overform, none partook of it *perfectly*. Hence, none of the other forms could be said to be perfect copies of it, and the allegedly higher form of resemblance, by which the Overform and its copies are similar, would simply not exist.

At first sight, once again, this too might seem to be implausible since the Overform and the other forms taken together would seem to be components of *one* system. Hence the oneness of this system would seem to be of a higher logical type than the logical type of the Overform (since the latter would be an element or member of the system). This would be true, I think, only if one utilized the now outmoded Russell hierarchy of logical types and if one could, in fact, assert that the Overform and the other forms (which are arranged in an ascending hierarchy) *are* one, or are components or elements of *one* system. I would simply deny both, plausible as they may seem: the first—the Russell hierarchy—because Professor F. B. Fitch has proved that it is itself self-referentially inconsistent;[12] and the second on the grounds that the Overform's nature is such that it necessarily cannot be rationally or intelligibly thought of as an element of *another* One or another system. Nevertheless, as I noted earlier, in at least Gödel's set theory the One can plausibly be viewed as causing or defining everything else that is an element of the universal set.

A word about the relation of Plotinus and Proclus to later thought is in order. Plotinus felt that because *Nous*—the Intellectual Principle—proceeds in some sense from the One, it must be essentially different from the One. This, however, does not follow. Later, Thomas Aquinas and also, I think, Saint Augustine argue that the three Persons of the Trinity—although they can be distinguished (only) relationally—are not essentially different because their essence is the same, namely, supreme overflowing goodness itself. What this means is that any one person of the Trinity cannot be distinguished from the others by an intrinsic property, but instead only by using ineliminable reference to the other persons. That is, the Father is not begotten from the Son, but the Son is begotten from the Father. And the Father and the Son do not proceed from the Holy Spirit, but the Holy Spirit does proceed from the Father and the Son.

The Anatomy of a Neoplatonist Metaphysical Proof

RONALD HATHAWAY

The Elements of Theology (Στοιχείωσις θεολογική) of Proclus Diadochus, the fifth century Neoplatonist commentator and philosopher, is the earliest extant rigorous metaphysical system in which every proposition is proved and is an element in the succeeding body of propositions.[1] Of the 217 proofs in Proclus' treatise, the proof of proposition or theorem 1 is the most significant and problematic. It is the first *element* in Proclus' system. The logic of the proof is more difficult to grasp than is implied by those who have tried to grapple with it. A better understanding of Proclus' sources in the proof, and the general model of reasoning at work in the proof illuminates many obscure aspects of this ancient example of the striving for logical rigor. In what follows I take a close look at the logical anatomy of Proclus' proof and draw general conclusions about Proclus' sources in the proof and about Proclus' general model of proof.

The title of Proclus' treatise, considering the fact that he wrote an extensive commentary on Euclid's *Elements* (Book I), apparently is what leads both L. S. Rosán and R. T. Wallis to contend that all of Proclus' proofs are consciously modeled on Euclid; and it was this view, with the addition of another common view—that Euclidean geometry is a formal axiom system—that prompted Bréton to try to formalize the logic of Proclus' proof.[2] Bréton's attempt at formalization is incomplete and raises many questions, some of which I note below; others are noted by Bréton himself. Why is this the case? My own analysis suggests that any treatment of the proof as a formal derivation is bound to be very difficult, and very likely is impossible in principle. At the outset it is important to note that even if Proclus had modeled his proof on Euclid, it does not necessarily follow that Proclus' system is reducible to a formal axiom system in Hilbert's sense.[3] Ian Mueller has criticized A. Szabó's view that Euclidean geometry is an axiom system in the modern sense, arguing cogently that Euclidean postulates are not assertions of existence-assumptions, but are statements that "license" the performing of certain imaginary cognitive operations with idealized physical bodies.[4] The modern axiomatized remnant of Euclidean geometry does not represent this part of the central core of Euclid's geometry.[5]

It is my contention that Proclus' proof of his first theorem presupposes a postulate-like assumption that licenses an infinitely continued operation. In this one respect, namely, in needing a postulate of this type, his proof does share an important feature with Euclidean geometry. However, it does not follow from this that Proclus consciously modeled his proof on Euclid. There is evidence that Proclus intended to make the *Elements of Theology* (*E.T.*) a non-Euclidean treatise. At the level of what he consciously intended, it seems that Proclus' model of reasoning in the *E.T.* is not Euclid. I thus reject the view held by Rosán and Wallis, with the qualification that the fact that the reasoning of Proclus and Euclid have some feature in common is of general significance. It highlights the point at which ancient metaphysical and mathematical reasoning intersect or *overlap*.

I

Proclus' first theorem is that "Every multitude partakes in some way of unity."[6] I consider the meanings of its component terms below. This proposition may sound trivial or, perhaps, axiomatic. However, if we substitute "set" for "multitude," at the risk of anachronism, the task of defining a set and the problems involved in proving that every set has a certain general feature might convince us that what Proclus is undertaking to do is far from trivial in its level of difficulty. Although I will argue against treating Proclus' "multitudes" as sets, we should approach Proclus' task—proving a truth at the foundation of his metaphysics—as one both ambitious in scope and potentially difficult.

A brief glance at the place of the *Elements of Theology* in the history of philosophy will help us to gain added perspective. It is the general consensus (Beutler, Lindsay, Dodds, Wallis[7]) that the *Elements of Theology* is the first (extant) rigorous metaphysical system, that is to say, a system of propositions each of which is proved. No one would dream of treating the long, tangled lines of argument in Aristotle's *Metaphysics* (many of which lack even a decisive conclusion) as attempts at rigor in this sense. The frequent pairing of Proclus with Spinoza[8] is appropriate, and one could add the names of Descartes (in the *Princi-*

ples) and perhaps Leibnitz. A lengthy digression would be needed to explore the topic, but it is possible that the recovery of the *Elements of Theology* in early modern times, especially after Patrizzi's Latin version in 1583, planted the seed of the rationalist program.

One striking difference between Spinoza and Proclus should nonetheless be noted. In his *Ethics* Spinoza states axioms and definitions, before enunciating propositions to be proved, revealing his debt probably both to Descartes and to Euclid. Proclus, on the other hand, enunciates proposition 1 in the *Elements of Theology* without stating any prior definitions, axioms, or postulates. He nonetheless assumes that his argument for proposition 1 is a proof, that is, that his premises are true and the argument is logically valid in a rigorous sense. Dodds, Proclus' great modern commentator, claims that most of Proclus' proofs are "formally correct."[9] Yet, prima facie must we not admit that they lack one of the cardinal features of Euclid's rigor as we ordinarily understand it, namely, the clear statement of *every* assumption that will play a logical, definitional, or operational[10] role in the system of proofs? On the face of it, Spinoza is indebted to Euclid and Proclus is not.[11]

This problem poses a number of perplexing questions and issues. Is Euclid in fact the model for Proclus' proofs? And if so, what does this mean for our grasp of the logic of his proofs, their "correctness," or validity? If their logic is the same as Euclid's, what is the logic on the type of rigor actually found in Euclid? If Proclus had other sources or models, did they share features with Euclidean reasoning or not? We cannot canvas in detail the ancient Pythagorean methods of proof, the arguments of Zeno of Elea, Plato's *Parmenides*, or Aristotelian and Stoic logics, but any one of these could conceivably have influenced Proclus (and, I shall argue, Zeno and Plato certainly did). I will briefly consider this problem of sources below. For the moment, it will help the reader if I state in advance what position I take with respect to this inquiry *ad fontes*. Although in his proof of Proposition 1 Proclus consciously intended to produce a nongeometrical and, therefore, non-Euclidean proof, his mind was so deeply imbued not only with Euclid, but with the entire general model of reasoning used by the Pythagorean geometers, Zeno, and Plato (on occasion), that he *unconsciously* adopted it. I will later identify more specifically what I mean by this "general model of reasoning."

An ancillary and neglected point relevant to any study in the history of ideas is that the existence of this kind of a gap between consciously and unconsciously adopted ideas shows that the whole thought of an author may be an unintended outcome, or an outcome in conflict with the author's intended outcome, despite the fact that his work gives every appearance of being wholly the product of conscious design. Some scholars give token recognition to this gap but they do not recognize the possibility that what we call the "thought" of an author is subject to "invisible-hand explanation."[12] The *Elements of Theology* is a good case for a test of a type of invisible-hand explanation, since *all* of its substantive content, if Dodds is correct,[13] is derived from preceding sources. The theory of explanation lying behind the traditional inquiry *ad fontes* is in need of much closer scrutiny. In what follows, I simply use Proclus' proof as a sample of the "gap" in question.

II

What does Proclus set out to prove in proposition 1? Πᾶν πλῆθος μετέχει πῆ τοῦ ἑνός can be taken to mean "every [all] multitude [mass] partakes in some way of unity." Because this translation differs from Dodds' in certain respects, and because the meaning of the component terms will be important in any analysis of the logic of Proclus' proof, I will comment on and justify the version offered. (πλῆθος) was used to refer to crowds of people or things, especially those of indefinite number or size. From this use it acquired the use that refers to a purely quantitatively large number of things. It always could connote either number or magnitude, however, and it is in this vague but common sense that Proclus uses the word. The vagueness of the term πλῆθος allows reference to something indefinitely large, that is, something of some large but unspecified size or number. It does not by itself refer to something of *infinite* size or number. Plato (*Parm.* 144A6) carefully uses πλῆθος ἄπειρον, not πλῆθος alone, to refer to an infinite multitude. It is significant that in his proof Proclus assumes that a πλῆθος is some kind of "whole" (ὅλον), namely, an indefinite "many of which the multitude [is composed] (πολλὰ ἐξ ὧν τὸ πλῆθος)."[14] Yet he never uses any of the available terms for "part" (μόριον, μέρος) to refer to what "makes up" a πλῆθος. In a sense, Proclus masks the problem of choosing how to regard these items. In another sense, he simply leaves the matter open to interpretation. Not only are we initially ignorant of what kinds of things (minds? disembodied souls? matter?) there can be multitudes of, but we do not even know whether a multitude is a "whole" like a number, a countable totality, or like a continuous magnitude, a divisible whole. Proposition 1, we must remember, is intended to lay a general foundation.

This unrestricted idea of πλῆθος intuitively seems close to our notion of a multitude, but the notion of a *mass* of something seems also connoted. By "mass" I do not mean the physicist's mass (inertial rest-energy of a body), but the general notion implied by phrases such as "mass of people" or, if we think of rock or water as indefinite collections of bits of rock or bits of water, such as "mass of rock" or "a mass of water." Because it is the normal and accepted synonym, I will use the term "multitude" rather than the term "mass" in what follows.

Bréton argues that the expression "every multitude" implies the universal quantifier.[15] Bréton is correct, but his claim raises a question: What does the quantifier range over? Some find it natural to treat Proclus' multitudes as sets.[16] Treating Proclus' multitudes as sets is not as "natural" as it may seem, though there are analogies between sets and multitudes. What makes the view unnatural are the following considerations. A minimal description of Cantor's notion of sets would be that sets are definite and distinct collections of definite and distinct members, that subsets of sets (or class inclusion) must be distinguished from members of sets (or class membership), and that there must be a role for empty sets, for unit sets and for infinite sets. When we examine Proclus' proof, we will find that: (1) his notion of the components of multitudes does not allow for a distinction between things that are members of multitudes and subsets of multitudes (i.e., it is impossible to distinguish subsets from members of sets); (2) his proof fails if there are empty or unit multitudes; and (3) Proclus' concept of the infinite is too weak to accommodate infinite sets. In addition, it is highly unclear what sorts of operations can be performed on Proclus' multitudes. The term πλῆθος has a cousin verb πληθύω that means "increase" in any of several ways, including "growth." This implies that a Proclus-multitude might become larger if its components grew; which is false of sets. As for *analogies* between multitudes and sets, it is possible that Proclus' later theory of "wholes" (Props. 66–69) offers analogies with a theory of sets. The only analogy that I will consider here is that between the unstated postulate that Proclus' proof presupposes and the Zermelo-Fraenkel Axiom of Choice (regarded as an axiom of constructibility of subsets). However, even there, I will not concede a *strong* analogy.

"Every multitude *partakes* . . . of unity." It is unnecessary to enter into the often arid controversies about the sense and import of the use of "to partake of" μετέχειν in Plato and his commentators. Damascius, Proclus' younger contemporary, remarks that "partake of" basically means "to have" (ἔχειν) something.[17] Whatever metaphysical elaboration Proclus and Damascius would add to this, Damascius' claim is an attempt to penetrate the meaning of the term. For our purposes, we may assume that if something "partakes of" unity, then that thing *has* unity, The text of Plato's *Parmenides* that seems to be the proximate source of proposition 1 (157C1–2: "The others are not wholly deprived of unity, but partake of it in a way") assumes that partaking of unity is possessing or having unity.[18] I assume that this point is in no way contentious, but obvious, as a semantic truth, no less to us than to Damascius.

"Every multitude partakes *in some way* of unity." Proclus' use of the expression "in some way" πῃ seems to imply that he has in mind Aristotle's observation that there are many ways in which one can say of something that it "is one," but nowhere—here or elsewhere in the *Elements of Theology*—does Proclus cite *Metaphysics* Iota or show that he intends to apply Aristotle's observation. In his proof, it will become clear that Proclus wishes to make a substantive claim about the two logically possible ways in which a multitude can have unity.

"Every multitude partakes . . . of *unity*." The expression rendered as "unity" is the definite expression "τὸ ἕν," so often rendered as "the One" in scholarly literature. It seems that Dodds is correct in preferring "unity" as a synonym of "τὸ ἕν." If the *Elements of Theology* is a general or, as we might say, a foundational work, then it should not begin by assuming the existence of something unknown and indefinable that bears "the One" as a name. Later in the work, admittedly, Proclus seems to use "τὸ ἕν" as the name of the "first cause" of all things. What is important is not whether "the One" is used as a name, but rather whether what this is the name of has properties that are imported *ad hoc* in the proofs in a whimsical way, or whether these properties are uncovered by means of the proofs themselves. If Proclus' intention is to build a foundational system without prior assumption, then the expression "τὸ ἕν" should bear its most obvious meaning and not function as the name of something whose identity and properties are unknown until a time when they are sneaked into his proofs. It may be objected that Proclus is so deeply committed to post-Plotinian Neoplatonic systems that there is simply no longer any question of an un-Neoplatonic use of "τὸ ἕν." This objection is at times based on the premise that Plato himself uses "τὸ ἕν" as the name of an entity (e.g., the Good) rather than as an expression to refer to unity. Controversy here is abundant and I will not enter into it, aside from noting that Owen and others have argued that "το ἕν" is Plato's expression for unity, and note that Aristotle is apparently the first to use the term "unity" (ἑνότης).[19] In any case, even if Proclus' use of "τὸ ἕν" is somewhat unclear, his proof of proposition 1 does not depend on anything other than the notion of unity. If Proclus' proofs are not consciously modeled in every respect on Euclid, Proclus was aware that one of the hallmarks of rigorous reasoning, of "clarity and articulateness," is the statement of "the common notions."[20]

These observations, I believe, will suffice to support my interpretation of Proposition 1 as the claim that "Every multitude partakes in some way of unity." It is, as I understand it, a straightforward and simple claim. Its proof, though deceptively short, is neither straightforward nor simple.

III

Proclus' proof of proposition 1 has the logical form of what he calls "a reduction to the impossible."[21] As it was employed in ancient times, the *reductio* was the oldest and, in some ways, the most powerful tool of argument known. It was used virtually from the origins of Greek geometry; was used by Zeno of Elea; is used by the "Parmenides" in Plato's dialogue of that name; is used by Euclid for certain important proofs; is well known to Proclus; and, if Szabó's suggestion is correct, provided the basis for the later development of the powerful method of "analysis" mentioned and used by Pappus.[22] The opening words of Proclus' proof are: "For if [a multitude] in no way partook [of unity]. . . ." Proclus assumes that the contradictory of the proposition to be proved and to be assumed for the sake of *reductio* is, "Not every multitude partakes in some way of unity." It follows that he must show only that something impossible is entailed by assuming that any given multitude in no way partakes of unity.

Because Proclus' actual proof is unschematically set out and is not broken into its smallest logical components, I have, for the reader's convenience, reproduced the proof in its original *sequence*; but I have broken it into manageable and logically (more or less) minimal components. I also intersperse occasional comments or queries, or note where a premise must be provided in more explicit form to help the reader foresee where difficulties will later emerge. The proof runs as follows, starting with the negation of the proposition to be proved, anticipating *reductio*.

1. Suppose that a multitude were in no way to partake of unity.[23]
2. "Neither the whole multitude nor each of the many making it up[24] will be one."
3. "Each of the many making up the multitude will be a multitude, and this [is the case; is true] to infinity."

4. "And of these infinite [multitudes] each will again be infinite multitude."

(4) is puzzling, since it is unclear how each of the (first level) infinite multitudes "will again be" infinite multitude, that is, what differentiates this contention from the trivial claim that each of the infinite multitudes *is* [an] infinite multitude. Note that (3) and (4) together seem to explain, if only partially, what is meant by (2). *Not being one* will be taken to mean *being infinite multitude* and also something else, namely, the infinite reiteration of whatever step it was that introduced *being infinite multitude* in the first place (or at the first level). This fact, that *not being one* is interpreted by Proclus as a complex predicate or characteristic which imports an indefinitely continued operation, will prove to be of central importance later. That is, we have here two uses or senses of "infinite" (ἄπειρον). One, referring to infinite collections, and another, referring to infinite generations by some step or steps, of infinite collections.[25]

5. A multitude partakes of unity either with respect to the whole multitude or with respect to each of the things in it.

Proclus speaks of the many that make up a multitude as being "in it." Notice that if a πλῆθος could be an undifferentiated mass or continuum, it would still make sense to speak of things "in" it as its *potentially* differentiable bits, although Proclus is silent about these different possibilities. (5) has the ring of a definition (of "partakes of unity"?) or an axiom. In any case, Proclus does not produce any argument for (5), and treats it as an indemonstrable truth. In the text, (5) occurs as part of a larger sentence, "[A multitude] that partakes of no unity in any way, *either with respect to the whole or with respect to each of the things in it,* will be infinite in every way and through and through." It is clear that "either with respect to the whole or with respect to each of the things in it" is a distinct assumption, and is understood to be logically exhaustive of the ways in which a multitude can partake of unity. The remainder of this larger sentence is equivalent to the following assumption:

6. A multitude that in no way partakes of unity will be infinite in every way (παντῇ ἄπειρον) and through and through (καὶ κατὰ πᾶν).

The logical implications of the infinite "through and through" will be discussed shortly. The literal force of καὶ κατὰ πᾶν is "and for all," that is, "and for every item" where each item is a suitably defined successor in a string of successors.

7. "For as regards each of the many, whichever one takes, it will either be one or not one."

The "for" (γάρ) introduces a new and independent argument for (6).

8. "If each of the many is not one, it would be either many or nothing."

One might expect Proclus to have first considered the case with respect to the whole multitude. The remainder of the proof considers only the case with respect to "each of the many" (τῶν πολλῶν ἕκαστον). This seems to leave a lacuna in his proof. Note that Proclus assumes that "one," "many," and "nothing" are logically exhaustive predicates.

> 9. "If each is nothing, then whatever is made up of these (τὸ ἐκ τούτων) is also nothing."

The proposition behind the consequent of (9) is almost certainly to be attributed to Zeno.[26] Proclus treats it as a truth not in need of proof.

> 10. "If each is many, on the other hand, each is made of an infinite times [succession] of infinites (ἀπειράκις ἄπειρον)."[27]

The term ἀπειράκις literally means "time without number," "indefinitely many times." The notion that Proclus evidently intends to capture is that of an infinite *succession* of steps carried through on an infinite number of entities, each both a component of a multitude and itself an indefinite multitude in turn. No proof of (10) is attempted. But why does Proclus think that (10) is true? In (6) he has already specified the general idea of a through-and-through infinite. In (10), he now assumes the carrying out in thought of the through-and-through operation in question. The appeal in (10), therefore, is to a postulate that licenses such an operation. Below I will consider how Proclus could have stated his assumptions here more clearly. Note that he could not *prove* the truth of (10) because it relies on a *postulate,* and on the intuitive carrying out of what is postulated. That is to say, a cognitive operation or experiment involving an infinite succession of steps is an essential part of the proof itself. The reliance on a postulate, though implicit, exhibits a resemblance between Euclid and Proclus. Proof (10) also illuminates why Proclus' proof is difficult or impossible to formalize. I will return to this point again.

> 11. "These things [viz., the consequents of (9) and (10)] are impossible."
> 12. "For it is impossible for something to be composed of nothing."

(12) is treated as a necessary truth; (12) would rule out, for Proclus, the concept of the empty or null set. This would constitute another strong reason against any attempt to treat Proclus' multitudes as sets.

> 13. "And nothing that is is made up of an infinite succession of infinites."

This is curious, for Proclus goes on below to prove (13). Since (13) is for him a logically necessary truth, we would expect him to write it in the form: "Nothing that is *can* be made up of an infinite succession of infinites." Perhaps Proclus assumes that since (13) is universally true, it must be true *at least* of everything that exists, whatever Proclus would include in his ontology.

> 14. "For there is nothing greater (*pleon*) than the infinite."
> 15. "And that which is made up of all [of certain items] is greater than each [item]."

These jointly are meant to constitute a proof of (13). These two propositions seem to correspond, at least loosely, to an ancient notion of the infinite criticized by Aristotle, namely, "that than which nothing is beyond ["outside"],[28] and to Euclid's axiom, "The whole is greater than the part."[29] I will argue later that the logical faults in Proclus' proof are concentrated here in his attempt to prove the truth of (13)—or what amounts to the same thing, his attempt to prove that (10) involves an impossibility.

16. "Therefore, every multitude in some way partakes of unity."

The conclusion follows by the principle of *reductio* arguments. Proclus' conclusion is not marked with either of the conventional Euclidean formulas, "Which was to be *proved*" for theorems, or "Which was to be *done*" for problems. Proclus was well aware of the importance of this distinction in Euclid.[30] Let us assume that he wished to avoid Euclidean conventions. Let us also note, however, that his proof may have "problematic" as well as purely "theorematic" aspects.

IV

Although many questions could be raised, there are two that I intend to address to Proclus' proof: (a) Is it "formally correct," as Dodds implies? (b) What feature, if any, does it share with Euclidean proofs?

Proclus assumes that multitudes can have unity in only two ways, either as wholes or through the unity of their components. He then argues that a multitude cannot have unity as a whole if its components lack unity. He assumes, without argument, that unity of components is a necessary condition of unity of a whole multitude.[31] In the case where the components are nothing, the whole is nothing.[32] The proof then turns on the case where the components are each many. In (3) and (4) he claims that a kind of infinite regress of infinites occurs in this case. What he means by saying that "each of the many . . . will be a multitude, and this to infinity," and "of these infinite [multitudes] each will again be infinite multitude," is then restated in (6), "[each such multitude] will be infinite in every way ($\pi\alpha\nu\tau\tilde{\eta}$ $\check{\alpha}\pi\epsilon\iota\rho\sigma\nu$) and through and through ($\kappa\alpha\grave{\iota}$ $\kappa\alpha\tau\grave{\alpha}$ $\tilde{\pi}\alpha\nu$)." It is the argument for this notion of through-and-through infinity that is at the heart of his proof.

What Proclus assumes, but does not clearly state, is that a necessary condition of the proof is the "thought experiment" of taking unity away from every successor component of every component of the multitude in question. This is the meaning of the phrase, "and this to infinity," and of the sign of iteration, "again" ($\pi\acute{\alpha}\lambda\iota\nu$), used in (4): "each of these infinites will again be infinite multitude." Zeno's argument against plurality, using the notion of through-and-through division,[33] uses a construction with the same general strategy, although Proclus does not rely on *division*. Proclus has abstracted from Zeno, it seems, the general notion of an infinitely extended through-and-through operation for suitably defined successors. Sinnige and others have shown how Zeno's strategy might well have developed with the use of the $\gamma\nu\tilde{\omega}\mu\omega\nu$ in early Pythagorean geometrical number theory.[34] Before we consider Proclus' debts to his predecessors, let us consider the validity of his proof.

That his proof fails should be obvious from an examination of his attempt to prove the impossibility of the consequent of (10), that is, that each component "is made up of an infinite succession of infinites (ἀπειράκις ἀπειρῶν."[35] This turns on his proof of (13): "And nothing that is is made up of an infinite succession of infinites." This depends on the truth of (14) and (15). Both of these are false, we would claim. Before saying why they are false, let us note that Proclus does not have a sufficiently strong conception of the infinite within his own tradition. Aristotle had criticized an older conception of the infinite as that than which nothing is greater. Aware of the use of the infinite in geometry, Aristotle suggests his own notion of the infinite as a progression or a power of progressing to something always greater.[36] Because Proclus' commentary on Euclid does not extend as far as X. 1, which introduces the so-called "Axiom of Archimedes," it is impossible to tell precisely what his attitude toward the method of exhaustion as used in classical theory of irrationals may have been.[37] Perhaps Proclus had a special reason for appealing to the older notion of the infinite, namely, that it permits us to conceive of the infinite as *complete*, which is implicit in Proclus' through-and-through operation. However, his conception of the infinite is insufficiently strong. Even if Proclus had anticipated the notion of infinite sets, both (14) and (15) are false as stated. It is false that there is nothing greater than the infinite. Some infinites are greater than others.[38] It is also false that whatever is made up of certain items is greater than *any* items, because an infinite set is equivalent to, not greater than, at least one of its proper subsets.[39]

Should I be charged with a *tu quoque*? Am I not guilty of doing what I forbade in interpreting Proclus' proof, namely, introducing talk about sets? My defense against the accusation would be that I am claiming only that the modern concept of infinite sets helps us to see with some precision why Proclus' proof fails, not that the notion of sets will enable us to fully *represent* Proclus' reasoning in the proof.

A different objection to my interpretation is that what Proclus means in (13) is that no existing thing *actually* consists of an infinite succession of infinites. This objection raises another question: What is the ontology—the list of types of entities of which proposition 1 is intended to be true? The base ontology in Neoplatonism is a hierarchy of minds, intelligible forms, disembodied souls, embodied souls, bodies, and the underlying matter of bodies. Is Proclus arguing, in effect, that none of these is actually an infinite succession of infinites? To air the controversy implied by this question goes beyond the bounds of my argument (indeed, how could the issue be settled?). The decisive reason for rejecting this objection is the fact that the *Elements of Theology* is a programmatic treatise that intends to provide the "elements" not only for a theological system or cosmology, but a unique "nonhypothetical science" that provides foundations for every other science. I will present evidence for this contention later. My present point is only that proposition 1 is a truth that must hold true of all entities, and this must include mathematical entities such as line segments. What Proposition 1 asserts is not restricted in its scope.

Proclus' first proof is invalid. However, this does not exhaust its potential significance for us. In particular, what debt, if any, does the proof have to Euclid? The preceding comments on the proof have already answered this question: Proclus presupposes a postulate that licenses the performance of a certain operation and, to this extent, resembles a part of the core of Euclidean geometry. Their general mode of reasoning is similar in using something like constructions. What is the real significance of this? Mueller has argued that one must not think of the Euclidean postulates as simply introducing veiled existence-assumptions, and contends that they are statements that have no truth values.[40] The first postulate, "Let it be postulated to draw a straight line from any point to any point," is neither true nor false, nor, lest anyone momentarily think so, is it a rule of inference of any kind. Euclid's famous constructions are built up on these licenses. Proclus was himself clearly aware of these "doings" or "producings" (ποιήσεις), "sectionings," and other operations in geometrical construction building.[41] Above I contended that the step of critical import in Proclus' proof was his assumption that the use of the predicate "is not one" introduces an infinitely iterated operation of some kind, one generating a series of entities and removing unity from every successor in the series. It might be said that Proclus uses a certain type of construction. It certainly is not a geometrical construction. How do I remove unity from a multitude according to Proclus' construction? I would take unity away from a building if I were to reduce it to a pile of bricks and mortar; but the individual bricks will have their unity. Since the unity of a multitude depends on the unity of its components, my act of removing unity from the building is still incomplete. For Proclus, the removal of unity is through and through, or involves everything that "makes up" the multitude. There are two logically distinct ways in which a multitude is "made up" of elements: it is made up of its immediate elements, but also is made up of all elements of these immediate elements, on whatever level. Proclus' operation is that of removing unity from the components of a multitude *on every level.*[42]

The notion of an operation that enables us to move from some feature of a component to the same feature for every successor reminds one of mathematical induction, which permits generalization for all successors where these are numbers. It is significant that the principle of mathematical induction itself is a postulate (of Peano) that cannot be proved. Perhaps more interesting than this is that the postulate that Proclus presupposes reminds us of the Zermelo-Fraenkel axiom of choice which allows the construction of all subsets of a given set.[43] This leads us to wonder what Proclus' postulate would look like if it were explicitly asserted. We might imagine it tentatively as follows: *Let it be postulated to remove unity from every component of a multitude.* I do not propose to draw any surprising conclusions from this rather vague postulate. Limiting myself only to what seems obvious, we might conclude that Proclus' proof is quasi-Euclidean in requiring a postulate at all, especially a postulate licensing an operation or mental construction. The postulate is strange in that it is really a postulate of deconstruction or of the deconstructibility of multitudes. The postulate is also exceedingly general and abstract in form. Proclus might well have contrasted his presupposed postulate with the standard constructions of geometry, which could usually be visually modeled or imagined as translated into manipulations of material objects. However, the central point remains: however sharp the contrast between ancient geometry and Proclus' proof (the "visualizable" and the truly "intelligible"), Proclus is not allowed logically to suppress his postulate. The fact that he fails to assert it or any definitions or axioms must have some explanation. What this is I will, in a moment, suggest.

With the laying bare of this postulate, I will assume that the anatomy of Proclus' proof is reasonably clear to us. What general conclusions *about the proof* can we draw? First, it should be clear now why Bréton found it difficult to formalize the proof. A standard formal derivation with finite steps and no postulate for generating infinite multitudes is bound to fail. A symptom of Bréton's difficulty is his rather surprising indecision as to whether Proclus' proposition 1 is an axiom or a theorem![44] This leads us to a second conclusion, namely, that the *status* of Proposition 1 is necessarily either (1) that of an *unproved* proposition, either false or true, or (2) that of an *unprovable* proposition, either true and necessary without proof or undecidable, or unprovable because false. If (1) is the case, proposition 1 could be true and *as yet* unproved. Or it is false. If its contradictory does not entail an impossibility, as my analysis implies, then its contradictory may be true (for all we know). Proclus' attempt to prove Proposition 1 by *reductio* might thus be thought of as similar to Saccheri's ill-fated attempt to prove Euclid's fifth postulate by *reductio* (ill-fated because it failed and significant because it led to the discovery of non-Euclidean geometries). That is to say, Proclus' attempt could lead philosophers conceivably to look for alternative metaphysical systems! If the Proposition's status is that of the second case (2), it could be unprovable simply because false, or unprovable and true. If unprovable and true, proposition 1 may not be a theorem but an *axiom* (as Bréton suggests), or perhaps a cryptic partial *definition,* as I have suggested (compare Note 16). On the other hand, if it is really a theorem in some system and unprovable, it could be an *undecidable* formula of the kind that Gödel's theorem proves must exist for suitably defined systems.

These two conclusions, about the formalizability of Proclus' proof, and about the status of his Proposition 1, are closely related and raise several questions. For instance, is there another proof of Proposition 1 that is either valid or formalizable? Is Proposition 1 in any way provable? If it is not provable, is this true because it cannot be made a theorem in any system? Or is this true only for the system of Proclus? These and other questions are raised here only as an agenda for future investigations.

V

In conclusion, I will consider the question about Proclus' intentions in his proof and in the *Elements of Theology* insofar as his debts to Plato shed light on this. About his debts to Plato, I wish to make only two claims: (1) that Plato anticipates Proclus' use of the infinite in his proof in a passage of the *Parmenides,* and (2) that Proclus' metaphysical system in the *Elements of Theology* is modeled on Plato's description of the "downward" half of the procedure of dialectic (*Republic* VI. 511B3–C2), the descent from a first "unhypothetical" (ἀνυπόθετον) starting point. About the nature of these debts, I further wish to claim that while Proclus knew Plato's *Parmenides* well, his own use of the infinite is probably not a conscious adaptation of Plato's argument; on the other hand, the *Elements of Theology* is probably consciously and intentionally modeled on Plato's programmatic remarks in *Republic* VI.

1. In an extended passage at *Parmenides* 158B–C, "Parmenides" asks us to think of "the things other than unity" *before they have acquired unity*.[45] Referring to these as "multitudes" (πλῆθη), he then goes on to construct a kind of thought experiment.

> Now if we choose to take in thought from such multitudes the least portion we can conceive, that portion also, if it does not possess unity, must be not one but a multitude. And if we go on in that way considering just by itself, the nature other than the form, any portion of it that comes into view will be without limit of multitude.[46]

Dodd notes that Proclus relies in some way on this passage, but denies that Proclus' proof is the same as Plato's argument in the passage.[47] Dodds is correct. Proclus' proof is not the same as the extended line of argument used by Plato. The *Parmenides* commentary gives no hint of any conscious borrowing from the passage.[48] The inference that anything that is not one is a multitude seems to echo Zeno's arguments against plurality, and since Proclus himself appears to use Zenonian assumptions, as already noted, and may have had direct access to the lost arguments of Zeno as well,[49] it is possible that a lost argument of Zeno is the common source for both Plato and Proclus.[50]

This question of Zeno as a source aside, the *Parmenides* passage proves that Plato also uses as a strategy of proof a kind of thought-construction in which an infinite sequence is built, each successor inheriting some feature. Plato's conclusion—that any portion of any given multitude will be "without limit of multitude" (lit., "infinite in multitude")—does not assume a through-and-through operation, and in this respect Proclus drives the argument further. But Proclus' conclusion is simply the generalization of the same operation for *every* component. There is no evidence in the *Elements of Theology* that Proclus made any conscious use of the *Parmenides* passage, and it seems natural to infer that we have here an example of an *unconscious* borrowing or, at best, a borrowing filtered through the *Parmenides* commentaries of Proclus' predecessors, for instance, that by Plutarch of Athens.

2. In his commentary on Euclid, Proclus defines as "elements" all those "theorems whose understanding leads to the knowledge of the rest."[51] Thus he regards Euclid I. 1 as an element of Euclid I. 2, and so on. By analogy, his own proposition 1 could be regarded as an element of proposition 2. Proclus' comment leaves the status of Euclid's definitions, postulates, and axioms unclear. Are they "elements" even though not theorems? Proclus later notes the problem about these sorts of "starting points" (ἀρχαί) and the distinction between them and "the things followed from the starting points" (τὰ ἑπόμενα ταῖς ἀρχαῖς).[52] Referring to definitions, postulates, and axioms, he comments that Euclid "divides them into

hypotheses, postulates, and axioms."[53] Proclus thus calls definitions "hypotheses."
A little earlier, he had made these remarks:

> The general arrangement of its [geometry's introductory] propositions we should
> explain somewhat as follows. Since this science of geometry is based, we say, on
> hypothesis and proves its later propositions from determinate first principles—*for
> there is only one unhypothetical science, the other sciences receiving their first
> principles from it*—he who prepares an introduction to geometry should present
> separately the principles of the science and the conclusions that follow from the
> principles, giving no argument for the principles but only for the theorems that are
> derived from them.[54]

In this passage, Proclus uses the term "principles" to refer not to the first theorems
in Euclid, but to all of Euclid's definitions, postulates, and axioms, that is, everything, for which Euclid gives no "argument." When Proclus says that Euclid's
geometry is "based, we say, on hypothesis and proves its later propositions from
determinate first principles," it is this body of *unproved* principles that he has in
mind. Clearly, Proclus is, therefore, using the term "hypothesis" here in a broader
sense than later, where it refers only to definitions in geometry. It is *because
geometry uses unproved principles* that it is said to be based on *hypothesis*.

Proclus' cryptic comment about a unique "unhypothetical science" now seems
clearer. The term "unhypothetical" (ἀνυπόθετον) for Proclus means "not based
on unproved propositions." An "unhypothetical science" would be a system of
propositions none of which is unproved. It would have no definitions, postulates,
or axioms. Its first theorem would be proved, but without the use of any unproved
propositions. Proposition 1 of the *Elements of Theology* is obviously meant to be
an example of such a theorem. The *Elements of Theology*, it seems we must
infer, is Proclus' attempt to work out the system of the unique unhypothetical
science.[55] In it no proposition is unproved and every proved proposition is an
element of some successor proposition (theorem).

Proclus' use of the term "unhypothetical" (ἀνυπόθετον) unmistakably points
toward its first striking use by Plato (at *Republic* 511B6). There its meaning again
depends on the meaning assigned to "hypothesis" (ὑπόθεσις). Important issues
depend on the meanings assigned to "ὑπόθεσις" in Plato's dialogues, and I will
not belabor the topic. But does it follow that Proclus is consciously pursuing
Plato's program in the *Republic* passage? I have purposely said only that this is
"probable." Proclus belongs to a tradition mediated by a lengthy development of
post-Plotinian hierarchical metaphysical systems, a tradition dominated by *Timaeus*
and then *Parmenides* exegeses.[56] This tradition regards *Republic* VI–VII as giving
clues to a correct interpretation of Plato's metaphysics. If *Republic* VI is Proclus'
"source" in the *Elements of Theology*, it may be so only in the sense that it was
the initial impetus and stimulus behind a long sequence of systems.

In conclusion, it seems that a central question emerges from this analysis of
the anatomy of Proclus' proof, one concerning the nature of the relationship
between ancient metaphysical and mathematical models reasoning. We found
Proclus' proof inadequate on two basic grounds; it use of a weak notion of the

infinite and its failure to state a postulate that is logically necessary. Now we find that Proclus probably intended to exclude unproved propositions like this from his system on principle. There is a tension between the Platonic "unhypothetical" model and the tendency of Euclidean rigor to force out every element, even those held at an intuitive level, until they take on an explicit form in the system. This tension between the nonhypothetical and the hypothetical routes of thinking—in Proclus' sense of these expressions—is like a distant mirror in which the aims of modern intuitionist and logicist metamathematical theories can be seen dimly reflected. The same tension, seen in another mirror a millenium earlier, appears in the controversy over the "objects" of διάνοια and ἐπιστήμη, their sameness or difference, on Plato's Divided Line.[57] The central question is: What is the nature of the irreducible *overlap* between ancient metaphysical and mathematical modes of reasoning?

As an added dividend, my analysis has provided a test of the usefulness of invisible-hand explanation in the history of ideas. We have found that although Proclus designed the *Elements of Theology* as an anti-Euclidean system, at least one element in his strategy of proof is Euclidean in its general role and is best explained by the historical influence of a complex Euclidean tradition. The *Elements of Theology* is an outcome that is partially explained by factors lying outside its author's conscious intention as well as by what the author intended.[58]

The Idea of False in Proclus

EVANGHELOS A. MOUTSOPOULOS

If, according to contemporary conceptions of the ways that lead to knowledge, it is possible to proceed to distinctions such as those established between notions like truth and rectitude or correctness, on one hand, and falsehood, error, or mistake[1] on the other, this analytical point of view does not always seem to have been obvious in ancient thought and in its medieval prolongations. Within this framework one has the impression that logical values are roughly limited to only two, that is, the positive and the negative. Parmenides had already connected being with truth, nonbeing with falsehood.[2]

On this basis, it was easy, as well as necessary, for Parmenides to proceed to a radical distinction between being and nonbeing (each one of them being considered as nonreducible to the other[3]) and, consequently, between truth and falsehood. Plato was the first to admit, in his so-called metaphysical dialogues, that this radical distinction is not absolutely valid, and that, in some way, the being is nonbeing, whereas nonbeing is being to a certain extent.[4] Against Parmenides' absolute dogmatism, Plato's epistemology, after his own metaphysical crisis,[5] orients him towards a moderate dogmatism whose skeptical aspects will be developed by Plato's successors at the Academy.[6] On the contrary, the Neoplatonists will largely inherit the fundamental dogmatic views of the theory.

Plotinus, namely, thinks of the possibility of conceiving the being as a non-being, and vice versa, when he refers to matter,[7] and this is, of course, in conformity with the purest Platonic tradition.[8] However, he also does so when he refers to the soul itself, which he considers to be the most dramatic hypostasis, since it is submitted to a certain distortion, and even to a certain separation,[9] one part of its being attracted by the Intellect, and the other tending towards matter which, in some respect, is a nonbeing.[10] In the same way, and in spite of the fact that they are suggested by dynamic structures of human existence, and are therefore endowed with some kind of reality,[11] products of imagination are nonbeings, according to Plotinus, and, consequently, belong to the group of erroneous contents of consciousness.[12] Nevertheless, Plotinus connects false opinion, a notion of purely Platonic origin,[13] with judgment whenever the latter deviates from its right way[14] because of its relation to imagination itself.[15]

Strictly conceived, deviation, erring, or wandering are the specific characters of error. However, Plotinus connects error to falsehood, although this is not always obvious in the *Enneads*.[16] The difference between the two notions seems to be better indicated in Proclus. This does not mean, of course, that any kind of detaching of the soul is erroneous, that is, that it leads to wrongness; for, when the soul tends towards the One, it is capable of grasping it "by detaching itself from imagination and opinion and indefinite knowledge . . . and by adapting itself to the Intellect."[17] Thus, falsehood depends on what cognition is able to detach itself from: (a) correct judgment or (b) conversely, those very attractions that cause its deviation from correctness. Proclus here refers not to two different and opposed eventual outcomes of thought, but to two entirely different levels of estimation of its value.

Error relies on some principle of unstructured or, at least, disorganized non-methodical deviation of thought from correctness. It is associated with the concept of plurality[18] as opposed to the principle of unicity on which correctness relies.[19] On the contrary, falsehood is defined as the reversal (*punctum contra punctum*) of every part or element of a given proposition or thought; a reversal that is supposed to be methodical enough to assure that the negation of what is reversed will appear as "true" and "likely."[20] Likelihood thus seems to be the *conditio sine qua non* of falsehood, whereas such a condition is not necessary to error, which denotes a certain freedom of thought.

Nothing is, of course, true or false in itself, but always in relation to something else. It is neither itself nor this "else," but its relationship to this "else" that makes it possible for it to be considered as true or false. Everything is true or false according to what it is related to.[21] Such a relation[22] should be understood as a "proposed"[23] connection that may be successful in one case, while being a failure in another. This seems to be the real meaning of Proclus' assertion that everything is true and that even if something partly contains falsehood (i.e., if at a certain point of view its correctness is damaged), it can be completely restored.[24]

Proclus probably does not mean by that that something is even partly true or false *in se*. This would neither bring us back to Parmenides' poem nor to Plato's theory of the mixed, for reasons differing, of course, in either case, and easy to understand.[25] On the contrary, assuming that truth and falsehood can coexist as far as good or bad usage of what is subsequently called true and false may be made in two different cases, it is not sufficient to declare something true or false in general.[26] On the contrary, it is necessary, just as Socrates did, to proceed to the evaluation of truth and falsehood inasmuch as each one of them is inherent in everyone's conception of true and false,[27] for ignorance is comparable to some temporary impotence of reason, which is equivalent to falsehood. This is proved by the omnipotence of reason itself.[28]

Imaginary data, for instance, should be interpreted as such, because whenever they are attributed to objective reality without any previous examination of their nature, they are falsified themselves.[29] However, Proclus believes that such data correspond to some kind of *idola tribus*,[30] and that they are related to passions.[31] Passions are relevant both to the rational[32] and to the irrational[33] soul. Paradoxical and peculiar divine processes,[34] as well as apparent movements of the stars,[35] are realities falsely interpreted by the human mind. The falsehood of such opinions clearly appears through an accurate control of noctical processes.[36]

A noetical process may lead to truth only when it is correctly and consequently based on a given principle.[37] However, such a principle might be chosen in advance in order to imply results or conclusions also chosen in advance.[38] In such cases of sophisms that are the result of deliberate and intentional processes, falsehood also appears as the result of an additive or subtractive alteration,[39] and as the effect of a substitution.[40] One here again meets the particular and specific mechanical character of falsehood considered as a lie (i.e., as the reversal, *punctum contra punctum*, of correctness), which has been mentioned before,[41] and which differentiates falsehood both from correctness and error. In conformity to this model, geometrical methodology offers criteria for controlling falsehood in geometrical constructions and proofs.[42] Even in a completely false thought, as has already been said,[43] there still remain some elements of truth[44] that form the potential, yet adequate, criteria of its falsehood.[45]

In order to draw a conclusion from the above observations, one may refer to a very significant text of Proclus, according to which the main cause of falsehood is inherent in multiplicity as opposed to unicity which, in its turn, is the cause of correctness. Multiplicity is associated here with the sensible world,[46] and hence, to corruption of the intellect which, under such conditions, is in constant revolt against itself.[47] More obviously than Plotinus, Proclus accepts, in this case, the model proposed by Plato's *Sophist,* of the being of nonbeing as reaching the nonbeing of being,[48] as being reflected on the functioning of thought itself. Thus, by referring to Plato, he applies, in a more concrete manner, the Parmenidean reduction of the "ontological" to the "epistemological" by reducing being to nonbeing, and vice versa which, according to Parmenides, are absolutely not reducible to each other.

Participation and the Structure of Being In *Proclus'* Elements of Theology

LEO SWEENEY, S.J.

The title of this paper, not surprisingly, indicates its contents. Accordingly, let us see what it means, beginning with "structure of being." Following Webster's Dictionary, we shall take "structure" to mean an arrangement of interrelated parts or constituents dominated by the general character of the whole they make up. "Being" can be synonymous with "reality," which, because equivalent to "unity" in Neoplatonism, would transcend "being" in a strict sense and thus encompass even the One Good as primal reality. Or it can signify "being" strictly, which in Neoplatonism is equivalent to "one-many" and, hence, is not applicable directly to the One. "Participation" in this context is the process by which (or the situation within which) what is lower is made real and becomes related to other realities (both peer and higher) by somehow receiving its intrinsic reality from what is higher.

Now, participation is not operative on the highest level of reality because the One neither participates in anything else nor is it participated in by anything directly (this point is explicitly made by Proclus).[1] Consequently, participation is not immediately operative in the structure of being when the last noun is understood as identical with "reality," which in Neoplatonism equals "oneness." But participation permeates the strata of "being" when intended technically by Neoplatonists as "one-many." Therefore, it directly accounts for the structure of "being" in this sense inasmuch as participation helps arrange beings[2] in and on definite levels of greater and less perfection, all of which are related to what is above and among themselves and all of which are characterized directly by "being" and mediately by "unity."

If the preceding two paragraphs are basically accurate, despite their tightly abridged and simplified version of being, participation, and other key notions, it will be instructive to study in Proclus what participation means and how participated perfections and participants arise. What follows is the result of rethinking and restating points made in my paper published more than a dozen years ago in a *Festschrift* (of which only a limited number of copies were printed and which has been out of print for several years), "The Origin of Participant and of Participated Perfections in Proclus' *Elements of Theology*" (*Wisdom in Depth: Essays in Honor of Henri Renard* [Milwaukee: Bruce, 1966], pp. 235–256). I hesitated to present a version of this paper again until rereading it during graduate courses in 1971 and 1979 entitled "Providence in Proclus" convinced me that the explanation given there of participation remains helpful but is so complicated (the complication arising from Proclus' own theory, I would like to think, rather than from my own intellectual density and awkwardness) that even if someone may have read the earlier and no longer extant version, he or she would have forgotten it or, at least, might be so puzzled by it as to welcome this current restatement.

This will consist in three parts: Participation as a Process, The Origin of Participated Perfections, and the Origin of Participants.[3]

PARTICIPATION AS A PROCESS

Here let us see in what participation as a process consists by listing its results and by briefly examining its extent. But first, a brief discussion of three Greek terms and their translations.

As Proclus describes participation (e.g., 182. 160. 5–10), it involves three different but closely related factors. The first is ἡ μέθεξις, which we shall customarily translate as "the process of participation," "the participative process," or simply, "participation." The second is τὸ μετεχόμενον, which literally means "that which is participated" or simply, "the participated." It is that which is received by the participant through the participative process, while simultaneously being also that which is given by the monad that is the source of the process and which is itself unparticipated. It is not really distinct from the monad (at least, not adequately so). It is not anything abstract but is a concrete reality or perfection— for example, henads are *ta metechomena* communicated by The One to beings; henads and beings are *ta metechomena* communicated by The One and The Being to intelligences; intelligences are *ta metechomena* communicated by The One, The Being, and The Intelligence to souls, and so on. Ordinarily we would translate the Greek expression as "the perfection participated" or "the participation" (the addition of the article sets the last apart from "participation" as a process, where no article is affixed to the noun). But whatever the translation (Dodd's is generally "the participated principle" or "the participated term"), it should be understood in the light of the aforementioned: it refers to a concrete perfection that is communicated by a monad to a participant and which, at best, is only mentally distinct from the monad and, sometimes, even from the participant. The third factor is τὸ μετέχον, "the participant."

Now let us return to our original question: In what does participation as a process consist? This we can answer by listing its results and by examining its extent.

One result of the participative process is that the perfection participated is present within the participant.[4]

> [140, 124, 7–13:] A participant which is suitably disposed is not baulked of its participation; so soon as a thing is ready for communion with them [henads or gods], straightaway they are present—not that in this moment they approached or till then were absent, for they are eternally unvarying. If, then, any terrestrial thing be fit to participate them, they are present even to it: they have fulfilled all things with themselves, and though present more mightily to the higher principles they reveal themselves also to the intermediate orders in a manner consonant with such a station, and for the lowliest orders there is a lowly mode of presence.
> [142, 126, 3–7:] While the gods are present alike to all things, not all things are present alike to them; each order is present in the degree of its capacity and enjoys them in the degree of its presence, which is the measure of its participation.

A second result is that the participant is filled, completed, perfected:

> [24, 28, 10–13:] The participant was incomplete before the process of participation and by that process has been made complete: it is therefore necessarily subordinate to the participation inasmuch as it owes its completeness to that process.
> [78, 74, 11–14:] That potency which needs some extraneous pre-subsistent actuation, the potency in virtue of which an item is potentially, is imperfect. For it needs the perfection which resides in another in order to become perfect by participating it.
> [98, 86, 29–31:] We mean by "cause" that which fills all things naturally capable of participating it, which is the source of all subsequents and by the fecund outpouring of its irradiations is present to them all.

Because the participation is present in and, thereby, completes the participant, this latter becomes similar to the source of the participation.

> [25, 28, 27–34:] Completeness is a part of the Good, and the complete qua complete imitates the Good. . . . The more complete is the cause of more effects in proportion to the degree of its completeness, for the more complete participates the Good more fully; that is, it is nearer to the Good; that is, it is more nearly akin to the cause of all; that is, it is the cause of more.
> [182, 160, 7–10:] If the process of participation makes the participant be like the participation and causes it to have the same nature, it is plain that a soul which participates and is annexed to a divine intelligence is itself divine, participating through the mediation of the intelligence the divinity immanent therein.[5]

Still another result of the participative process needs to be explicated and stressed. Participation also involves the fact that the participation literally becomes *part of* the participant.[6]

[12, 14, 7–11:] To hold that things proceed from a cause which would be superior to the Good and yet which would not exercise some force upon them is a strange view, for thus it would forfeit its title to the name of cause. For some thing must in every case pass over from the cause to the effect; and especially is this true of the first cause, from which all depend and through which each being is. But if things participate in this supposed superior cause, as they have in the Good, . . .

[23, 26, 28–32:] Or else [the unparticipated] will give something of itself, which the receiver participates, while what is given is constituted as a participation. But every participation, becoming a property of that which participates it, is secondary to that which in all is equally present and has filled them all out of itself.

[188, 164, 5–6:] Any participation gives to the participant either itself or some part of itself: unless it furnished one or the other, it would not be participated.

In the light of those quotations, the participational process terminates in the perfection participated somehow becoming literally a part of the participant.[7] Its terminus is not solely the likeness or resemblance that the latter has to the source of the perfection. Neither is it any sort of presence within the participant of the perfection. Rather, the participation is so present as somehow to be an integral part of the participant. The process contributes to its very constitution.

A final point remains to be made. How widespread is participation in Proclus' universe? What existents are constituted by it? How many are composites of participant/participation(s)? Absolutely all, except the One or Good (4. 4. 9 sq.; 8. 8. 29 sq.).[8] Even though the Monad of each series lower than The One (e.g., The Intelligence with respect to intelligences, The Soul with respect to souls, and so on) is itself described as Unparticipated in relation to members of its own series (101. 90. 17 sq.), still each is the source of participations received in and, thus, fashioning those members (63. 60. 1 sq.). Moreover, each such monad, as well, of course, as each member in its series, participates the One (100. 90. 1 sq.).[9] The Proclus cosmos is, then, permeated by participation from top to bottom.[10] Beings participate henads (props. 138, 162); intelligences participate beings and, through them, henads (props. 161, 163); souls participate intelligences and, through them, beings and henads (props. 164, 202); sensible bodies participate souls and, through them, intelligences, beings, and henads (props. 129, 165).

Such seem to be the points on participation as a process that are necessary to know as a key to understanding the structure within which Proclus fits being, and as a preparation for discussing the genesis of the participations and of the participant. It is a process by which a perfection comes to be present within the participant, which it thereby completes and fulfills as a constitutive part. It directly affects all existents except The One and matter.

Now on to the discussion of origins.

THE ORIGIN OF PARTICIPATED PERFECTIONS

There are at least two key texts in the *Elements* on how participations originate, the first of which is Proposition 23. As depicted in passages immediately adjacent to it, Proclus' universe is made up of four strata of reality: bodies, souls, intelligences, and henads (20. 22. 1 sq.).[11] Each stratum has at its head an existent from which it has proceeded, to which it reverts, upon which it depends, and which is called its "monad" (21. 24. 1 sq.). Thus, bodies are headed by Nature (= the World Soul), souls by The Soul, intelligences by The Intelligence, and henads by The One (21. 24. 22 sq.). Just as one stratum transcends another (e.g., souls are prior to bodies, intelligences to souls, henads to intelligences), so too their monads transcend one another. Thus, The One is beyond The Intelligence, which, in its turn, is beyond The Soul, which is beyond Nature (20. 22. 1 sq.).[12] Each of these monads is unparticipated—that is, "it is common to all that can participate and is identical for all and, hence, it is prior to all" (23. 28. 5–7).

It is of these monads, these unparticipateds, that Proclus speaks in the first key passage.

> [23, 26, 22–32:] Every unparticipated produces out of itself participations, and all participated hypostases tend upward to unparticipated realities.[13]
>
> For on the one hand the unparticipated, having the status of a monad (as being its own and not another's, and as transcending the participants), generates what is capable of being participated. For either it must remain fixed in sterility and isolation and so lack a place of honor; or else it will give something of itself, which the receiver participates, while what is given is constituted as a participation.
>
> On the other hand, every participation, becoming a property of that which participates it, is secondary to that which is equally present in all and has filled them all out of itself.

What can be offered as comments on those lines? Clearly, they are a broad affirmation that participations are caused by an unparticipated monad and they provide information both on the cause and on the participations. The monad causes them *from itself* ("produces out of itself," "will give something of itself"). Their origin from within the cause is somewhat intelligible in view of the fact (gathered from immediately subsequent propositions) that production of effects comes about because the cause is perfect (25. 28. 21 sq.): it has complete and superabundant power (27. 30. 25 sq.). Despite this self-bestowal, though, a cause remains steadfast and immobile while producing (26. 30. 10 sq.); consequently, it is not depleted or rendered imperfect by its causality (26. 30. 22). The fact that the monad is common to all and yet transcends all (23. 28. 5)[14] accounts for its being unparticipated; but the fact that it is the source of participations enables one also to say that it is participated mediately.[15]

On the other hand, the participations become constitutive parts of the participants and, thus, are less perfect than the unparticipated (23. 26. 31), although they generally are more perfect than the participant that they fill and complete (24. 28.

8). As immediate effects of a monad, they simultaneously remain in it, proceed from it, revert to it (props. 30, 31, 35).

In the second capital text Proclus qualifies the earlier statement by adding that the participations that an unparticipated causes are of two sorts.

[63, 60, 1 sq.:] Every unparticipated produces two orders of participations, the one in things which participate only for a time, the other in things which participate always and connaturally.[16]

For what is always participated is more like the unparticipated than what is participated for a time only. Consequently, what is everlastingly participated will be set up before what is only intermittently participated, since the former *qua* everlasting is more akin and like the unparticipated, although *qua* participation it does not differ from the for-a-time-only participation. These intermittent participations are not, then, the sole class of participations, since prior to them are the everlasting and continuous participations, through which they too are linked with the unparticipated in an ordered sequence of procession. Nor are the everlasting participations the sole class, since they have an inexhaustible power (because they are eternal) and thus are able to produce others—namely, the intermittent participations.[17] With these, though, downward production ceases.

From this it is apparent that the unities with which The One irradiates beings are participated, some enduringly, others for a time; and in like manner intellective participations are of two kinds, and the ensoulments produced by souls, and similarly the participations of Forms too.

Obviously, Proclus describes the two kinds of participations through their participants. This is his methodology because, as he states in later propositions, participations are known through what participates them (123. 108. 25–27; 123. 110. 4 sq.; 162. 142. 1–3) and this because the differences in participants arise from differences in the perfections participated (142. 126. 1 sq.). But (to return to prop. 63), there are two kinds of participants: the continuous and the intermittent. Therefore, we know there are two kinds of participations caused by the unparticipated. Proclus adds the important detail that the constant, everlasting participations cause the intermittent ones (63. 60. 10–12), which accordingly the unparticipated causes mediately.[18]

Have we any additional information on those participations? Yes, if we interpret Proposition 64 as restating its predecessor. Although this interpretation has the authority of E. R. Dodds,[19] reflection after initially publishing this paper in 1966 has led me to work out another interpretation. But before setting forth this more recent exegesis, let me indicate what (following Dodds) I had written previously and which is still informative.

What Proposition 63 described as enduring, continuous participations (hereafter, "the first sort") and as intermittent ones (hereafter, "the second sort"), proposition 64 depicts as hypostases complete in themselves and as irradiations that have their hypostasis in something other than themselves (64. 60. 20–22) because they are incomplete in themselves (*ibid.*, 1. 26). The first sort "make the participants belong to them, for being complete they fill the participants with themselves and establish them in themselves, and for their hypostasis they have no need of inferior beings" (*ibid.*, lines 28–31). The second sort "belong to their participants, for being incomplete they require a substrate for their reality" (*ibid.*, lines 26–28).

The participant of this latter kind can exercise such strong influence because they are simultaneously participating participations of the first sort (but issuing from a monad of a lower sort than that from which the irradiations proceed). These participations, of course, fill those participants with themselves, establish them in themselves and, thus, constitute them as independent existents capable of receiving irradiations from higher monads. Thus, a demon is fundamentally constituted by the soul and intelligence it participates (= first sort of participations). But as so set up, it can also receive an occasional irradiation from the henad participated by that soul and intelligence.[20] That irradiation is a participation of the second sort—a unity "with which The One irradiates beings [but] participated for a time only" (63. 60. 13–14), a unity that is incomplete in itself and that belongs to the demon providing it a temporary substrate (64. 60. 26–28). Similarly, a human soul is basically constituted by the soul it participates but, as so constituted, it can also receive intermittent irradiations from an intelligence. A plant, once constituted by participating life, also receives irradiations of soul. In brief:

> [64, 62, 5–12:] It is apparent that some henads proceed self-complete from The One, while others are irradiated states of unity; that some intelligences are self-complete entities, while others are intellectual perfections; that some souls belong to themselves, while others belong to the ensouleds as mere phantasms of souls. And so not every unity is a god but only the self-complete henad; not every intellectual property is an intelligence but only those whose proper reality is to be such; not every irradiation of Soul is a soul but there are also reflections of souls

Such, then, is the information with which Proposition 64 complements Proposition 63 when the two are read (following Dodds) as making the same points. Before setting forth our more recent approach to them, let us first discuss three other Propositions (81, 9, and 10) that illumine them somewhat.

Proposition 81 helps clarify Proposition 63, especially with respect to the intermittent participations that a monad produces. In interpreting Proposition 81, let us use one of the examples from the penultimate paragraph: a human soul in relationship to The Soul it continuously participates and to the intelligence that intermittently irradiates it. Considered in itself, that intelligence is a participation of the first sort because it has filled its direct participant with its own store of unity, intelligibility, intelligence (coming to it from a henad, being, and the Intelligence—[163. 142. 9 sq.; 175. 152. 19 sq.]) and, accordingly, is a hypostasis complete in itself. But it also is participated by a human soul occasionally and without directly becoming a part of it. It is, in this context, a "separate" participation."

Now to Proposition 81:

> [81, 76, 12–21:] Every perfection which is participated separately [in our example, the intelligence] is present to the participant [the human soul] through a power which

is inseparable from [= immanent to] the participant and which the participation [the intelligence] implants there.

For if it is itself something separate from the participant and not contained in it, something which has its own hypostasis, then they need a mean term to connect them, one which more nearly resembles the participation than the participant does and yet actually resides in the latter. For if the former is separate, how can it be participated by that which contains neither it nor any emanation from it? Accordingly, a potency or irradiation, proceeding from the participation [= the intelligence] to the participant [= the human soul], will link the two; and this power will be that through which the process of participation occurs and will be other than the participation and the participant.

This Proposition emphasizes several points seen previously. Through the participational process a perfection comes to be present in the participant and becomes a part of it. This happens either directly or mediately—that is, through a power and irradiation which the directly participated perfection causes. Rather obviously, the direct and indirect participations are identical with the first and second sorts of participants encountered in Propositions 63 and 64.[21]

As a final clarification, let us review what our author says concerning self-sufficiency (props. 9–10). How does what is self-sufficient (τὸ αὔταρκες) differ from what is not? The former furnishes well-being to itself, the latter needs another's help; the former has the cause of its goodness present within itself, the latter has its cause separated from it: it needs an extraneous cause and receives the completion of its reality and activity from without (9. 10. 18–23). Both are good through participation; yet the former has its goodness from and in itself, the latter from another (*ibid.*, lines 25–28). Consequently, "what is self-sufficient in entity or activity is superior to what is . . . dependent upon another entity for the cause of its perfection" (*ibid.*, lines 14–16). Yet, although it has its good from and in itself, still the former does participate and is filled with goodness and, thus, is inferior to The Good (10. 10. 29–34).

What relationship do Proclus' remarks on self-sufficiency have with Propositions 63 and 64? Both sets appear to be affirming the same thing from different points of view. For the self-sufficient to furnish well-being to itself, to have the cause of its goodness present within itself, to have its good from and in itself, does not eliminate The Good (and whatever other monad may be involved) as the source and cause of the perfections participated since what is self-sufficient, as well as what is not, *is a participant*. Nor does it exclude the fact that the participated perfection is a part of what is self-sufficient, as well as of what is not: both participate perfections which, consequently, help constitute them. Rather, the question is, How do those perfections pertain to them? If directly and immanently, the existent is self-sufficient. If indirectly and extrinsically, the existent is not: it does not have the perfection itself but an irradiation and power from it, with the result that the existent depends upon that separate perfection as a factor in its *intrinsic* makeup.

In this interpretation, then, the self-sufficient is equivalent to the first sort of participation: a perfection everlastingly participated, having its own hypostasis and dominating the participant it fills and establishes with itself. What is not self-sufficient is identical with the second sort of participation: the power or irradiation of a perfection intermittently and mediately participated and having a hypostasis and substrate in another, which dominates it because of its incompleteness.[22]

Thus far, these paragraphs have disclosed my initial reading of Propositions 63 and 64, complemented by information from Propositions 81, 9, and 10, according to which each is describing the same two sorts of participations in different words. That is to say, the unparticipated monad causes two sorts of participations—the first directly, the second through the first. The first is constantly present to its participant, which it fills with itself and thus dominates; it is a self-complete and self-sufficient hypostasis, having the perfection in question as an immanent cause. The other is a mere irradiation or power issuing from the former and intermittently received by a participant that provides it a substrate and which, thus, dominates it. Its participant is also a participation of the first sort, but one caused by a monad of a series lower than that from which the irradiation arises.[23] Properly understood, then, a participation of the second sort is both caused by and received in participations of the first sort. Perhaps Diagram One will help.[24]

Diagram One

If Props. 63 and 64 present the same doctrine, then:

#63:
   participations are

   a) permanently in
      the participant

   b) transiently in
      the participant

#64:
   participations are

   a) self-complete
      hypostases

   b) in other
      hypostases

This resultant arrangement:

$$O \rightarrow o^1 \rightarrow o^2 \rightarrow o^3 \rightarrow o^4 \rightarrow o^5$$
$$B \rightarrow b_1 \rightarrow b_2 \rightarrow b_3 \rightarrow b_4 \rightarrow b^5$$
$$N \rightarrow n_1 \rightarrow n_2 \rightarrow n_3 \rightarrow n_4 \rightarrow n^5$$
$$S \rightarrow s_1 \rightarrow s_2 \rightarrow s_3 \rightarrow s_4 \rightarrow s^5$$

*In the second portion of this Diagram, "O" stand for The One, "o" for a henad, "B" for The Being, "b" for a being, "N" for The Intellect, "n" for an intellect, "S" for The Soul, "s" for a soul. The arrows in each horizontal series indicate that its members are produced by the monad without participation occurring. The dotted vertical lines indicate that each existent in those lines is produced through participation—e.g., The Being participates henad #1, The Intellect participates in henad #2 and being #1.

There is, however, another way of interpreting Propositions 63 and 64, according to which the latter Proposition divides participations (= participated perfections) into existents that are self-complete hypostases and those that reside in hypostases other than themselves, whereas Proposition 63 lists two subdivisions of this second sort of participations by positing that these other-completed hypostases are found in their participants either permanently or intermittently. In this interpretation the initial members of each horizontal series of existents are not participated in by anything; for example, in Diagram Two such members are henads 1 to 12, Being and beings 1 to 2, Intellect and intellects 1 to 2, Soul and souls 1 to 2: all of these are self-complete hypostases.[25] The subsequent members of each horizontal series are other-completed hypostases (e.g., henads 11 sqq., beings 3 sqq., intellects 3 sqq., souls 3 sqq.) and this residence in existents other than themselves can happen (in the light of Prop. 63) either permanently or intermittently.

Diagram <u>Two</u>

If props. 63 and 64 do not represent the same doctrine, then:

#64:
  participations are

  a) self-complete existents
     or hypostases   self-sufficient (Props. 9-10)

  b) in other
     hypostases   and

#63:   self-constituted (prop. 40)

     1) permanently in
        participant

     2) transiently in   not: self-sufficient and
        participant   self-constituted

This resultant arrangement:

$$O \to \underset{1}{o} \to \underset{10}{o} \to \underset{11}{o} \to \underset{12}{o} \to \underset{13}{o} \to \underset{14}{o} \to \underset{15}{o} \to \underset{16}{o}$$

$$B \to \underset{1}{b} \to \underset{1}{b} \to \underset{2}{b} \to \underset{3}{b} \to \underset{4}{b} \to \underset{5}{b} \to \underset{6}{b}$$

$$N \to \underset{1}{n} \to \underset{1}{n} \to \underset{2}{n} \to \underset{3}{n} \to \underset{4}{n} \to \underset{5}{n}$$

$$S \to \underset{1}{s} \to \underset{1}{s} \to \underset{2}{s} \to \underset{3}{s}$$

Such, then, are two possible and plausible readings of Propositions 63 and 64, which deal with how the participations themselves arise. Each has advantages. But one's personal preference for one or the other interpretation does not essentially affect one's understanding of the propositions in which Proclus discloses how the participants themselves are produced. To these let us now turn.

THE ORIGIN OF PARTICIPANTS

Proposition 72 is the first of three capital texts on the participant and its genesis.

> [72, 68, 17–29:] In the participants whatever has the position of substrate proceeds from more complete and more universal causes.
>
> For the cause of more effects is more powerful, more universal and nearer to The One than the cause of fewer. But whatever sets up the prerequisite substrates for others is the cause of more since they preestablish suitably receptive conditions even for the presence of forms. Hence, those characteristics of the substrates are, as found in causes, more universal and complete.
>
> From this it is apparent why matter, taking its origin from The One, is in itself devoid of form: and why body, even though it participates Being, is in itself without participation in soul. For matter, which is the substrate of all, proceeds from the cause of all;[26] and body, which is the substrate of ensoulment, is derived from a principle more universal than soul in that after its fashion it participates Being.

The point Proclus is trying to make in these lines is rather awkwardly expressed. Perhaps seeing them in their immediate context will help. In propositions 70 and 71 Proclus moves from cause to effect, from the source to participations and participants: "A higher cause begins to operate upon secondary existents before a lower cause, is present concomitantly with the presence of the latter, and is still present and operative when the consequent has ceased to operate" (70. 66. 14–16). Consequently, the irradiations[27] from a higher cause are present in the participant before those issuing from a lower cause and remain there after those from a lower cause have withdrawn (*ibid.*, lines 11–13). As a result, the irradiations proceeding from a higher cause become a kind of substrate for those from a lower cause, which they receive and ground: "There is thus an order of precedence in the participative process: the same recipient is bombarded by successive rays from above, the more universal causes affecting it first, and the less universal ones supplementing these by the bestowal of their own gifts upon the participants" (71. 66. 30–68, 8; also see *ibid.*, lines 12–16).

In Proposition 72 our author seems to move from effect to cause in that from knowing what a substrate is, one also knows what sort of cause it has. The cause of more effects is more powerful and more universal than the cause of fewer; but the cause of what serves as a substrate is the cause of more effects than the cause of what the substrate receives; therefore, the cause of a substrate is more powerful, more universal, and higher than the cause of what perfects the substrate.[28]

What is especially important and relevant is that in Proposition 72 Proclus speaks of matter, which is the absolutely first substrate, and which is participant only and not a combination of participant/participation, such as is any material body. And on this point he is clear. Prime matter comes from The One. That which is the substrate of all comes from the causes of all. Although an inanimate body is without soul, still it participates being and, thus, originates directly from Being.[29] But matter, because it is without form and being, originates from that which is above form and being.[30] Or, as he says elsewhere, that which merely is suitable receptivity for participation of causes (39. 42. 4–5),[31] and which is the privation of forms, comes from the Good (57. 56. 36–37). What is actually one but is only potentially being does not have as its cause Being but The Not-Being which is superior to Being and which is one (138. 122. 17–20).[32]

Perhaps Diagram Three will help.

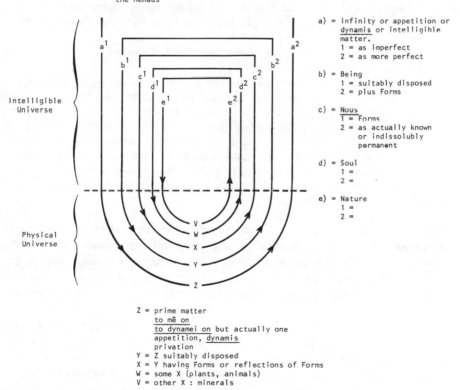

Diagram <u>Three</u>

AIM: To show the extent of causality in Proclus' universe
how far down causality of various Monads extends;
how permeating it is.

THE ONE-GOOD-LIMIT, from which all else comes
the henads

Intelligible Universe

Physical Universe

a) = infinity or appetition or
dynamis or intelligible
matter.
1 = as imperfect
2 = as more perfect

b) = Being
1 = suitably disposed
2 = plus Forms

c) = <u>Nous</u>
1 = Forms
2 = as actually known
or indissolubly
permanent

d) = Soul
1 =
2 =

e) = Nature
1 =
2 =

Z = prime matter
<u>to mē on</u>
<u>to dynamei on</u> but actually one
appetition, <u>dynamis</u>
privation
Y = Z suitably disposed
X = Y having Forms or reflections of Forms
W = some X (plants, animals)
V = other X : minerals

*To understand how extensive the One's causality is in Proclus' universe, it helps to conceive Diagram Three as tridimensional. Also, the line, $a^1 Z a^2$, marks the outside boundary of the One's causal overflow, which also extends throughout the entire intelligible and physical universes and (so to speak) lies under the causal contribution of Being (i.e., $b^1 Y b^2$) and of other lower monads. *Re* the right-hand column in the diagram: the second stage of a segment in the column is identical with the first stage of the following segment—e.g., b^1 is equivalent to a^2, c^1 to b^2, and so forth. The segments d and e are incomplete because Proclus seems not to have spoken of them in detail in the *Elements*.

The second key text, which is a composite of relevant lines from propositions 99 and 100, speaks of both participants and participations, although not without ambiguity.

> [99, 88, 20–34:] Every unparticipated arises *qua* unparticipated from no cause other than itself but is itself the first principle and cause of all participations [in its series]. Thus the first principle of each series is always without origin.
>
> For if it is unparticipated, it has primacy in its own series and does not proceed from other principles, since if it received from an external source that character in respect of which it is unparticipated, it would no longer be first in that series. If it is inferior to others and proceeds from them, it proceeds from them not *qua* unparticipated but *qua* participant. For those principles from which it has taken its rise are of course participated by it, and the perfections which it participates, it does not possess primally; but what it is as unparticipated, this it is primally. Accordingly, *qua* unparticipated it is uncaused. *Qua* caused it is a participant,[33] not unparticipated; *qua* unparticipated, it is a cause of participations and is not itself a participant of others.

> [100, 90, 2–3 and 7–16:] All unparticipateds are dependent from the one First Principle of all things. . . .
>
> All the unparticipated monads are referred to The One because all are analogous to The One. . . . In respect of their common origin from the latter, none of them is a first principle but all have as their first principle The One;[34] each, however, is a first principle *qua* unparticipated. As principles of a certain order of things they are dependent from the Principle of all things. For the Principle of all things is that which all participate, and this can only be the primal cause; the rest are participated not by all but by a certain some. Hence also that cause is absolutely The Primal, while the rest are primal with respect to a certain order but when considered absolutely are not primal.

These lines seem in obvious contrast with the first key text of this section. In Proposition 72 Proclus is concerned almost solely with participants and views the universe from the bottom up, so to speak. Here, though, he is concerned mainly with monads as unparticipated and his remarks on them as participants are almost incidental (and, certainly, somewhat ambiguous). He views the universe here from the top down.

In what does that ambiguity consist? It centers around the second point noted here.) Precisely as unparticipated, a monad causes and explains itself. This self-causality appears not to be identical with self-sufficiency (props. 9–10) and self-constitution (prop. 40 sq.), since what is self-sufficient and self-constituted do participate. In fact, these latter *are* participations that are self-causing only insofar as the perfection participated is itself present within them and not a mere irradiation from it. But a monad is self-causing and -explaining precisely because the perfection that is uniquely its own and that it contributes as participations to the series it heads (e.g., beingness re Being, animation re Life, etc.) is from itself—it is not received as a participation from an external source but originates from within. Otherwise, it would not be first in that series, it would not be the source therein of those unique participations. 2) Accordingly, if "it is inferior to others and proceeds from them, it proceeds from them not *qua* unparticipated but *qua* participant." This is the ambiguous sentence. Conceivably, something can be caused as a participant because it receives participations from its cause or, secondly, because as prior to and a substrate for those participations, it itself arises also from that cause.

Which meaning does Proclus intend here? It is difficult to decide, although the words immediately subsequent to those just quoted seem to point to the first: "it proceeds from them . . . *qua* participant, *for those principles from which it has taken its rise are of course participated by it, and the perfections which it partici-pates* it does not possess primally." But Proposition 100 provides material for an inference pointing to the second meaning. All unparticipated monads are depen-dent upon and ultimately reduced to The One, their common origin and First Principle. Their procession from it as participants can hardly be solely with re-spect to the participations they receive from it since such participations are abso-lutely primal and would, in this supposition, be without any participant at all. A participation can help provide a substrate to a subsequent participation (71. 66. 30 sq.), but it can hardly be a substrate *to itself*. Consequently, all other unpartici-pated monads (and, of course, the series they initiate) proceed as participants in the sense that the One establishes them prior to any participations and causes in them what serves as a substrate for all participations—namely, that which Proposition 72 calls "matter," the underlying receptable for all perfections, the privation of and desire for all forms, what is actually one but is merely potential being, what is in itself an indeterminate and infinite power looking to future development (props. 90–92; refer again to Diagram Three).

The final text discloses the role each henad or god plays with the One in respect to the participant.

> [137, 120, 31–122, 6:] Each henad co-operates with The One in producing its own participant.
>
> For as The One is constitutive of all, so it is the cause both of the participations which are the henads and of the beings dependent upon them. At the same time each henad produces and irradiates its dependent. The One makes each dependent be, simply; the henad makes each be of the same nature as itself.[35] Thus, the henad imposes its own determinate character upon the being participating it, in which it entitatively displays its own supra-entitative property.

Earlier (props. 120–122) Proclus had spoken of the gods as causes of partici-pations. An agent's activity parallels and conforms to his nature or reality; but a god by nature is not an intelligence but a prior-to-intelligence, is not a being but a prior-to-being: he *is* goodness; consequently, his activity is not intellection but a function prior to intellection (το προνοεῖν) and to being (τὸ προεῖναι): the bestowal of goods upon subsequents, the communication of participations upon participants (120. 104. 31 sq.). These participations each henad bestows without itself assuming any relationship to the participants, without itself becoming de-pendent on them (122. 108. 13–17). Moreover, that bestowal occurs sponta-neously, naturally, inevitably, necessarily since it is in virtue of being what they are that they make all things good. . . . By their very being or, rather, by their very priority to being, they irradiate goods upon beings. For being nothing but goodnesses, they furnish by their very being goods to all without stint [*ibid.*, lines 14–17, and 6–11].[36]

In proposition 137, though, our author speaks of the gods with reference to the participant itself. Working together with the One, the henad helps cause the being which immediately participates it (135. 120. 1 sq.) by making it be connatural with itself, by manifesting on the level of being the character that it has supraentitatively and primally. Thus, a "paternal" henad implants paternity in its being-participant (151. 132. 26 sq.), a "generative" henad implants generativity (152. 134. 6 sq.), and so on down the line of the other henadic characters spoken of in Propositions 153–158.[37]

On the other hand, while a god makes its participant "be of the same nature as itself," The One "makes it be simply." What does that striking statement mean? First of all, our author does not intend that The One makes it be *being*: such is the function of The Being. This latter monad accounts for the presence of form in matter (57. 56. 12–13) or, in other texts, of limit in infinity (89. 82. 1 sq.; 102. 92. 1–2, 7–8), and such is "being": a combination of form/matter, of limit/infinity. But The One brings it about that what as yet is merely potential being not only is actually one (138. 122. 17–18), but also *is* simply. Does this signify that The One causes matter, the absolutely primal substrate, the participant of henads (and ultimately of all else, too), *to actually exist*? I think not, because every effect in Proclus' universe is, at bottom, identical with its cause: although an effect proceeds from and thus is somehow distinct from its cause, still it also remains in, and thereby is the same as, its cause (30. 34. 12 sq.). Causality consists in the higher deploying *itself* on a lower level, where it is less perfect and more multiple than before, but where it remains itself under the camouflage of imperfection and multiplicity.

Apparently, matter would be no exception to this general rule. Radically, it *is* The One descending to a lower and pluralized level. It *is* The One emerging into evolving cycles of explicitation and differentiation. We can say that The One, in contrast with the henads, makes matter *be* simply insofar as under its influence what we call matter comes to deploy on a lower level, which the henads then make connatural to themselves and, thereafter, fill with themselves. In this interpretation, then, "to be simply" is not "to actually exist" since this latter demands that what now is, before was in no way. Accordingly, Proclus appears not to have had a genuine doctrine of creation. Not only does The One produce necessarily rather than voluntarily and freely, but the product is not really distinct in any genuinely adequate way from the producer and, therefore, the product is not caused to actually exist. That which is is now *where* it was not before, is now in a different state and under a different guise than it was before, is now different from *what* it was. But that which now is *was* before. The One no more causes it to exist then or now than it causes itself to exist.[38]

SUMMARY AND CONCLUSION

Despite this seeming lack of a doctrine of creation, though, Proclus' *Weltan-schauung* as outlined in *Elements of Theology* is not a mere cosmology but a genuine cosmogony. At the head of each stratum of reality within the universe stands an unparticipated monad which is the cause of all participations within its stratum. In Dodd's (and my earlier) interpretation, these are either constantly participated perfections (which are self-complete and self-sufficient hypostases and are causes immanent to their participants), or they are perfections only inter-mittently participated (which are mere powers or irradiations issuing from the former and which have their hypostases and substrates in their participants) (see Diagram One). In my more recent interpretation, though, the two sorts of partici-pations just mentioned express two ways in which participations reside in other-completed hypostases and are contrasted with those that are self-complete exis-tents or hypostases (see Diagram Two).

In either interpretation one must face this question: Where does the monad itself acquire those perfections? From itself. With respect to the characteristic which is uniquely its own and which is the basis for the unique participations it bestows upon all members of its series, it is primal, it is unparticipated, it has no external cause.

With the exception of The One, though, every monad (as well, of course, as the members of its series) is a participant with reference to higher monads, whence it receives not only participations but also derives its status as participant. In the last analysis, all else has proceeded from and reverts to The One, which is the primal monad and which is unparticipated without itself being a participant of anything higher. It causes matter—the underlying stuff of all substrates—to be simply; not by making it actually exist, but by that which is absolutely one and totally perfect stepping down onto levels of gradually increasing multiplicity and imperfection.

In Proclus' cosmos then, there are at least two sorts of causality operative, both of which are spontaneous, natural, necessary. The one (= vertical) is a process of participation: participations come to be present in participants, which they complete and perfect as integral parts. The other (= horizontal) is not: the participations themselves and their participants originate simply (and mysteriously) by proceeding from their monads.[39] There issues from the two causalities a tightly structured hierarchy of reality stretching from the One-Good-Limit at the top to matter, the deployment of the One itself at the very bottom.

Notes

ON LOGICAL STRUCTURE AND THE PLOTINIC COSMOS

1. A. E. Taylor, *Plato, the Man and His Work* (London: Methuen, 1963, first published in 1926), p. 293.
2. The translation used throughout is that of MacKenna. Namely, Plotinus, *The Enneads* translated by Stephen MacKenna, Second edition (London: Faber and Faber, Ltd., 1917–1930).
3. See especially the author's *Whitehead's Categoreal Scheme and Other Papers* (The Hague: Martinus Nijhoff, 1974), especially chapter 1.
4. On virtual classes and relations, see especially the author's *Belief, Existence, and Meaning* (New York: New York University Press, 1969), chapter 6, and *Semiotics and Linguistic Structure* (Albany: The State University of New York Press, 1978), chapters 1 and 2.

SOME LOGICAL ASPECTS OF THE CONCEPT OF HYPOSTASIS IN PLOTINUS

1. The general view is that there are three hypostases: One, *Nous*, and Soul. A. H. Armstrong, in his "Introduction" to the Loeb edition of Plotinus' *Enneads* (London and Cambridge, Mass.: Harvard University Press, 1966) vol. I, p. xxii, suggests that nature is a fourth distinct *hypostasis*, although

Plotinus "is reluctant to admit it." In his earlier work, *The Architecture of the Intelligible World in the Philosophy of Plotinus* (Cambridge: Cambridge University Press, 1940), p. 102, Armstrong proposed five Plotinian hypostases: One, Nous, Soul, Logos, and Nature; he states that "The *Logos* is a fourth hypostasis even more clearly than nature, and a hypostasis, moreover, whose own structure is complex." John M. Rist, in his *Plotinus: The Road to Reality* (Cambridge: Cambridge University Press, 1967), especially in chapter 7, argues against Armstrong and takes the view that there can be only three hypostases; so also John N. Deck, *Nature, Contemplation and the One: A Study in the Philosophy of Plotinus* (Toronto: University of Toronto Press, 1967), p. 56, but seems rather uncertain about excluding nature, p. 66. R. T. Wallis appeals to *Enneads* II. 9. 1. 57–63, to indicate that in Plotinus' view "Logos is not a separate Hypostasis but expresses the relation of an Hypostasis to its source, its products, or both, cf. III. 2. 2. 15ff," *Neoplatonism* (New York: Charles Scribner's Sons, 1972), p. 68. For Plotinus' own testimony that the primal hypostases are (i) three, see V. 1. [10] 1; and (ii) only three, II. 9. [33], 1–2: One, *Nous*, and Soul.

2. There are key passages in the *Enneads* which refer to the basic features of *hypostasis,* and we may single out four: (i) as power a *hypostasis* is infinite and nonspatial (VI.3.8. 35ff; VI.9.6. 10–12); (ii) *hypostasis* remains unaffected by what it produces, and as such it is "undiminished giving," suffering no diminution of substance (III.8.8.46–48 and 10.1–19); (iii) a *hypostasis* creates without inclination, will, or movement (V.1.6.25–27; V.3.12. 20–29); (iv) a *hypostasis* has no knowledge of its products; the One qua hypostasis transcends knowledge altogether (VI.7.39. 19–33); yet the lower hypostases know only the causal principles they contain within themselves (IV.4.9. 16–18; V.8.3. 26–27). See also Wallis, *Neoplatonism,* pp. 62–63.

3. Deck, *Nature, Contemplation and the One,* pp. 9–11.

4. *Ibid.,* p. 9. John Rist follows a somewhat different formulation from Deck, who appeals to demonstrate from causality. His understanding that the One is the first hypostasis is stated as follows: "The One does not concern itself. But the *result* of willing itself is its production of the second hypostasis, for it wills itself to be such as to produce it. Creation is as free, no more and no less, than the One itself. As for pantheism it is irrelevant." See his *Plotinus,* p. 83. While Deck emphasizes the argument from cause to establish the One as *hypostasis,* Rist stresses the ontological analysis of the nature of the One qua "willing itself."

5. Deck, *Nature, Contemplation and the One,* p. 66. His meaning, however, is not made clear.

6. Deck's claim that the titles are Porphyry's own seems to rest on his misreading of the text. See Porphyry, *On the Life of Plotinus,* ch. 4, in *Enneads* (Loeb edition) vol. I. Porphyry does not say that he supplied the titles, only that he used the ones that had prevailed: "These were the writings, to which, since he gave them no titles himself, each [of the few people who had received copies] gave different titles for the several treatises. The following are the titles which finally prevailed. I add the first words of the treatises, to make it easy to recognize from them which treatise is indicated by each title" (Armstrong's translation [Loeb edition], vol. I, p. 13). The word for title is *epigraphē.* See also, Porphyry, ch. 25, 32–37.

7. Armstrong's translation of the title Porphyry preserved: Περὶ τοῦ ἑκουσίον καὶ θελήματος τοῦ ἑνός, (ch. 26 [Leob edition] vol. I, p. 85).

8. E. Bréhier's text. Plotin, *Ennéades,* (Paris: "Les Belles Lettres," 1924–38), vol. VI², p. 153.

9. S. MacKenna, *The Enneads,* English translation, 3rd edition revised by B. S. Page (London: Faber and Faber, 1962), p. 608.

10. Compare III.8.10, where Plotinus speaks also of life as founded in "roots": οἷον ἐν ῥίζῃ ἱδρυμένης.

11. Wallis claims that "Plotinus' aversion to formal systems . . . is shown by his continual qualification of his accounts of spiritual being by such Greek works as *hoion* or *hosper* ('so to speak')" (*Neoplatonism,* p. 41). Evidently, Wallis questions the possibility that *hoion* is a technical expression. If Wallis's claim is granted, then all conceptual terms used by Plotinus to explicate the One are reducible to "so-to-speak" expressions. It may be objected that the expression "so to speak" is too weak to render Plotinus' meaning or capture the seriousness of his arguments and the tone of his exposition. There is an important passage where the expression *to hoion* is used in a conspic-

uously technical sense: VI.8.11. Plotinus states there that for the whole inquiry to determine the meaning of μὴ ὑποστάν as related to "the question just raised," we need to think of the following concepts: ἢ τοῦ τί ἐστιν εἶναι ἢ τοῦ οἷον ἢ τοῦ διὰ τί ἢ τοῦ εἶναι. After stating what the last two mean, he says that τὸ δὲ οἷόν ἐστι ζητεῖν τί συμβέβηκεν αὐτῷ ᾧ συμβέβηκεν μηδέν (lines 9–10).

12. For comparable examples of the use of *hoion,* see VI.8.7.31–32: Ὑπὲρ δὴ ταῦτα τοῦ ἀγαθοῦ αὐτοῦ ὄντος οἷον ἄλλο παρ' αὐτὸ ἀγαθὸν ζητεῖν ἄτοπον. A comparative study of the uses of *hoios* in the Platonic texts may prove useful on this point. See, for instance, *Ion* 537C and 538A and also *Gorgias* 454D.

THE ONE, OR GOD, IS NOT PROPERLY "HYPOSTASIS":
A Reply to Professor John P. Anton

1. See pp. 24–33 of this volume. The article was also previously published in *The Review of Metaphysics* 21:2 (December, 1977), pp. 258–271; hereafter, "Anton." All page references are to the *Review* article.

2. John N. Deck, *Nature, Contemplation and the One* (Toronto: University of Toronto Press, c. 1967); hereafter *NCO.*

3. Professor Anton is, of course, aware of this doctrine—too obvious to be missed—from his own reading of Plotinus. But he does not appreciate its overriding significance. "Though the One is beyond *ousia* and thus beyond predication, still it is the case that he [Plotinus] makes it the object of discourse" (Anton, p. 25). There seems to be here scarcely a suspicion of the adjustments required when a philosopher makes the "beyond predication" an "object of discourse." The absence of this whole dimension makes it possible for Anton to write an entire article demonstrating that "correct discourse" about the One "demands" that the One *is something*—in this case, that the One *is the first hypostasis*! (Anton, p. 33–Conclusion).

4. Professor Anton does not attend sufficiently to the doctrine that the One is not dual: "The One gave itself its own subsistence and necessarily so" (Anton, p. 31); ". . . the original activity of the One which is presupposed by its *ousia*" (p. 33; ". . . in control of itself" (p. 30). These and similar phrases are quoted or supplied by him absolutely without correctives.

5. Just as Anton did not feel the force of "beyond predication," so in the same paragraph (Anton, p. 25, para. 1) he fails to appreciate (although he quotes), "beyond being." For him Plotinus believes that it is impossible to make contradictory statements about the One because the "thesis that contradictions are not possible when we speak of Being . . . is fundamental to all classical ontology." *Beyond* being!

    (To wander much further afield, I would be prepared to defend, sometime, that the principle of contradiction (noncontradiction?) is not nearly so sacred to the Plato of the Sophist, to Plotinus, or even to Aristotle as it is to, say, Leibnitz—and also that the ordinary logical notion of contradiction is too crude, at any rate, to be of value in serious metaphysics.)

6. Professor Anton, for whom the "concept" of hypostasis is important (and apparently univocal) in Plotinus, shows concern about the *number* of hypostases, and says that they are three and only three (p. 24, n. 1). In doing so, he represents me as "being rather uncertain about excluding Nature." What I had done was virtually to quote *Plotinus* (in passing, and in another connection): "Soul, by descending into plants, makes another hypostasis" (*NCO,* p. 65, referring to V.2.1. 24–26). But I am not terribly interested in whether Nature is or is not another hypostasis. I am very interested, as Plotinus himself was, in the delineation of the sameness-and-difference, continuity-and-discontinuity, between Soul and Nature.

7. If Plotinus were to have an *ex professo* doctrine of hypostasis (I do not see that he has), and if that doctrine were correctly rendered by Professor Anton, that is, if "*hypostasis*" were really to mean, for Plotinus, what is *in*finite and *non*spatial, what is *un*affected by what it produces, what creates *without* inclination, will, or movement, what has *no* knowledge of its products, "*hypostasis*" still would not name what the One is in its own nature. "*Hypostasis*" would connote only, and strictly

from the outside, what the One *is not*. It could not refer to an internal negation; the One is above that. It would be what the Scholastic textbooks used to call an "extrinsic denomination." "The One is the first *hypostasis*" would be a case of *via negationis* or *via remotionis*.

PLOTINUS' THEORY OF THE ONE

1. "According to the time of writing—early manhood, vigorous prime, worn-out constitution—so the tractates vary in power." Porphyry, "On the Life of Plotinus and the Arrangement of his Work," from Plotinus *The Enneads,* trans. Stephen MacKenna, with an Introduction by Professor Paul Henry, S. J., 4th rev. ed., (New York: Random House, 1969), p. 5.
2. Almost all commentators have recognized at least two different ways Plotinus has of speaking of The One, though they do not characterize them in the same way always. Leo Sweeny, S. I. "Infinity in Plotinus," *Gregorianum* 38 (1957), 515–535, suggests that infinity is predicated of The One extrinsically in virtue of its *dynamis,* but intrinsically of its Non-Beingness. The non-being of the One is particularly emphasized by Jean Trouillard, "Plotin et le Moi," *Horizons de la personne,* eds. A. Jagu et al. (Paris: Les Editions Ouvrieres, 1965), p. 75. John M. Rist, "Theos and the One in Some Texts of Plotinus," *Mediaeval Studies,* 24 (1962), 169–180, recognizes that while the One transcends being, it does not transcend causality. Rene Arnou, *Le Desir de Dieu dans la Philosophie de Plotin* (Paris: Librairie Felix Alcan, n.d.), p. 178, describes in some detail both immanental and transcendental modes of discourse in reference to The One. Another author emphasizes the One as the synthesis of both modes of discourse: "So ist das Eine die Einheit von Sein und Nichtsein, von Rationalem und Irrationalem, von Allem und Nichts." Fritz Heinemann, *Plotin: Forschungen uber die plotinische Frage, Plotins Entwicklung und sein System* (Leipzig: Felix Meiner, 1921), p. 253. Finally A. H. Armstrong has emphasized recurrently both the positive and negative elements of the One in Plotinus and their incompatibility. Cf. especially A. H. Armstrong, "Platonic Mysticism," *Dublin Review* 216 (April, 1945), 130–143; and also his *The Architecture of the Intelligible Universe in the Philosophy of Plotinus: An Analytical and Historical Study* (Cambridge: The University Press, 1940), pp. 1–47.
3. *Enn.* V.5.6, p. 408. ". . . ἀνάγκη ἀνείδεον ἐκεῖνο εἶναι. ἀνείδεον δὲ ὂν οὐκ οὐσία · τόδε γάρ τι δεῖ τὴν οὐσίαν εἶναι · τοῦτο δὲ ὡρισμένον · τὸ δὲ οὐκ ἔστι λαβεῖν ὡς τόδε · ἤδη γὰρ οὔκ ἀρχή, ἀλλ᾽ ἐκεῖνο μόνον, ὅ τόδε εἴρηκας εἶναι . . . οὐδὲν δὲ τούτων ὂν μόνον ἄν λέγοιτο ἐπέκεινα τούτων. ταῦτα δὲ τὰ ὄντα καὶ τὸ ὄν · ἐπέκεινα ἄρα ὄντος. τὸ γὰρ ἐπέκεινα ὄτος οὐ τόδε λέγει—οὐ γὰρ τίθησιν—οὐδὲ ὄνομα αὐτοῦ λέγει, ἀλλὰ φέρει μόνον τὸ οὐ τοῦτο." Trans. Richard Harder, Plotins Schriften, Band IIIa, (Hamburg: Felix Meiner, 1956), V.5.6. p. 82, 84. Cf. also *Enn.* V.6.6. p. 419; III.6.6. p. 207; IV.4.16, pp. 299–300; III.8.9, p. 248; III.8.10, p. 249; V.5.4, p. 406; V.5.5, p. 407; V.5.12, p. 413; V.5.13, p. 414; VI.7.16, p. 574; VI.7.38, p. 591; VI.7.40, p. 593; VI.7.41, p. 594; VI.8.9, pp. 602–603; VI.8.10, p. 604; VI.8.11, p. 605; VI.8.12, p. 605; VI.8.19, p. 612; VI.2.3, p. 473; VI.2.17, p. 486.
4. *Enn.* VI.7.17, p. 576. "ἔδει δὲ τὸ πρῶτον μὴ πολὺ μηδαμῶς εἶναι · ἀνήρτητο γάρ ἂν τὸ πολὺ αὐτοῦ εἰς ἕτερον αὖ πρὸ αὐτοῦ." Harder, IIIa. VI.7.17, p. 296. Cf. also *Enn.* V.5.4, p. 406; V.5.6, p. 408; V.5.11, p. 412; VI.8.8, p. 601; VI.8.11, p. 605; VI.8.17, p. 610; VI.2.9, p. 480.
5. *Enn.* V.5.13, p. 413. "εἰ οὖν μήτε τὸ οὐκ ἀγαθὸν μήτε τὸ ἀγαθὸν ἔχει, οὐδὲν ἔχει · εἰ δ᾽οὐδὲν ἔχει, μόνον καὶ ἔρημον τῶν ἄλλων ἐστίν." Harder, IIIa. V.5.13, p. 100. Cf. also *Enn.* V.5.11, p. 412; V.5.13, p. 414; II.9.1, p. 132.
6. *Enn.* VI.7.40, p. 593. "οὐ γὰρ ἐνεργήσας πρότερον ἐγέννησεν ἐνέργειαν · ἤδη γὰρ ἂν ἦν, πρὶν γενέσθαι · οὐδε νοήσας ἐγέννησε νόησιν · ἤδη γὰρ ἂν ἐνενόηκει, πρὶν γενέσθαι νόησιν. ὅλως γὰρ ἡ νόησις, εἰ μὲν ἀγαθοῦ, χεῖρον αὐτοῦ. . . ." Harder, IIIa. VI.7.40, p. 350. Cf. Also *Enn.* V.6.6, p. 418; III.8.11, p. 250; VI.7.17, pp. 574–575.
7. *Enn.* III.8.11, p. 250. " . . . ὁ τοιοῦτον παῖδα γεννήσας νοῦν, κόρον καλὸν καὶ παρ᾽ αὐτοῦ γενόμενον κόρον. πάντως τοι οὔτε νοῦσ ἐκεῖνος οὔτε κόρος, ἀλλὰ καὶ πρὸ νοῦ καὶ κόρου · μετὰ γὰρ αὐτὸν νοῦς καὶ κόρος, δεηθέντα καὶ κεκορέσθαι καὶ νενοηκέναι. . . ." Harder, IIIa. III.8.11, p. 32. Cf. also *Enn.* VI.7.32, p. 586.

8. Cf. *Enn.* V.6.2, p. 416; V.8.7, p. 428.

9. *Enn.* VI.6.10, p. 549. ". . . καὶ ἕκαστον μὲν τοῦ ἐν μετέσχεν, ἵνα ἓν ᾖ ἔστι δὲ ὄν παρὰ τοῦ ὄντος, ἐπεὶ καὶ τὸ ὄν παρ' αὐτοῦ ὄν ˙ ἓν δὲ παρὰ τοῦ ἕν. . ." Harder, IIIa. VI.6.10, p. 184.

10. *Enn.* VI.6.9, p. 548.

11. *Enn.* VI.7.40, p. 593. "εἰ δέ τις καὶ τοῦτο ἅμα νοοῦν καὶ νοούμενον ποιεῖ καὶ οὐσίαν καὶ νόησιν συνοῦσα τῇ οὐσία καὶ οὕτως αὐτὸ νοοῦν θέλει ποιεῖν, ἄλλου δεήσεται καὶ τούτο πρὸ αὐτοῦ. . . ." Harder, IIIa. VI.7.40, p. 352.

12. *Enn.* VI.7.33. p. 587. ". . . τὸ δὲ ὄντως ἢ τὸ ὑπέρκαλον μὴ μεμετρῆσθαι εἰ δὲ τοῦτο, μὴ μεμορφῶσθαι μηδὲ εἶδος εἶναι, ἀνείδεον ἄρα τὸ πρώτως καὶ πρῦτον καὶ ἡ καλλονὴ ἐκεῖνο, ἡ τοῦ ἀγαθοῦ φύσις." Harder, IIIa. VI.7.33, p. 332. Cf. also *Enn.* V.5.6, p. 408; VI.7.17, p. 575; VI.7.17, pp. 575–576; VI.7.32, p. 586; VI.8.11, p. 605.

13. *Enn.* VI.7.38, p. 591. "τί οὖν γνώσεται; << ἐγώ εἰμι >>. ἀλλ' οὐκ ἔστι. διὰ τί οὖν οὐκ ἐρεῖ << τὸ ἀγαθόν εἰμι >>; ἢ πάλιν τὸ << ἔστι >> κατηγορήσει αὐτοῦ. ἀλλ' οὐ τὸ << ἀγαθὸν >> μόνον ἐρεῖ ˙ [τι προσθείς] << ἀγαθὸν >> μὲν γὰρ νοήσειεν ἄν τις ἄνευ τοῦ << ἔστιν >> εἰ μὴ κατ' ἄλλου κατηγοροῖ ˙ ὁ δὲ αὐτὸν νοῶν ὅτι ἀγαθὸν πάντως νοήσει τὸ << ἐγώ εἰμι τὸ ἀγαθόν >> . . ." Harder, IIIa. VI.7.38, pp. 344, 346. Cf. also *Enn.* V.5.13, p. 413; V.5.13, p. 414.

14. *Enn.* V.6.2, p. 416. "ἔδει δὲ πρὸ τοῦ νοεῖν τέλειον εἶναι παρ' αὐτοῦ τῆς οὐσίας. ᾧ ἄρα τὸ τέλειον ὑπάρξει, πρὸ τοῦ νοεῖν τοῦτο ἔσται ˙ οὐδὲν ἄρα δεῖ αὐτῷ τοῦ νοεῖν ˙ αὔταρκες γὰρ πρὸ τούτου ˙ οὐκ ἄρα νοήσει. τὸ μὲν ἄρα οὐ νοεῖ, τὸ δὲ πρώτως νοεῖ, τὸ δὲ νοήσει δευτέρως." Harder, IIa. V.6.2, p. 78. Cf. also *Enn.* V.6.3, p. 417; V.6.4, p. 417; V.6.5, p. 418; V.6.6, p. 418; V.6.6, p. 419; III.8.9, p. 247; III.8.11, p. 250; V.5.13, p. 414; VI.7.35, p. 588; VI.7.37, p. 591; VI.7.38, p. 591; VI.7.39, p. 592; VI.7.40, p. 593; VI.7.41, p. 594; VI.8.11, p. 605.

15. *Enn.* VI.8.9, p. 603. ". . . αὐτὴν δὲ μείζονα παντὸς τοῦ θέλειν οὐσαν τὸ θέλειν μετ' αὐτὴν θεμένην." Harder, IVa. VI.8.9, p. 28.

16. *Enn.* VI.8.8, p. 601. "τούτων γὰρ αὐτὸς ἀρχή ˙ καίτοι ἄλλον τρόπον οὐκ ἀρχή; ἀποτιθεμένοις δὴ πάντα καὶ τὸ ἐπ' αὐτῷ ὡς ὕστερον καὶ τὸ αὐτεξούσιον . . ." Harder, IVa. VI.8.8, p.22.

17. *Enn.* VI.5.1, p. 533. "ποῦ γὰρ ἂν εἴη ἔξω τοῦ ὄντος περιπεπτωκός, ἢ πῶς ἂν τις ἐν τῷ μὴ ὄντι ἐξεύροι αὐτό; ἀλλὰ δῆλον ὅτι ἐν τῷ ὄντι ἐκεῖνο, ἐν ἑαυτῷ ἂν εἴη ἑκάστῳ οὐκ ἀπέστημεν ἄρα τοῦ ὄντος, ἀλλ' ἐσμὲν ἐν αὐτῷ οὐδ' αὖ ἐκεῖνο ἡμῶν ˙ ἓν ἄρα πάντα τὰ ὄντα." Harder, IIa. VI.5.1, pp. 46, 48.

18. *Enn.* VI.8.16, p. 609. "ἔτι τοίνυν, εἰ ἔστι μάλιστα, ὅτι [πρὸς] αὐτὸν οἷον στηρίζει καὶ οἷον πρὸς αὐτὸν βλέπει καὶ τὸ οἷον εἶναι τοῦτο αὐτῷ τὸ πρὸς αὐτὸν βλέπειν, οἷον ποιοῖ ἂν αὐτόν. . . ." Harder, IVa. VI.8.16, p. 46. Cf. also *Enn.* VI.8.8, p. 602; VI.8.13, p. 606; VI.8.13, p. 607; VI.8.20, p. 612; VI.8.20, p. 613; III.8.10, p. 248; V.5.12, p. 413.

19. *Enn.* VI.8.20, p.—612. "οὐδὲ γὰρ φοβητέον ἐνέργειαν τὴν πρώτην τθεσθαι ἄνευ οὐσίας, ἀλλ' αὐτὸ τοῦτο τὴν οἷον ὑπόστασιν θετέον. εἰ δὲ ὑπόστασιν ἄνευ ἐνεργείας τις θεῖτο, ἐλλιπὴς ἡ ἀρχὴ καὶ ἀτελὴς ἡ τελειοτάτη πασῶν ἔσται. καὶ εἰ προσθείν ἐνέργειαν, οὐχ ἓν τηρεῖ. εἰ οὖν τελειότερον ἡ ἐνέργειαμτῆς οὐσίας, τελειότατον δὲ τὸ πρῶτον, πρώτη ἂν ἐνέργεια εἴη." Harder, IVa. VI.8.20, p. 56. Cf. also *Enn.* V.6.6, p. 418; III.8.10, p. 248; VI.8.10, p. 604; VI.8.13, p. 606; VI.8.16, p. 609; VI.8.16, p. 610; VI.8.20, p. 613; VI.1.26, p. 466; V.5.3, p. 406.

20. *Enn.* VI.8.7, p. 601. ". . . ἡ οἷον οὐσία αυνοῦσα καὶ οἷον συγγενομέθη ἐξ αἰδίου τῇ ἐνεργεία ἐξ ἀμφοῖν αὐτὸ αὐτὸ ποιεῖ [καὶ ἑαυτοῦ καὶ οὐδενός]." Harder, IVa. VI.8.7, p. 22.

21. *Enn.* V.5.12, p. 413. ". . . τὸ δὲ πρεσβύτερον οὐ χρόνῳ, ἀλλὰ τῷ ἀληθεῖ, ᾧ καὶ τὴν δύναμιν προτέραν ἔχει ˙ πᾶσαν γὰρ ἔχει ˙ τὸ γὰρ μετ' αὐτὸ οὐ πᾶσαν, ἀλλ' ὅση μετ' αὐτὸ καὶ ἀπ' αὐτοῦ. ὥστε ἐκεῖνος καὶ ταύτης κύριος. . . ." Harder, IIIa. V.5.12, pp. 98, 100. Cf. also *Enn.* V.5.10, p. 411; VI.8.9, p. 602; VI.8.10, p. 604; VI.8.18, p. 611; VI.8.20, p. 613; VI.8.21, p. 613.

22. *Enn.* VI.1.12, p. 455. ". . . εἰ δὲ κατ' οὐσίαν ἡ δύναμις, ἤ τις δύναμισ. . . ." Harder, IVa. VI.1.12, p. 130.

23. *Enn.* III.8.10, p. 248. "Τί δὴ ὄν; δύναμις τῶν πάντων ˙ ἧς μὴ οὔσης οὐδ' ἂν τὰ πάντα,

οὐδ'ἀν νοῦ ζωὴ ἡ πρώτη καὶ πᾶσα." Harder, IIIa. III.8.10, p. 26. Cf. also *Enn*. III.8.10, p. 249; VI.8.8, p. 601; VI.8.9, p. 602; VI.8.11, p. 604.

24. *Enn*. VI.8.20, p. 613. "τί οὖν αὐτοῦ ὅ μὴ αὐτός; τί οὖν, ὃ μὴ ἐνεργεῖ; καὶ τί, ὃ μὴ ἔργον αὐτοῦ." Harder, IVa. VI.8.20, p. 58.

25. *Enn*. VI.8.16, p. 609. "τοῦτο δ' ἐστὶν ὑποστήσας αὐτόν, εἴπερ ἐνέργεια μένουσα καὶ τὸ ἀγαπητότατον οἷον νοῦς." Harder, IVa. VI.8.16, p. 46.

26. *Enn*. VI.8.18, p. 611. "οἷον γὰρ γὸ ἐν θῷ, πολλαχῇ μεῖζον ἢ τοιοῦτον, τὸ ἐν ἑνὶ ἐκένψ . . . οὐ μὴν ἀλλοειδὲς τὸ σκεδασθὲν εἴδωλον ὁ νοῦς. . . ." Harder, IVa. VI.8.18, p. 52.

27. *Enn*. VI.7.18, p. 576. ". . . καὶ ἐπὶ νοῦ δὴ τοῦ ἀληθινοῦ ἀνάγκη λέγειν τοῦ πρώτου ἐκείνου, ὅτι ἀγαθόν ˙ καὶ δῆλον ὅτι καὶ εἶδος ἕκαστον ἀγαθὸν καὶ ἀγαθοειδές." Harder, IIIa. VI.7.18, p. 298. Cf. also *Enn*. III.8.11, p. 250.

28. *Enn*. VI.6.14, p. 553. "ἓν μὲν εἶναι τοῦ ἓν παρουσία, δύο δέ, δυάδος, ὥσπερ καὶ λευκὸν λευκοῦ καὶ καλὸν καλοῦ καὶ δικαίου δίκαιον. . . ." Harder, IIIa. VI.6.14, pp. 198, 200.

29. *Enn*. VI.8.14, p. 608. ". . . τὸ ὄντως καὶ τὸ πρῶτον, ἀμιγὲς τύχαις καὶ αὐτομάτῳ καὶ συμβάσει, αἴτιον ἑαυτοῦ καὶ παρ' αὐτοῦ καὶ δι' αὐτὸν αὐτός ˙ γὰρ πρώτως αὐτὸς καὶ ὑπερόντως αὐτός." Harder, IVa. VI.8.14, p. 42. Cf. also *Enn*. VI.8.16, p. 609; VI.8.16, p. 610; VI.8.20, p. 612; VI.8.20, p. 613; VI.8.21, p. 613.

30. *Enn*. VI.7.39, p. 592. ". . . ἀλ' ἁπλῆ τις ἐπιβολὴ αὐτῷ πρὸς αὐτὸ ἔσται." Harder, IIIa. VI.7.39, p. 346.

31. *Enn*. VI.8.18, p. 611. Beginning with the phrase "showing forth," the last clause reads as follows: ". . . μαρτυρεῖν τὸν οἷον ἐν ἑνὶ νοῦν οὐ νοῦν ὄντα. . . ." Harder, IVa. VI.8.18, p. 52. Cf. also *Enn*. VI.8.16, pp. 609–610.

32. *Enn*. VI.8.13, p. 606. "εἰ γὰρ δοίημεν ἐνεργείας αὐτῷ, τὰς δ' ἐνεργείας αὐτοῦ οἷον βουλήσει αὐτοῦ—γὰρ ἀβουλῶν ἐνεργεῖ—αἱ δὲ ἐνέργειαι ἡ οἷον οὐσία αὐτοῦ, ἡ βούλησις αὐτοῦ καὶ ἡ οὐσία ταὐτὸν ἔσται. εἰ δὲ τοῦτο, ὡς ἄρα ἐβούλετο, οὕτω καὶ ἔστιν." Harder, IVa. VI.8.13, p. 36. The entire thirteenth chapter of VI.8 contains many references to the presence of will in the One. Cf. also *Enn*. VI.8.9, p. 603; VI.8.15, p. 608; VI.8.16, p. 609; VI.8.21, p. 613.

33. *Enn*. VI.8.20, p. 612. "Τί οὖν; οὐ συμβαίνει, εἴποι τις ἄν, πρὶν ἢ γενέσθαι γεγονέναι; εἰ γὰρ ποιεῖ ἑαυτόν, τῷ μὲν ἑαυτὸν οὔπω ἐστί, τῷ δ' αὖ ποιεῖν ἐστιν ἤδη πρὸ ἑαυτοῦ τοῦ ποιουμένου ὄντος αὐτο." Harder, IVa. VI.8.20, p. 56.

34. *Enn*. VI.8.20, p. 612. ". . . καὶ οὐκ ἔστιν ὡς πρὶν γενέσθαι ἦν ˙ τότε γὰρ οὐκ ἦν πρὶν γενέσθαι, ἀλλ' ἤδη πᾶς ἦν." Harder, IVa. VI.8.20, p. 56.

35. *Enn*. VI.8.20, pp. 612–613. "ἐνέργεια δὴ οὐ δουλεύσασα οὐσία καθαρῶς ἐλευθέρα, καὶ οὕτως αὐτὸς ταρ' αὐτοῦ αὐτός. Καὶ γὰρ εἰ μὲν ἐσῴζετο εἰς τὸ εἶναι ὑπ' ἄλλου, οὐ πρῶτος αὐτὸς ἐξ αὐτοῦ ˙ εἰ δ' αὐτὸς αὐτὸν ὀρθῶς λέγεται συνέχει, αὐτός ἐστι καὶ ὁ˙ παράγων ἑαυτόν, εἴπερ, ὅπερ συνέχει κατὰ φύσιν, τοῦτο καὶ ἐξ ἀρχῆς πεποίηκεν εἶναι." Harder, IVa. VI.8.20, p. 56.

36. *Enn*. VI.8.20, p. 613. ". . . τὸ πεποιηκέναι ἑαυτὸν τοῦτο νοείτω τὸ σύνδρομον εἶναι τὸ πεποιηκέναι καὶ αὐτό ˙ ἓν γὰρ τῇ ποιήσει καὶ οἷον γεννήσει ἀϊδίῳ τὸ εἶναι." Harder, IVa. VI.8.20, pp. 56, 58.

37. *Enn*. V.5.13, p. 414. καὶ οὖν καὶ ἡμεῖς μηδὲν τῶν ὑστέρων καὶ τῶν ἐλαττόνων προστιθῶμεν, ἀλλ' ὡς ὑπὲρ ταῦτα ἰὼν ἐκεῖνος τούτων αἴτιος ᾖ, ἀλλὰ μὴ αὐτὸς ταῦτα. καὶ γὰρ αὖ φύσις ἀγαθοῦ οὐ πάντα εἶναι οὐδ' αὖ ἕν τι τῶν πάντων. . . ." Harder, IIIa. V.5.13, p. 100, 102.

38. Cf. *Enn*. VI.8.12, p. 605.

39. *Enn*. VI.7.17, p. 575. "πρὸς ἐκεῖνο μὲν οὖν βλέπουσα ἀόριστος ἦν, βλέψασα δ' ἐκεῖ ὡρίζετο ἐκείνου ὅρον οὐκ ἔχοντος. εὐθὺς γὰρ πρὸς ἕς τι ἰδοῦσα ὁρίζεται τούτῳ καὶ ἴσχει ἐν αὐτῇ ὅρον καὶ πέρας καὶ πέρας καὶ εἶδος ˙ καὶ τὸ εἶδος ἐν τῷ μορφωθέντι, τὸ δὲ μορφῶσαν ἄμορφον ἦν." Harder, IIIa. VI.7.17, pp. 292, 294. Cf. also *Enn*. III.8.11, p. 250; VI.7.16, p. 574; VI.7.17, pp. 575–576; VI.7.25, p. 581; VI.7.32, p. 586; VI.7.33, p. 587; VI.8.13, p. 606; VI.8.14, p. 607.

40. Cf. *Enn*. VI.7.28, p. 583; VI.7.33, p. 587.

41. *Enn*. 7.32, p. 586. "οὐδὲν οὖν τοῦτο τῶν ὄντων καὶ πάντα ˙ οὐδὲν μέν, ὅτι ὕστερα τὰ ὄντα, πάντα δέ, ὅτι ἐξ αὐτοῦ." Harder, IIIa. VI.7.32, p. 328. Cf. also *Enn*. VI.8.16, pp. 609–610; VI.2.9, p. 479.

42. *Enn.* V.5.7, p. 409. "οὕτω δὴ καὶ νοῦς αὐτὸν ἀπὸ τῶν ἄλλων καλύψας καὶ συναγαγὼν εἰς τὸ εἴσω μηδὲν ὁρῶν θεάσεται οὐκ ἄλλο ἐν ἄλλῳ φῶς, ἀλλ' αὐτὸ καθ ἑαυτὸ μόνον καθαρὸν ἐφ' αὑτοῦ ἐξαίφνης φανέν, ὥστε ἀπορεῖν ὅθεν ἐφάνη, ἔξωθεν ἢ ἔνδον, καὶ ἀπελθόντος εἰπεῖν <<ἔνδον ἄρα ἦν καὶ οὐκ ἔνδον αὖ>>." Harder, IIIa. V.5.7, p. 88.

VERTICAL CAUSATION IN PLOTINUS

1. John M. Rist, *Plotinus: The Road to Reality* (London: Cambridge University Press, 1967).
2. A. H. Armstrong, "Plotinus," Part III of *The Cambridge History of Later Greek & Early Medieval Philosophy*, ed. A. H. Armstrong (London: Cambridge University Press, 1970).
3. My reference to Plotinus' noumenatics must be distinguished from what I shall later call Plotinus' doctrine of the noumenal world. "Noumenatics" refers to Plotinus' contemplation, intellection and intelligible object account; "noumenal" refers to the notion found in Early Modern Rationalists. As I shall use them, the two words are closely related but they are not quite the same, as I shall distinguish between Plotinus' noumenatic account and his proper account of the noumenal world.
4. My interpretation thus parts company with Rist's interpretation in *Eros and Psyche* (Toronto: University of Toronto Press, 1964). Rist recognizes in Plotinus' philosophy a hierarchy of types of persons on the road to unity with Intellect. First is the lover, a person who at least has the predilection to become unified with something other than himself. Second is the music-lover, one who studies the science of harmonies and proportions. Higher still is the lover of wisdom, whose highest study is that of mathematics (τὰ μαθήματα). Having recognized this hierarchy, however, Rist does not see any essential connection between arithmetic, and the like, and union with Intellect: "In view of the general tone of Plotinus' work and of the age in which he lived, we can attribute this continued interest in mathematics solely to Plotinus' unwillingness to diverge from the Platonic method as he knew it" (p. 90).

   Rist's conclusion is based upon his almost exclusive emphasis throughout the book on Plotinus' noumenatics. I maintain, in contrast, that music theory and mathematical training is essential for Plotinus because the concepts, proof procedures, and the like, which are thereby learned are the very means by which Intellect is to be articulated in its most basic form. As to the fact that "Plotinus does not put as much emphasis as Plato on the exact sciences" (p. 90), I refer to the closing remarks of my introduction and to the fact that, in view of the grounding which our ordinary concepts have in Intellect's structure (see page 56), Plotinus can maintain that those concepts provide a means for the "vulgar" to attain a derivative union with Intellect.
5. See Leibnitz's *New Essays Concerning Human Understanding*, Book IV, chapter 3. For instance: "When one has certain confused ideas . . . as one ordinarily does, it is not to be wondered at if one does not see the means for solving [philosophical] questions. It is as I have remarked before, that a person who has not ideas of the angles of a triangle except in the way in which one has them generally, will never think of finding out that they always equal two right angles . . . and when we farther consider what belongs to the nature of [real things] . . . we are transported, so to speak, into another world, that is to say, into the *intelligible world of substances*, whereas before we have been only among the *phenomena of the senses*" Leibniz, *Selections*, ed. Philip P. Wiener (New York: Charles Scribner's Sons, 1951), p. 464.
6. Plotinus' theory of perception maintains that in performing conceptual activities on occasions of sensation, we thereby *make* a world of perceived objects, in a manner analogous to a craftsman using his tools to make a craft object. I shall say more about this view as I proceed, but I shall not discuss it at length or defend my interpretation of Plotinus' theory of perception in this essay.
7. Given his theory of perception (see Note 6, above), Plotinus holds that phenomenal bodies are not real causes at all—not even of our sensations. Not being causes, they are not "metaphysically concrete," as it were. They are "well-founded" rather than real as such.
8. Plotinus rejects a temporal or dispositional reading of capacities in *Ennead* II.5 except insofar as it is applicable in a derivative way in talk about phenomenal bodies (see Armstrong's introduction to

that treatise in his Loeb Classical Library translation). Plotinus thus says that "this part of the [species] soul, the capacity to undergo, is not body but a certain Form" (III.6.4.31); and that "the capacity to undergo is a cause of undergoings" (III.6.4,44).

9. The distinction between undergoings and activities thus has nothing to do with the latter occurring in an immaterial entity distinct from the body in some Dualistic fashion. It is misleading at best to say, for example, that for Plotinus an "immaterial soul 'inside'" does the perceiving. See Henry J. Blumenthal, "Plotinus' Adoption of Aristotle's Psychology, Sensation, Imagination and Memory," in *The Significance of Neoplatonism,* ed. R. Baine Harris (Albany: State University of New York Press, 1976), pp. 41–58; see especially pp. 47–48.

10. Plotinus' use of the Stoic doctrine of cosmic sympathy also has its home in the theory of vertical causation. Gordon G. Clark, for example, interprets Plotinus' doctrine of cosmic sympathy as claiming that one body can act upon another body without benefit of a connecting causal chain. Clark calls this mode of horizontal causation "action at a distance" ("Plotinus' Theory of Sensation," *The Philosophical Review* 51 (1942), p. 357–382; p. 364). But more precisely for Plotinus, the doctrine of cosmic sympathy claims that everything occurs of necessity "when" and "where" it occurs in the eternal universe and, derivatively, in the phenomenal universe. It is in virtue of this alone that one can classify one body as an agent and another as a patient without discerning an intermediate causal chain.

11. The eternal and nonproductive (in a horizontal sense) character of what I call vertical causation is remarked on by John H. Randall in "The Intelligible Universe of Plotinus," *Journal of the History of Ideas* 30 (1969), pp. 3–16; p. 13; and, A. H. Armstrong in *Cambridge History* (pp. 252–253). R. T. Wallis gives an account of apparently similar views in Proclus to Plotinus' views on the distinction between horizontal and vertical or real causes in *Neoplatonism* (Gerald Duckworth and Company Ltd., 1972, p. 126). And Rist even proposes that what I would call phenomenal matter and noumenal matter may be distinguished for Plotinus in terms of whether or not the "matter" is being considered as being temporal or as being eternal (*Road to Reality,* p. 118).

2. It is at this point that Proclus especially departs from Aristotle's classic account of relative-to's in *Categories.* Aristotle claims that the correlatives perception and perceptual object differ from other correlatives, like slave and master, in that they need not occur together. That is, while perceptions and actually perceived things may always occur only together, the same is not true for perceptions, and percept*ible* objects. In short, Aristotle argues, "the perceptible holds prior to perception" (7b36). But Plotinus disagrees. The perceptual world is strictly relative to our discernments of it for Plotinus (see Note 6). Recall, in particular, Plotinus' claim that *perceptible* air, earth, fire, and water are *not* the *elements* called by the same names. Plotinus thereby rejects Aristotle's argument to the effect that the perceptible is prior to perception (and to the percei*ved* as well) because the elements are prior to the perceptive animal (8a10).

13. The idea that Aristotelian-type categories apply to the perceptual world while the Platonic categories apply to the real world is noted by Merlan in *Cambridge History,* p. 38. That Aristotelian-type categories are, ultimately, derivative from the Platonic categories for Plotinus is discussed by John P. Anton in "Plotinus' Approach to Categorical Theory" (*Significance,* pp. 83–89, esp. p. 88). I shall not discuss the precise character of this derivativeness thesis in this essay.

14. The interdependence of Intellect's "seeing" with sames and differents is discussed by Rist in "The Indefinite Dyad and Intelligible Matter in Plotinus," *Classical Quarterly* 12 (1962), pp. 99–107, esp. pp. 101–102. The source of Plotinus' view that real or intelligible motion is to be explicated in terms of differentiation may be Plato's *Parmenides,* where Plato defines motion as "always being in a different" (146a). The idea that the "matter" of Intellect is the Dyad is suggested by Merlan (*Cambridge History,* p. 27), and Rist identifies the Dyad in Plotinus with the very "urge to contemplate" ("Indefinite Dyad," p. 102).

15. This analogy between contemplation and geometrical derivations is, in fact, grounded in text. Plotinus offers as a prime example of engaging in contemplation a geometer theorizing about lines (III.8.4.8–11).

16. Plotinus thus maintains that as one proceeds from considering the contemplation of nature to that of Soul and finally to that of Intellect, the contemplation becomes more unified or simple (ἐνούμενα) (III.8.8.1–8).

THE ONTOLOGICAL BASIS OF PLOTINUS' CRITICISM OF ARISTOTLE'S THEORY OF CATEGORIES

1. This was only one of several titles given to the treatise, as we will see. The abbreviation *CAG* below stands for *Commentaria in Aristotelem Graeca,* vol. 23 (Ed. Academia Litterarum Regia Borussica, Berolini: G. Reimeri, 1882–1909), MacKenna's translation of the *Enneads* is followed here. (Plotinus, *The Enneads,* trans. by Stephen MacKenna, Second Ed., London: Faber and Faber, 1917–1930).
2. Plotinus challenges this view and relates the treatise to *Metaphysics,* as is evident from his references to this work.
3. Simplicius *CAG* VIII mentions the names of these commentators.
4. *CAG* IV. 2. 5. 16–24.
5. The characterization is Simplicius' *CAG,* pp. 16, 18.
6. According to Simplicius, Plotinus was the last and the sharpest critic of Aristotle's categories, *CAG,* pp. 2–5.
7. Also, parts of his *Isagōgē* relate to the categories, especially the sections on genus, species, and differentia.
8. From another point of view, even Plotinus could be called an Aristotelian, if Porphyry's remark that much of Aristotle's *Metaphysics* is incorporated in the *Enneads* is correct. *Vita,* MacKenna translation of *Enneads,* p. 14.
9. It is understandable that the Stoic doctrine, as more materialistic, receives Plotinus' more severe criticism.
10. Cf. *Metaphysics* 1053b; also *Physics* 689a. 11–21.
11. *Timaeus* 27d–28e.
12. *Ibid.,* 29b and 48e.
13. *Ibid.,* 48c d.
14. *Sophist* 254c 255c.
15. As given here the "genera of being" are to found in VI. 2, especially chapters 7 and 8. For the other genera, see VI. 3. 1–27.
16. However, even κόσμοσ νοήτοσ lacks the absolute unity of the One.
17. The example is Aristotle's *Metaphysics* 1024a. 33–6.
18. *Ibid.,* 1024b. 5.
19. *Ibid.,* 1024b. 809.
20. *Topics* 102a. 32–3.
21. It is correct that Aristotle refers to categories as genera, but to my knowledge he never used the expression "genera of being."
22. *Categories* 1b. 25.
23. Porphyry *CAG* IV, pp. 139–140, reluctantly accepts the last four categories of the Aristotelian list.
24. Dexippus, *CAG,* wrote three treatises answering Plotinus' aporias on Aristotle's categories.
25. Simplicius, *CAG,* pp. 16–18.
26. *CAG* IV, pp. 56–7.
27. According to Simplicius, *CAG,* pp. 16–17.
28. The labeling is mine, but the commentators after Porphyry speak of these alternative interpretations as a commonplace.
29. Simplicius, *CAG,* pp. 11–12, for example.
30. *Ibid.,* pp. 16, 18–19.
31. Porphyry, *CAG,* pp. 25–30, 85; and *Isagōgē 1a. 9–14.*

PLOTINUS AND SELF-PREDICATION

1. R. E. Allen, "Participation and Predication in Plato's Middle Dialogues," in ed. R. E. Allen, *Studies in Plato's Metaphysics* (New York: Humanities Press, 1965), p. 43.

2. This idea was developed by Sandra Peterson Wallace in "A Reasonable Self-Predication Premise for the Third Man Argument," *Phil. Rev.* 82 (1973), pp. 451–70.
3. Gregory Vlastos, "A Note on 'Pauline Predications' in Plato," *Phronesis* 19 (1974), pp. 95–101.
4. Vlastos, "Note," p. 95.
5. It seems appropriate to refer to this type of predication as epsilon predication.
6. Vlastos, "Note," p. 96.
7. Vlastos, "Note," p. 96.
8. This is also Lloyd's conclusion. Cf. A. C. Lloyd, "Neoplatonic Logic and Aristotelian Logic," *Phronesis* 1 (1955–1956), pp. 58–72, 146–60, p. 159.
9. Cf. Lloyd, "Logic," p. 62.
10. Cf. John Deck, *Nature, Contemplation, and the One,* (Toronto: Univ. of Toronto Press, 1967); R. T. Wallis, *Neoplatonism* (New York: Scribner, 1972); John Fielder, "Chorismos and Emanation in the Philosophy of Plotinus" in ed. R. B. Harris, *The Significance of Neoplatonism* (Norfolk, International Society for Neoplatonic Studies, 1976).
11. Deck, "Nature," p. 73.
12. Deck, "Nature," p. 116.
13. Wallis, "Self-Predication," p. 93.

OMNIPRESENCE, PARTICIPATION, AND EIDETIC CAUSATION IN PLOTINUS

1. Émile Bréhier, *The Philosophy of Plotinus,* translated by Joseph Thomas (Chicago: University of Chicago Press, 1958), p. 111.
2. All references to Plotinus are to the critical edition of Paul Henry and Hans-Rudolf Schwyzer (Paris and Brussels: Desclée de Brouwer, 1951–1973). Unless otherwise indicated, all translations in this paper are those of the author.
3. On the need for appropriate principles in (scientific) inquiry, see Aristotle *Posterior Analytics* A. 2. 71b23–72a6.
4. This description clearly draws heavily from the *Timaeus,* particularly 27d5–28a4 and 52a1–b1.
5. Cf. Bréhier's "Notice" to VI. 4–5 in his edition of *Plotinus* (Paris: Société d'édition "Les Belles Lettres," 1924–1938), especially VI.1, pp. 165, 171, and 173. My reconstruction agrees in certain details with that sketched by John Fielder in "Plotinus' Reply to the Arguments of *Parmenides* 130a–131d," *Apeiron* 12 (1978), pp. 1–5.
6. Alan Donagan, "Universals and Metaphysical Realism," in ed. Charles Landesman, *The Problem of Universals* (New York: Basic Books, 1971), pp. 98–118, 105.
7. Ibid.
8. The translation here is adapted from that of W. D. Ross in ed. Richard McKeon, *The Basic Works of Aristotle* (New York: Random House, 1941), p. 707; cf. also, the passage at M. 5 on p. 896.
9. The translation here is adapted from that of E. S. Forster in his Loeb edition of the treatise (Cambridge, Mass.: Harvard University Press, 1955), p. 309.
10. Cf. the discussion of ποίησις and πρᾶξις in René Arnou, Πρᾶξις ετ Θεωρία: *Étude de détail sur le vocabulaire et la pensée des Ennéades de Plotin,* nouvelle édition (Rome: Presses de L'Université Grégorienne, 1972), pp. 27–37.
11. All translations from III. 8 are adapted from the translation of A. H. Armstrong in his Loeb edition of *Plotinus* (Cambridge, Mass.: Harvard University Press, 1966–.).
12. See Armstrong's note on this passage in his Loeb edition of *Plotinus,* ibid., volume III, p. 368, note 1.
13. *Plato and Parmenides: Parmenides' "Way of Truth" and Plato's "Parmenides,"* translated, with an introduction and running commentary, by Francis MacDonald Cornford (London: Routledge & Kegan Paul, Ltd., 1939), p. 194. For a good introduction to the Neoplatonic reading of the *Parmenides,* see the introduction to Proclus, *Théologie Platonicienne,* texte établi et traduit par H. D Saffrey et L. G. Westerink (Paris: Société d'édition "*Les Belles Lettres,*" 1968–.), especially volume I, pp. lxxv–lxxxix.
14. It seems to be a distinguishing characteristic of various forms of metaphysical idealism (and, as w·

shall see, Plotinus' system involves some form of metaphysical idealism) to conceive of psyche or mind or consciousness as essentially a locus of relation, a medium for the reconciliation of opposites and the uniting of things that are different; cf. the quasi-Hegelian arguments of T. H. Green and Hastings Rashdall discussed in A. C. Ewing, *Idealism: A Critical Survey,* 3d ed. (London: Methuen & Co. Ltd., 1974), pp. 399–403.

15. The essential negativity of the *psyche* in the context of Proclus' metaphysics and, more generally, within the Neoplatonic tradition is the central subject of Jean Trouillard's *L'Un et l'âme selon Proclos* (Paris: Société d'édition "Les Belles Lettres," 1972).

16. Other recent discussions of productive contemplation include John N. Deck, *Nature, Contemplation, and the One: A Study in the Philosophy of Plotinus* (Toronto: University of Toronto Press, 1967), and Joseph Moreau, *Plotin ou la gloire de la philosophie antique* (Paris: J. Vrin, 1970), chapters X and XI.

17. Cf. III.7[45].12.19–22, where Plotinus maintains that when *psyche* leaves the activity of discursive contemplation and returns to the unity of *noesis* "time is abolished," which fact shows that it is the life of the *psyche* that generates time (οὗτος ὁ βίος τὸν χρόνον γεννᾶ).

18. The translation here is adapted from that of Armstrong in his Loeb edition of Plotinus.

19. Cf. MacKenna's inspired rendering, "Time in its ceaseless onward sliding produces parted interval," in Plotinus, *The Enneads,* translated by Stephen MacKenna, 4th ed. (New York: Pantheon Books, 1969), p. 540.

20. For an extended treatment of this aspect of VI.4–5, see my "The Doctrine of Reception According to the Capacity of the Recipient in *Ennead* VI.4–5," *Dionysius* III (December, 1979), pp. 79–97.

21. Bréhier, *The Philosophy of Plotinus,* p. 111.

22. *Ibid.,* p. 117.

23. *Ibid.,* pp. 123–129.

24. *Ibid.,* pp. 109–111.

25. For a contemporary discussion of this basic idealistic problem, see Nicholas Rescher, *Conceptual Idealism* (Oxford: Basil Blackwell, 1973), pp. 177–180.

CANTOR'S SETS AND PROCLUS' WHOLES

1. Alan Calder, "Constructive Mathematics," *Scientific American* 241 (October, 1979), 146–171, and bibliography, p. 186; Felix E. Browder, "The Relevance of Mathematics," *American Math. Monthly* 83 (1976), 249–254; Ernest Snapper, "The Three Crises in Mathematics: Logicism, Intuitionism, and Formalism," *Mathematics Magazine* 52 (1979), 207–216.

2. Evangelos Stamatis, "Peri tēs theōrias tōn Synolōn para Platōni," *Praktika tēs Akademias Athenōn* (1958), 298–303.

3. Proclus, *In Primum Euclidis Elementorum Librum Commentarii,* ed. G. Friedlein (Leipzig, 1873); trans. Glenn R. Morrow, *Proclus' Commentary on the First Book of Euclid's Elements* (Princeton, 1970).

4. Sir Thomas Heath, *History of Greek Mathematics,* 2 vols. (Oxford, 1921), vol. II, pp. 530–536.

5. Proclus, *Elements of Theology,* ed. and trans. E. R. Dodds (Oxford, 1934).

6. Georg Cantor, *Allgemeine Mengenlehre* (Leipzig, 1883).

7. Stamatis, "Peri tēs theōrias," 298–303.

8. Heath, *Greek Mathematics* I, 326–327; and cf. Note 1 supra.

9. Calder, "Constructive Mathematics"; Browder, "Relevance of Mathematics"; Snapper, "Three Crises in Mathematics."

10. For the Z-F axioms, see A. A. Fraenkel, Y. Bar-Hillel, and A. Levy, *Foundations of Set Theory* (Amsterdam: North Holland Press, 1973).

11. Snapper, "Three Crises in Mathematics," p. 208.

12. Plato's "Late Learners," *Sophist* 251C–D.

13. The alternative logicist scheme of Whitehead and Russell requires another extralogical axiom, the axiom of reducibility. This, in effect, asserts a context that is not Neoplatonic. Consequently, I will use set theory in the Zermelo-Fraenkel version.

14. Plato *Republic* VII. 528A2–E1: "But this subject [stereometry] does not appear to have been investigated yet" (Shorey's translation).
15. *Republic* VII. 531D1–5.
16. Aristotle *Posterior Analytics* I.27. 87a30–35; 11.77a30–35.
17. Cf. Note 8, supra.
18. Cf. Note 3, supra.
19. R. Courant and H. Robbins, *What Is Mathematics?* (Oxford, 1941).
20. Courant and Robbins, *What Is Mathematics?* p. 108.
21. *Ibid.*, pp. 108–119.
22. Boethius, *de trinitate.* 1ff.
23. Courant and Robbins, p. 111.
24. Robert S. Hartman, *The Structure of Value* (Carbondale, Ill., 1967). See also R. S. Brumbaugh, "Formal Value Theory: Transfinite Ordinal Numbers and Relatively Trivial Practical Choices," *Journal of Human Relations* (1973).
25. For Dodds's edition, see Note 3, supra. Stamatis works from the edition of Creuzer (Frankfurt, 1822), also citing the *Refutation of Proclus' Elements of Theology* by Bishop Nicholas of Methone, ed. J. Th. Voemel (Frankfurt, 1822).
26. Stamatis translates with the following equivalents: Cantor's *menge* = Proclus' *holon*; Cantor's *regel* = Proclus' *eidos*; Cantor's *element* = Proclus' *meros*; Cantor's *object* = Proclus's *meros*. For philosophical purposes, these equivalences require some further qualifications, though they work well mathematically.
27. Stephan Körner, *Categorial Frameworks,* London (Blackwell, 1970), appendix A.
28. For the difference between systems with continuity and with definiteness, see my "Metaphysical Presuppositions and the Study of Time," International Soc. for the Study of Time, *Proceedings III* (New York, 1978), pp. 7–9.
29. Cf. R. S. Brumbaugh, "Logical and Mathematical Symbolism in the Plato Scholia," *Journal of the Warburg and Courtauld Institute,* (1961), 45–58; 1965, 1–13; 1968, 1–11.
30. See Note 24, supra. There is an excellent comparison of Plato's forms and Cantor's sets in a monograph by John Faris, which came to my attention after the present paper was written. (John Faris, *Plato's Theory of Forms and Cantor's Theory of Sets,* Belfast, 1968) Faris' work shows, I think that Proclus has taken up a position of his own, one closer to Plato than Cantor's is.

THE MATHEMATICS OF MYSTICISM: PLOTINUS AND PROCLUS

1. *Enneads* III.8.8 (351d); III.89 (352b); V.4.1. (516b–c); VI.8.9 (743c). Cf., with respect to the following summary and argument, my "Proclus on the One," *Idealistic Studies* (1973);229–237.
2. Damascius, *Dublitationes,* 43.
3. *Ibid.*, 38. I. 79, 20ff.; 41. I. 83, 26ff.; 42. I. 85, 8ff.; 107. I. 278, 24ff.
4. *Corpus Platonicum Medii Aevii,* ed. R. Klibansky; *Plato Latinus III, Parmenides usque ad finem primae hypothesis nec non* Procli *Commentarium in Parmenidem, pars ultima inedita,* eds. R. Klibansky and C. Labowsky, trans., G. E. M. Anscombe and L. Labowsky (London: Warburg Institute), 1953.
5. That Proclus thinks Plato intended the first hypothesis to be the correct one is illustrated by the following passages from his *Commentary:* "The alternative remains, that the discussion of the One is either in this [the first] hypothesis, or nowhere. But the latter is unlikely . . . ," (p. 65 [26–28]) ". . . so he shows that that most glorious One is neither expressible nor knowable. Now he rightly pronounces the final negation" (p. 71 [29–30]). "For by means of a negation Parmenides has removed all negations. With silence he concludes the contemplation of the One" Anscombe and Labowsky translation (London: Warburg Institute, 1953) (p. 77[4–5]). It is indeed hard to accept Proclus' view as a correct interpretation of Plato since the latter seems to dismiss the first hypothesis as leading to an untenable position. Professor Robert S. Brumbaugh has argued in detail that Plato's proof in the *Parmenides* is an indirect proof by elimination (*Plato on The*

One, New Haven, Conn.: Yale University Press 1961); if this is correct, as I think it is, then one must reject, as not being Plato's the mystical Proclusion interpretation of the first hypothesis.

6. Proclus, *Commentary,* London: Warburg Institute p. 45 (lines 13–14). Subsequent page references in the text will all refer to this work cited in Note 4, above.

7. In "Proclus on The One," *Idealist Studies* 3 [1973].

8. Compare my "Self-Reference and the Philosophy of Science" read at the *6th International Congress for Logic, Methodology, and Philosophy of Science,* Hanover, Germany, August, 1979.

9. For reasons analogous to those presented in Sections I–III, I also feel that Wittgenstein's conclusion to the *Tractatus* is unsatisfactory (6.54): "My propositions serve as elucidations in the following way: anyone who understands me eventually recognizes them as nonsensical, when he has used them—as steps ["means"]—to climb up beyond them. (He must, to to speak, throw away the ladder after he has climbed up it.)"

"He must transcend these propositions, and then he will see the world aright."

"What we cannot speak about we must pass over in silence." I simply cannot accept this. When the "steps" we have used to get to a certain point (mysticism) are nonsensical or invalid, then our presence at that point is unjustified; the need for our being there has just not been demonstrated.

10. Professor J. N. Findlay has provided some admirable efforts in this direction through his investigation into the logic of such notions. Cf. "The Diremptive Tendencies of Western Philosophy," *Philosophy East and West* 14(1964), 167–178; "The Logic of Mysticism," *Religious Studies* 2(1967), 145–162; "The Logic of Ultimates," *Journal of Philosophy* 64(1967), 571–583; *Ascent to the Absolute* (London: George Allen & Union Ltd., 1970).

11. Cf. Gregory Vlastos, "The Third Man Argument in the Parmenides," *Philosophical Review* 63(1954), 330.

12. Cf. F. B. Fitch, *Symbolic Logic* (New York: The Ronald Press, 1952), the appendix entitled "Self-Reference in Philosophy."

THE ANATOMY OF A NEOPLATONIST METAPHYSICAL PROOF

1. *Proclus, The Elements of Theology:* A Revised Text with Translation, Introduction and Commentary by E. R. Dodds (Oxford, 1963). Hereafter cited as *E.T.* According to Proclus' own explanation (*In Euclidis El.,* ed. G. Friedlein [Teubner, 1873], pp. 71, 22–73, 14; cf. *A Commentary on the First Book of Euclid's Elements,* trans. Glenn R. Morrow [Princeton, 1970], pp. 59–60), the meaning of στοιχείωσις in writings with that title presupposes the notion of "element" (στοιχεῖον) "that determines the arrangement of the elements in Euclid's work." Interestingly, Proclus here defines an "element" as something "ranked as the more primary *type* (τὰ ἀρχοειδέστερα) of members of an argument [proof] leading to a conclusion, *as postulates are elements of theorems*" (*In Euc. El.* 73. 8–9). If Proclus intended to restrict the meaning of "element" with this illustration, the relation of postulate to theorem, where the element is different in "type" or "form" from what it is an element of, then *E.T.,* which consists only of theorems and their proofs, would not conform to his Euclidean model. However, he earlier had defined "element" more simply as "what proves," e.g., as in Euclid "The first theorem is an element of the second" (*In Euc. El.* 72. 24–26). (I follow Morrow in translating τὸ κατασκευόηον as "what proves," although the sense of the term as used in geometry would more naturally suggest "what solves by construction"; since this is the relation between *Elements* I. 1 and I. 2, the implication is again that Proclus understands elementhood as involving postulates and constructions). The general question here is whether *E.T.* does or does not conform to a Euclidean model as Proclus himself understood the model. On the place of *E.T.* as the first rigorous metaphysical system, cf. R. Beutler, *Reale Encyclopädie,* XXIII. 1, col. 198, "Die einzige systematischen Darstellung der neuplatonische Metaphysik, die uns erhalten ist"; J. Lindsay, "Le système de Proclus," *Revue de Metaphysique et Morale* 28 (1921), pp. 497–523; R. T. Wallis, *Neoplatonism* (London, 1972), p. 146.

2. L. J. Rosán, *The Philosophy of Proclus: the Final Phase of Ancient Thought* (New York, 1949), pp. 36–37, *E.T.* "Is consciously modelled on the *Elements of Geometry* by Euclid"; Wallis, *op.*

cit., *E.T.* follows "the procedures of Euclidean geometry"; Stanislas Bréton, "Le Théorème De l'Un Dans Les Éléments De Théologie De Proclus," *Revue des Sciences Philosophiques et Theologiques* 58 (1974), pp. 561–583. The literature on *E.T.* is filled with expressions like "logical deduction" (Wallis, p. 211), "successions logiques" (Lindsay), and so on, which omit any reference to Euclid; this alone might explain Bréton's attempt to think of the proof as free of any geometrical aspects; cf. his *Philosophie et Mathématique chez Proclus* (Paris, 1969).

3. Ian Mueller, "Euclid's *Elements* and the Axiomatic Method," *British Journal for the Philosophy of Science* 20 (1969), pp. 289–309. Cf. David Hilbert, "Axiomatic Thinking," *Philosophy Math* 7 (1970), pp. 1–12.

4. Mueller, *op. cit.*, pp. 290–291, "Grammatically, at least, these postulates are not existence assertions like their modern counterparts." Euclidean proofs are "thought experiments" involving "An idealized physical object which can be represented in a diagram" (p. 291). Proclus alludes to a view (*In Euc. El.* 80. 15–81, 4) that a problem, as distinguished from a theorem in Euclid's sense, asks under what conditions "something exists," which implies that the postulates are among certain existence *conditions*. But to say that something is an existence condition is not to say that it is an assertion of existence of anything; besides, the view in question was far from universally held.

5. Jaakko Hintikka and Unto Remes, *The Method of Analysis: Its Geometrical Origin and Its General Significance* (Dordrecht, 1974), seem to support this contention, but continue to treat the postulates at the core of Euclidean ἔκθεσις and auxiliary constructions as assertions of existence ("the existential assumptions that the postulates *in effect* are" [italics added], p. 4). The position contested by Mueller is represented by A. Szabó, *Anfänge der griechischen Mathematik* (München–Wien, 1969).

6. *E.T.*, pp. 2, 1. All references to *E.T.* are to Dodd's page and line numbers of the Greek text. No term, such as "proposition" or "theorem" is affixed by Proclus to the numbered statements to be proved in *E.T.* For problems of translation of the first numbered statement to be proved, cf. *infra*, pp. 5–9 and Notes, 14–19.

7. Cf. Note 1, *supra*. The content of *E.T.* seems wholly derivative (Dodds, p. xxv; followed by Wallis, p. 211). Proclus' originality, therefore lies in his systematic procedure or attempted rigor.

8. Cf. Jean Trouillard, *L'Un et l'ame selon Proclus* (Paris, 1972), p. 155; Thomas Whittaker, *The Neo-Platonists* (Cambridge, 1918), p. 161; Wallis, *op. cit.*, p. 146.

9. Dodds, *E.T.*, p. ix: "Lapses even from formal correctness of reasoning may be detected here and there, though less frequently than one might have expected." Dodd's judgment is somewhat surprising in view of the obscurity of many of Proclus' assumptions.

10. The role corresponding to the postulates in Euclid that permit constructions, but also to the type of infinitely continued operation intuitively presupposed by Proclus' proof of proposition 1. For Proclus' definitions of Euclidean axioms, definitions, and postulates (adapted from Aristotle), cf. *In Eucl. El.*, pp. 76, 6–77; 2 = Morrow, pp. 62–63. Proclus' definition of a postulate as a statement that is "Unknown and nevertheless is accepted without the student's granting it" places the difficult to grant fifth postulate in the foreground, omitting any reference to the *role* of the postulates in Euclidean constructions.

11. In the Euclid commentary, Proclus clearly distinguishes the unproved principles from the theorems and problems that follow them (*In Eucl. El.*, pp. 75, 5–26). Was *E.T.* written before the Euclid commentary? Dodds, p. xvii, following Freudenthal in all essentials (*Hermes* 16 (1881), pp. 214ff.), pronounces *E.T.* "definitely . . . relatively early." Below I cite evidence independent of chronology which proves that the Dodds-Freudenthal early dating of *E.T.* need have no direct bearing on Proclus' reasons for omitting unproved principles in *E.T.* (*infra*, pp. 23–25). The same evidence proves that Proclus was consciously avoiding certain ingredients of the Euclidean system namely, precisely all unproved propositions.

12. Cf. Robert Nozick, *Anarchy, State, and Utopia* (Oxford, 1974), pp. 18–22.

13. Dodds, p. xxv. A test of the usefulness of invisible-hand explanation would be to find an element in Proclus' strategy of proof that goes *counter* to the intentional design of *E.T.* as a whole, but which can be explained by certain historical facts.

14. *E.T.*, p. 2, 2–3. The occurrence of συντίθεσθαι at 2. 13 is used to supply the verbal idea. I assume

throughout that the relation between the "many" and the "multitude" is, loosely, that of composition or componenthood. For the ancient use of πλῆθος, cf. Liddell-Scott-Jones (9th ed., 1966), 1417–1418 for examples. Although at times abstract and general, Proclus' notion of multitude is nontechnical. Dodd's version, *E.T.*, p. 3, "Every manifold in some way participates unity," which unavoidably recalls Kant's *"ein Mannigfaltiges"* in the Critique of Pure Reason, seems intended to suggest something technical (but what?). *LSJ* give "quantity" as one meaning of πλῆθος, but the uses cited still connote an unstipulated amount, *some* quantity of *something*.

15. Bréton, *art. cit.*, p. 562. Following M. L. Roure, Bréton translates proposition 1 into symbolic notation as: *Ux̂ · ax ⊃ (bx v cx)*. The disjunct is supposed to capture the logic behind "in some way partakes of unity" (as it turns out, for Proclus there are only two ways in which a multitude, which Bréton variously renders as "ensemble," "multiplicité," and "pluralité", can partake of unity). Bréton's vacillation over the meaning of πλῆθος can lead to logical confusions, as when he once refers to the "whole" in question as a *"totalité"* (p. 571), which restricts multitudes to those whose components are discrete, countable things. Consider Pappus' remark that "In the case of the continuous quantities. . . , the contrary of whole is part, the term 'whole' being applicable to continuous things only, just as the term 'total' is applicable only to discrete [i.e., countable] things," in *The Commentary of Pappus on Book X of Euclid's Elements*, Arabic text and translation by William Thomson (Cambridge, Mass., Harvard University Press, 1930), p. 66. Proclus distinguishes two kinds of wholes in the Euclid commentary, those divisible into like and those divisible into unlike parts (*In Eucl. El.*, p. 144, 18–145, 25), which is consistent with Pappus' restriction of "whole" to continuous magnitudes since Proclus is here discussing geometrical figures. However, it is doubtful that Proclus would restrict his multitudes in *E.T.* either to magnitudes or to countable totalities. It helps to think of Proclus' multitudes as masses the components of which can be differentiated according to some as yet *unspecified procedure*.

16. Bréton, *art. cit.*, pp. 562–564, alludes to the view without attempting a formal treatment; the view was suggested much earlier by Evangelos Stamatis, Περὶ τῆσ θεωρίας τῶν Συνολῶν παρὰ Πλατῶνι Πρακτικὰ τἐς Ακαδεμίας Αθενῶν (1958), pp. 298–303, as noted and developed by Robert Brumbaugh, "Cantor's Sets and Proclus' Wholes." For expositions of set theory, cf. Abraham A. Fraenkel, "Set Theory," *The Encyclopedia of Philosophy* (1967), vol. 7, 421ff., and *Abstract Set Theory* (Amsterdam, 1966); also W. V. O. Quine, *Set Theory and Its Logic* (Revised ed., Harvard Cambridge, 1978). Because I do not consider all the merits of this view below, I will here simply note that if there is some resemblance between Proclus' need to refer to his sample multitude as a "whole" (*E.T.*, p.2, 2) and Cantor's 1895 definition of a set as a "collection into a whole" (*Zusammenfassung zu einem Ganzen, in Gesammelte Abhandlungen* (Berlin, 1932), p. 282), then one might also compare the *claim* made by Proclus' first proposition (that all multitudes partake of unity) with Cantor's 1899 "Letter" to Dedekind, in which he speaks of a set as being thought of as "being collected to '*one* thing'" (*ibid.*, p. 443). In his first proposition (i.e., *theorem*) Proclus is trying to *prove* what Cantor assumed as part of a definition or essential condition of a set. The problem of determining the precise status of Proclus' first theorem goes beyond analogies between "multitudes" and sets to the foundations of set theory.

17. Damascius Diadochus, *Dubitationes et solutiones de primis principiis*, ed. C. A. Ruelle (Paris, 1889), 126, 11–12, "The term (ὄνομα) 'partaking' means . . . 'having' (σεμαίνει τὸ μετέχειν . . . τὸ ἔχειν). Dodds's version, "participates unity" seems awkward and ungrammatical, despite the advantages to which he refers (viz., in translating μεταχόμενον).

18. Cf. Dodds, *E.T.*, p. 188. The legal or political metaphor locked away in much of Plato's metaphysical vocabulary is overlooked. The root meaning of μέθεξισ is joint ownership of possession by many of one thing, as κοινωνία at *Rep.* 476 is an "association" of bodies and actions with forms, or forms with forms. It is only after Plotinus, who makes the realm of forms also a realm of Life and Mind, uneasily distinguished from each other, that μέθεξισ clearly takes on a connotation of "participation" in an activity. For one essential phase of this in Plotinus, cf. J. M. Rist, "Plotinus and the Value of the Human Person," unpublished, 1978, p. 5.

19. G. E. L. Owen, "Notes on Ryle's Plato," *Ryle: A Collection of Critical Essays* (New York: Anchor, 1970), p. 342, is content to use either "the One" or "Unity" for "τὸ ἕν" in *Parm.* Plato had other ways of referring to unity, (e.g., Parm. 129B7 ὅ ἐστιν ἕν, 158A5 αὐτὸ ἕν, 158C6 τὸ

εἶδος [sc. τὸυ ἑνός]); since Owen follows Ryle in treating the former expression as referring to "one of Socrates' Forms," all of these expressions would be namelike. Cf. Aristotle *Phys*. IV. 13. 222a19; *Met*. 1023b36. "τὸ ἕν" seems to function as a name in proposition 13, if the "is" at 16. 8 is of identity and not predication. For a treatment of inconsistencies that follow from Proclus' treatment of names of his highest principle, cf. Carl Kordig, "Proclus on the One," *Idealistic Studies* 3 (1973), pp. 229–237.

20. Proclus, *In Eucl. El*. p. 74,13–16. Axioms are most credible (p. 76, 9–12), followed by definitions or "hypotheses" (p. 76, 12–17) and postulates (p. 76, 17–21). For an interesting discussion of ancient disputes about the Euclidean definitions, cf. Thomas L. Heath, *Euclid's Elements* (New York: Dover 1956), vol. I, pp. 155–194.

21. Cf. *In Eucl. El.*, pp. 254, 21–256, 8.

22. An example of a Pythagorean *reductio* proof is found appended to Book X of the *Elements*. *Euclidis Elementa X cum Appendice post Heiberg*, ed. E. S. Stamatis (Leipzig: Teubner, 1972), vol. III, App. 27, pp. 231,10–233,13. Cf. Heath, *A History of Greek Mathematics* (Oxford, 1921), vol. I, p. 168. Euclid uses *reductio* in Book II. 8 and III. 1. For Zeno of Elea and Plato, it is the standard rigorous form of argument, and is used by Aristotle as well. For Szabó's suggestive remarks, cf. Hintikka and Remes, *op. cit.*, "Working Backwards and Proving by Synthesis", p. 128. Proclus sees no connection between the method of analysis and reduction to impossibility proofs. In the passage where he says that Plato "taught this method [analysis] to Leodamas" (*In Eucl. El.*, p. 211, 21–22), he clearly distinguishes it from the latter (p. 212, 1–4).

23. Literally "For if it were in no way to partake" (εἰ γὰρ μηδαμῇ μετέχοι).

24. The notion of many *making up* a multitude has to be supplied from the context, and the occurrence of συντίθεσθαι at 2, 13. Dodds's "nor any of its several parts" is an overtranslation. No term for *"part"* (μέρος, μόριον) occurs in the proof.

25. Cf. *infra*, (10) and also my Note 35 of this essay. How does Proclus justify "*'m* is not one ⊃ *m* is infinite multitude"? He assumes that unity of components is a necessary condition of the unity of the multitude made up of those components (cf. *infra*, p. 15 and Note 31); so he infers that "*m* is not one" means that *m* is radically divisible, that is, divisible for *every* component c_n of level *n*, $n \rightarrow \infty$. Cf. *infra*, pp. 12–13, 15–16.

26. (9) could be inferred from Zeno, DK B2 (cf. Vlastos' version, "Zeno of Elea," *art. cit.*, p. 369–370) or, more directly, from the Zenonian argument reported by Aristotle, *GC* 316a14–34, 325a8–12, and Simplicius, *In Phys.*, p. 139, 24–140, 26 (= Lee 2; cf. Vlastos, *ibid.*, pp. 371–372): if what is is "divisible through and through" (παντῇ ὁμοίος . . . διαίρετον), then one possibility is that "It will be dissolved into nothing and consist (συστήσεται) of nothing" (Lee, p. 12, 13), and "If indeed it consists, again it consists of nothing" (Lee, p. 12, 17–18).

27. Not, as Dodds translates, "an infinity of infinites." For the use of ἀπειράκις, cf. Aristotle, *De an*. 407a14 = "infinitely many times" and *LSJ*.

28. *Phys*. 207a1–2, The infinite "Is not what has nothing outside it, but what always has something outside it (οὗ ἀεί τι ἔξω ἔστει)", trans. Robertson-Hardie. Aristotle improves on this rough formulation at 207a7–8: "That is infinite such that for any amount they take there is always something outside to take." This, of course, is still rough and is true only of infinite things, such as magnitudes, substances, series, place, and time. Aristotle's technical term for his own view of the infinite as ἀδιέξοδον (207a14), "what cannot be gone through."

29. *El*. I. C. N. 5.

30. *In Eucl. El.*, p. 77, 7–81, 22, esp. 81, 5–18.

31. Note that this again rules out the concept of an empty multitude, which could have unity but no components. Presumably, this assumption also would mean that for Proclus the unity of a multitude, however strong (e.g., the collection of all Platonic Forms), is not logically independent of the unity of its components. For the gap in Proclus' proof, cf. my remarks on (8), p. 128, *supra*.

32. (9).

33. Cf. *supra*, Note 26, and William E. Abraham, "The Nature of Zeno's Argument Against Plurality in DK 29 B1", *Phronesis* XVII (1972), pp. 40–53.

34. Theo Gerard Sinnige, *Matter and Infinity in the Presocratic Schools* (Assen, 1968), pp. 70–83; B. L. Van der Waerden, *Science Awakening* (Oxford, 1961), pp. 98–99. It is an important insight of Sinnige that γνώμαν can refer to any repeatable (constructible) pattern, not merely a "carpenter's square" (cf. Kirk and Raven, *The Presocratic Philosophers* [Cambridge: Harvard Univ. Press, 1963] pp. 243–244) and not "Any number which when added to a figurate number gives the next number" (Ross, *Aristotle Physics,* pp. 542–545). What is important is that the patterns are repeated according to postulates, that is, rules of construction. It was Zeno's special genius to apply these gnomonic constructions where they have paradoxical implications.

35. The sense of ἀπειράκις ἀπείρων is this: (1) If no component of a given multitude m, $C_N \to \infty$, has unity, then any component c_n is an infinite multitude; (2) and since we can apply the same reasoning as often as we like, we get infinite times many infinite multitudes, or for short, "infinitely many infinites" [in succession].

36. Cf. *Phys.* 207b11–15.

37. Cf. Heath, *Elements,* vol. III, pp. 15–16.

38. A. A. Fraenkel, *Abstract Set Theory* (Amsterdam, 1966), sec. 5, th. 2; Quine, *op. cit.,* p. 201, 28. 17 = Cantor's theorem.

39. Fraenkel, *op. cit.,* p. 29. I assume that we may here think of subsets as "making up" a set, though obviously not precisely in the same way that a set's members "make up" the set (any set has more subsets than members).

40. Mueller, *art. cit.,* pp. 290–291 with Notes 3–4.

41. *In Eucl. El.,* pp. 78, 20–79, 2. His comments are worth citing in part: "The discovery of theorems does not occur without recourse to . . . intelligible matter. In going forth into this matter and shaping it, our ideas are plausibly said to resemble acts of production (γενέσεσιν); for the movement of our thought (τῆς διανοίας ἐμῶν κίνησιν) in projecting its own ideas is a production, we have said, of the figures in our imagination (Φαντασία) and of their properties. But it is in imagination that the constructions (συστασεῖς), sectionings, superpositions, comparisons, additions, and subtractions take place, whereas the contents of our understanding (τὰ δὲ ἐν τῃ διανοιᾶ) all stand fixed, without any generation or change" (trans. Morrow, p. 64). Proclus distinguishes the contents in thought, the movement of thought, and the place, imagination, in which thought carries out these movements. He does not restrict the constructivist role of thought to Euclidean problems becuase he treats construction (κατασκευή) as one of the essential "parts" of theorems also (*In Eucl. El.,* p. 203, 1–4).

42. Cf. *supra,* Notes and 25, 35.

43. Bréton, *art. cit.,* p. 564. An axiom in need of proof is not an axiom. Bréton says that proposition 1 "prend les allures d'un théorème," which approaches saying that it is not a real theorem or is not proved, with which I would agree. The more interesting claim is that proposition 1 is for some reason *unprovable.*

44. *In Eucl. El.,* p. 76, 9–12.

45. *Parm.* 158B2, B8–9.

46. *Parm.* 158C2–7.

47. *E.T.,* Commentary, p. 188.

48. *In Parm.,* ed. Cousin, cols. 1292–94.

49. Proclus' testimony that Zeno's work contained forty arguments (*In Parm.,* col. 694, 23–25), repeated or confirmed by Elias (*In Cat.,* 109,6; cf. DK 29 A15) may be evidence that Proclus had Zeno's work, although for lack of stronger confirmation this is not generally credited.

50. The possibility is, of course, entirely conjectural. The immediate ancestors of Proclus' Proposition and proof could as well have been earlier Neoplatonist commentaries on the *Parmenides* like the one by Plutarch of Athens (*In Parm.,* cols. 1058, 21–1061,20). What is striking, however, is that Plato's strategy and intentions in *Parm.* 158 and Proclus' strategy in *E.T.* are clearly not the same if we consider the whole context in each case.

51. *In Eucl. El.,* p. 72, 3–4.

52. *In Eucl. El.,* p. 76, 1.

53. *In Eucl. El.,* p. 76, 4–6.

54. *In Eucl. El.*, p. 75, 5–14.
55. Dodds, *E.T.*, p. x, seems to have anticipated my view here when he writes that *E.T.* may be regarded "As an attempt to supply the comprehensive scheme of reality desiderated by Plato in the seventh book of the *Republic*," but he links *E.T.* with *Rep.* VII instead of *Rep.* VI, as I do.
56. Cf. my argument for this in "The Neoplatonist Interpretation of Plato: Remarks on its Decisive Characteristic," *The Journal of the History of Philosophy* VII (1969), pp. 19–26.
57. Cf. F. M. Cornford, "Mathematics and Dialectic in the *Republic* VI–VII," *Mind* N.S. 41 (1932), pp. 37–52, 173–190; R. Hackforth, "Plato's Divided Line and Dialectic," *The Classical Quarterly* Jan.–Apr. (1942), pp. 1–9. Proclus seems to distinguish metaphysical from mathematical reasoning by means of the role played by imagination in the latter. Cf. A. Charles, "L'imagination, miroir de l'ame selon Proclus," *Actes du Colloque de Royaumont* 69 (1971), pp. 441–451. But then how would Proclus characterize the *movement* of the mind implied in his own proof of proposition 1? Issues in the foundations of mathematics seem inevitably to press in on us. Proclus seems to be closer to Brouwer than to Russell and Frege, as Julia Annas argues is the case for Plato's theory of foundational principles, *Aristotle's Metaphysics Books M and N*, translated with introduction and notes by Julia Annas (Oxford, 1976), p. 43.
58. Cf. Note. 13.

THE IDEA OF FALSE IN PROCLUS

Note: Passages from the *Commentary in Euclid's Elements' First Book,* hereafter *In Eucl.,* numbered according to the edition by Friedlein, are given here in the English translation of Glenn Morrow, *Proclus, A Commentary on the First Book of Euclid's Elements* (Princeton, N.J.: Princeton University Press, 1970). All the remaining translations, except *Enn.* III. 6. 7, are mine.

1. Cf. E. Moutsopoulos, *Cognition and Error* (in Greek) (Athens: 1961), pp. 37 sq.; "Vers un élargissement du concept de vérité: le presque-vrai," *Annales de la Fac. des Letteres et Sc. Hum. d'Ais, 40, 1966,* pp. 189–196; *Knowledge and Science* (in Greek) (Athens: Univ. Press, 1972), pp. 134.; Du "faux" dans l'art, *Actas del II Congreso Nacional de Filosofia (Cordoba, Arg, 1971)* (Buenos Aires: Ed. Sud-americana, 1973), pp. 335–338; and *Annales d' Esthetique,* 9–10, 1971, pp. 39–43.
2. *PARM.,* Fr. B 3 (5) (D-K., I, 231): "for, thinking is identical to being."
3. ID., fr. B 7 (D-K): "It will never be conceded that nonbeings be."
4. Cf. *Soph.* 241a; cf. E. Moutsopoulos, *The Ontological Status of Art in Plato's "Sophist"* (in Greek) (*Athens:* 62, 1958), pp. 369–378. Cf. Proclus, *In Alcib.* 108. 3, (trans. Westerink): "it is false to assert . . . that there really is a nonbeing, as Plato's inspired interpreters use to say."
5. Cf. P. M. Schuhl, *L'oeuvre de Platon* (Paris: Hachette, 1954), pp. 117 sq.
6. Cf. L. Stefanini, "La Scepsi platonica," *Giorn. Crit. Filos. Ital.,* 1931, pp. 241–247; E. Moutsopoulos, "From Dogmaticism to Skepticism. The Importance of the Academy and the Role of the Stoa," *Stasinos,* 1974, pp. 157–166.
7. Cf. *Enn.* III. 6. 7: "Matter has no reality . . . it is mere indetermination . . . and so has no title to the name of Being. It will be more plausibly called a nonbeing, and this not in the sense that movement and station are Not-Being (i.e., as merely different from Being) but in the sense of veritable Not-Being, so that it is no more than the image and phantasm of mass, a bare aspiration towards substantial existence; it is stationary but not in the sense of having position, it is in itself invisible . . . a phantasm unabiding and yet unable to withdraw . . . so absolute its lack of all Being." Cf. Plato, *Tim.* 52b (trans. MacKenna): "it is palpable without sensation, through some spurious thought . . . it is nothing at all."
8. Cf. *Rep.* VII. 514a sq.
9. Cf. *Enn.* I. 1. 9: "The compound fears its own dissolution, and, when being dissolved, it is with pain and ache."; IV. 4. I; IV. 5. I.
10. Cf. *Enn.* IV. 4. 3; cf. J. Trouillard, *La purification plotinienne* (Paris: P.U.F., 1955), pp. 186 sq.

Chr. Rutten, *Les categories du monde sensible dans les "Enneades" de Plotin* (Paris: Les Belles Lettres, 1961), pp. 37 sq.

11. Cf. E. Moutsopoulos, "Dynamic Structuralism in the Plotinian Theory of Imagination," *Diotima* 4 (1976), pp. 11–22; "The Problem of the Imaginary in Plotinus" (in Greek), *Scient. Ann. of the Fac. of Philos., Univ. of Athens,* 19 (1968–1969), pp. 94–174, namely pp. 150 sq.

12. Cf. A. Levi, "Il concetto dell'errore nella filosofia di Plotnio," ed. Torino, di "Filosofia," 1951 (Studie Ricerche di storia della filosofia), p. 9.

13. Cf. Plato *Gorg.* 472e; *Rep.* VI. 506c–510b; *Theet.* 187b sq; *Phil.* 36c; *Laws* I. 631c–d; 645e; 653a. Cf. P. Kucharski, *Les chemins du savoir dans les derniers dialogues de Platon* (Paris: P.U.F., 1949), p. 14, n. 1. Cf. in general J. Stenzel (Eng. trans.), *Plato's Method of Dialectic* (Oxford: Clarendon Press, 1940), and F. M. Cornford, *Plato's Theory of Knowledge* (London: 1935), Routledge & Kegan Paul, 1960, pp. 110 sq.

14. Cf. *Enn.* I. 8. 15: "False opinions are generated for the soul whenever it deserts the true itself"; I. 1. 9: "for, a false opinion generates many evils by itself."

15. Cf. *Enn.* I. 1. 9: "The so-called intellection of false is an image"; cf. *ibid:* "if the opinative faculty and intellection are activities of the soul, how can they be impeccable?"

16. Cf. *Enn.* I. 1. 9, where it is supposed that erroneons thought "(opinion) does not wait for the judgment of intellection; on the contrary, we act after conviction on behalf of the worst; this namely occurs in the case of sensation."

17. Cf. *In Tim.* I. 247. 10–15 (trans. Diehl): "When the soul detaches itself from imagination and opinion, and from varying and indefinite knowledge, and adapts itself to its own thought. . . ." Cf. *In Eucl.* 12. 2–9 (trans. Friedlein). Cf. J. Trouillard, *L'Un et l'a me selon Proclos* (Paris: Les Belles Lettres, 1972), pp. 26–29; cf. *In Alcib.* –77–278 (trans. Westerinck); *Element Theol.,* theor. 31 (trans. Dodds); cf. J. Trouillard, *Introduction Proclos, Elements de théologie* (Fr. trans.) (Paris: Aubier, 1965), p. 39.

18. Cf., for instance, *In Parmen.* 995. 36 (trans. V. Cousin): "error . . . moves around according to such an itinerary . . ., as well as in the intellect, such a variety of thoughts"; *ibid.,* 996. 6 (Cousin): "it is said that whatever moves towards multiplicity moves in an erroneous way."

19. Cf. *ibid.,* 988. 38.

20. Cf. *ibid.,* 914. 34 (Cousin): "it is false to merely extend inversion to everything." Cf. *ibid.,* 728. 35; 856. 26; 857. 6; 1040. 31; 1039. 31.

21. Cf. *ibid.,* 978. 17 (Cousin): "one should not wonder if something which proves to be true (in one case) would prove false when applied to another."

22. Cf. *ibid.,* One should insist upon the importance of the repeated terms "upon . . . upon."

23. Cf. *ibid.,* "proposed."

24. Cf. *ibid.,* 975. 15 (Cousin): "it has been proved that not only everything is true, but also that whatever is false in it may be completely cured." Cf. *infra.* and Note 43.

25. Cf. *supra.* and Note *3,* on nonreducibility of being and non being; cf. *supra.* and Note 2, on identifiability of being and thinking, in *Parmenides.* On Plato's theory of the mixed, cf. N. I. Boussoulas, *L'etre et la composition des mixtes dans le "Philèbe" de Platon* (Paris, P.U.F., 1952); cf. E. Moutsopoulos, *La musique dans l'oeuvre de Platon,* pp. 360 sq.

26. Cf. *In Parm.* 654. 17 (Cousin): "it either only reveals the truth or only controls the false." Cf. *infra.* and Notes 32 and 39. In geometry, theorems are true or false; problems are possible or impossible. Cf. *In Eucl.* 330. 15 (trans. Friedl).

27. Cf. *ibid.,* 654. 19–22 (Cousin): "by searching whether each one's opinion is true or not, whether sensation is knowledge or not . . ., to what extent are true opinions partially invalid, and by testing again and proving that they are unsound."

28. Cf. *ibid.,* 951. 39: "in its development, the argument proves that ignoring such things and failing to dominate them is pure falsehood."

29. Cf. *ibid.,* 893. 22 (trans. Cousin): "what is given through sensation is something imaginary and unconceivable; it should remain such (within the soul) as it has been received from the very beginning, so that false and nonbeing may not occur (through it) . . . (error) proceeds only from the soul."

30. Cf. In *Alcib.* 243. 13 (trans. Westerink): "the crowd is the cause of false opinion; for (it inspires to us) evil images since our young age."
31. Cf. *ibid.*, (trans. Westerink): "it even causes various passions."
32. Cf. *In Tim.* III. 341. 8 sq. (trans. Diehl): "and these . . . passions affect the irrational soul; it however occurs that they also affect the rational soul."
33. Cf. *In Alcib.* 175. 14 (trans. Westerink): "even the soul, by being perturbated by false opinion and by accepting help from knowledge according to its own habit, generates an even falser opinion and fallacy."
34. Cf. *In Plat. Theol.* (Aem. Portus) 55. 27.
35. Cf. *Hypotyposis* (trans. Manutius) 18. 5; cf. *In Eucl.* 40. 13 (trans. Friedlein): "optics . . . which explains the illusory appearances presented by objects seen at a distance." cf. *ibid.*, 248. 8 (trans. Friedlein).
36. Cf. *ibid.*, 352. 22 (trans. Friedlein): "by proving that they (sc. "certain Hypotheses") are erroneous or superfluous," *ibid.*, 248.8 (Friedlein): "and so prepares the way for the refutation of unfounded objections"; *ibid.*, 70. 13 (Friedlein) "setting the true beside the false and adapting its refutations of error to seductions we may encounter" (see Note 42); *ibid.*, 247. 21 (Friedlein): "for refuting error."
37. Cf. *In Eucl.* 247. 21 (trans. Friedlein): "it is a mark of scientific and technical skill to arrange in advance for the undoing of those who attack what is going to be said and to prepare the positions from which one can reply so that the previously demonstrated matters may later serve not only for establishing the truth, but also for refuting error."
38. Cf. *ibid.*, 70. 13: τοῦ ἔλεγχον τῆς ἀπάτης συναομόσας. The parallel use of φεῦδος and ἀπάτη underlines the moral dimension of the notion. Cf. *In Alcib.* 166. 9 (trans. Westerinck): "he drives falsehood away from his life and, at the same time, does not clearly confess that he is fond of commanding and of authority"; *ibid.*, 190. 3 (Westerink): "due to the falsehood that surrounds him, he has not received the principles of research."
39. Cf. *In Eucl.* 69. 28 (Friedlein): "If you add or take away any detail whatever you are not inadvertently leaving the way of science and being led down the opposite path of error and ignorance?"
40. Cf. *ibid.*, "against"; *ibid.*, 253. 17 (Friedlein): "we must also note in this connection that many conversions are made fallaciously and are not true."
41. Cf. *supra.* and Notes 19 and 20.
42. Cf. *In Eucl.* 59. 3–6 (Friedlein): "Hence geometry also furnishes criteria whereby we can discriminate between statements that follow from its principles and those that depart from them. The various tropes for refuting fallacies when they occur have this function"; *ibid.*, 70. 10–13 (Friedlein): "[Euclid's book entitled *Fallacies*] enumerates in order the various methods of refutation and for each of them provides exercise for our understandings by a variety of theorems, setting the true beside the false and adapting its refutation of error to the seductions we may encounter"; *ibid.*, 212. 19–23 (Friedlein): "An 'objection' prevents an argument from proceeding on its way by opposing either the construction or the demonstration. Unlike the proposer of the case, who has to show that the proposition is true of it, he who makes an objection does not need to prove anything; rather it is necessary [for his opponent] to refute the objection and show that he who uses it is in error."
43. Cf. *supra.* and Note 24.
44. Cf. *In Tim.* III. 341. 8 (trans. Diehl): "even those who have false opinions also display some true opinion; it is through the latter that they are proved to have false opinions." Cf. *ibid.*, III. 340. 9 (Diehl) "to have a false opinion."
45. Cf. *supra.* and note 26.
46. *In Tim.* III. 340. 8–11 (trans. Diehl): "due to sensations, the opinative faculty is distorted, opinates falsely and becomes multiple; . . . it is thus filled with false opinions; it thus splits out, just as sensation, and rebels against itself."
47. Cf. *ibid.*
48. Cf. *Soph.* 241a. Cf. E. Moutsopoulos, "The Ontological status." Cf. *supra.* and Note 4.

PARTICIPATION AND THE STRUCTURE OF BEING
IN PROCLUS' *ELEMENTS OF THEOLOGY*

1. See Props. 116, 102, 13 sq.; 123, 108, 27–28. See Note 9, below. Born in Byzantium in either A.D. 410 or 412. Proclus studied at Alexandria in Egypt rhetoric and Roman law, afterwards mathematics and philosophy (the last under Olympiodorus the Peripatetic). Moving to Athens ca. 430, he continued his study of philosophy in the Platonic Academy under Plutarch of Athens and, especially, Syrianus. Shortly after the latter's death, Proclus assumed the leadership of the Academy until his death on April 17, 485. See T. Whittaker, *The Neo-Platonists* (Cambridge, England: University Press, 1928), pp. 157–159; L. J. Rosan, *Philosophy of Proclus* (New York: Cosmos, 1949), pp. 12–13 and pp. 13–35 (the last is a translation of Marinus' biography of Proclus); P. Bastid, *Proclus et le crépuscule de la pensée grecque* (Paris: J. Vrin, 1969), pp. 5–18; G. Martano, *Proclo di Atene: L'ultima voce speculativa del genio ellenico* (rev. ed. of *L'uomo e Dio in Proclo* [1952]; Napoli: Giannini, 1974), pp. 7–28.

2. For our purposes, "beings" in Proclus' *Elements* are all existents below the level of the One and henads and, thus, would comprise the levels of Being, Life, *Nous*, Soul, and Nature. For various listings, see Notes 11 and 12, below.

3. For the Greek text we shall use E. R. Dodds, *Proclus, The Elements of Theology* (Oxford: Clarendon Press, 1933; 2nd ed., 1963). In our references to this edition, the first number refers to the proposition, the second to the page, the third to the lines. As often as is conveniently possible, we shall put direct references to Proclus in the body of the paper itself so as to cut down the number of Notes. Whenever quoted, the Greek text will be put in the Notes.

   In our English translation we have been helped by Dodds, *ibid.*, and by Moerbeke—see ed. C. Vansteenkiste, O.P., "Procli Elementatio Theologica Translata a Guilielmo do Moerbeke," *Tijdschrift voor Philosophie* 13 (1951), 263–302 and 491–546; also Jean Trouillard, *Proclos' Eléments de théologie* (Paris: Aubier, 1965).

4. The monad that is the source of the perfection can also be said to be present in the participant but solely through the perfection.

   See Propositions 18 and 25 as instances of the wide variety of verbs Proclus uses for "to produce" or "to cause." They seem to have only minor shades of difference in meaning. On "procession" and other aspects of causality in Proclus, see P. Bastid, *Proclus*, p. 216 sqq.; J. Trouillard, "L'antithèse fondamentale de la procession selon Proclus," *Archives de Philosophie* 34 (1971), 435–449; idem, *L'un et l'âme selon Proclos* (Paris: Les Belles Lettres, 1972), pp. 78 sqq. and 91 sqq.; idem, "La *monē* selon Proclos," *Le néoplatonisme* (Paris: Centre National de la Recherche Scientifique, 1971), pp. 229–240; W. Beierwaltes, *Proklos: Grundzüge seiner Metaphysik* (Frankfurt am Main: Klostermann, 1965), pp. 118 sqq.

5. Likeness holds an important place generally in Proclus' causal doctrine. It is responsible for an effect's procession from its cause (see 29. 34. 3 sq. and, especially, the strong statement in line 6: "It is likeness which generates the product out of the producer"), as well as its reversion back to it (32. 36. 3 sq.).

6. This point is already implied in the fact that the participation is present in the participant.

7. The fact that the participation must somehow be part of the participant does not conflict with Props. 64, 81, or similar passages. The perfection participated can either itself reside in the participant or remain separate and yet produce an irradiation or offshoot which inheres in it. This point will be developed later in "The Origins of Participated Perfections."

8. Also matter must be excepted since of itself it is participant and nothing else. It is below participation, The One is above participation. In my more recent interpretation, schematized in Diagram Two, the henads, too, are not composites of participant/participation but are participations or participated perfections only.

9. What does Proclus intend by saying elsewhere (116. 102. 13 sq.; 123. 108. 27–28) that The One is unparticipated? Basically, this: that although it is the source of participations for subsequents, still

it is not itself a participation nor is it a participant of anything (99. 88. 32–33); that (as is true of every monad in relationship to the series it initiates) "it is common to all that can participate and is identical for all and, hence, is prior to all" (23. 28. 5–7); that "it has primacy in its own series and does not proceed from other principles" (99. 88. 24–25).

Besides those passages listed in the body of the article, the One is said to be participated in the following: 25. 28. 31–32; 109. 96. 23; 114. 100. 24.

10. Always, of course, excepting The One and matter, as well as henads in my more recent exegesis (see Note 8). On henads see Prop. 137 (discussed below as the final key text in the section, "The Origin of Participants"); G. Martano, *Proclo*, pp. 131 sqq.; P. Bastid, *Proclus*, pp. 254–271.

11. Also see 14. 16. 9 sq., where the lowest three strata are listed. The henads are not mentioned in either Props. 20 or 14, but they are in 21. 24. 29 sq. and 6. 6. 26–28 (my interpretation here differs from Dodds, *op. cit.*, p. 196). Abundant attention is given to the One-Good in early passages—see Props. 4, 5, 8, 11, 12, and 13.

12. This ordering of the monads occurs rather frequently in the *Elements*. Besides Prop. 20, see Props. 57, 62, 63, 64, 109, 129, and 139. In the foregoing Propositions, the second monad (Intelligence) is equivalent to Being-Intelligence; in Props. 160–165 Being is separated from Intelligence, with this resultant list: The One, Being, Intelligence, Soul, bodies.

There are, though, at least two other arrangements of monads, the first of which is: The One, First Limit, First Infinity, Being, Eternity, Time (Props. 90–94). The other arrangement is: The One (as well as gods or henads), Being, Life, Intelligence (Props. 39, 101, 105, 138). On the triad Being, Life, and Intelligence, see E. R. Dodds, *op. cit.*, pp. 252–254; L. J. Rosan, *Philosophy of Proclus*, pp. 97–98; Pierre Hadot, "Être, vie, pensée chez Plotin et avant Plotin," *Les Sources de Plotin*, tome V of *Entretiens sur l'antiquité classique* (Vandoeuvres-Genève: Fondation Hardt, 1960), pp. 105–158; *idem, Porphyre et Victorinus* (Paris: Études Augustiniennes, 1968), pp. 213–236 and 260–271; P. Bastid, *Proclus*, pp. 354–364; R. T. Wallis, *Neoplatonism* (New York: Scribner's Sons, 1972) pp. 66–67, 124–125, 130–133; S. Gersh, *Kinēsis Akinetos: Spiritual Motion in the Philosophy of Proclus* (Leiden: Brill, 1973), pp. 20–22 and 78–80; *idem, From Iamblichus to Eriugena* (Leiden: Brill, 1978), pp. 47, 87–88, 143 sqq.; G. Martano, *Proclo*, pp. 161–165; W. Beierwaltes, *Proklos*, pp. 93 sqq.

13. Lines 22–24: Πᾶν τὸ ἀμέθεκτον ὑφίστησιν ἀφ' ἑαυτοῦ τὰ μετεχόμενα, καὶ πᾶσαι αἱ μετεχόμεναι ὑποστασεις εἰς ἀηεθέκτους ὑπάρξεις ἀνστείνονται. Note that for ὑφίστησιν (line 22) Proclus substitutes ἀπογεννᾶ (line 26) and δώσει (line 28).

Following Moerbeke's lead (see C. Vansteenkiste, *op. cit.*, p. 275), I transliterate rather than translate ὑποστάσεις. On the meaning of the term in various authors, see Heinrich Dörrie, "Hypostasis: Wort und Bedeutungsgeschichte," *Nachrichten der Akademie der Wissenschaften in Göttigen*, (1955), 35–72. The noun, ὕπαρξις, means, I think "that which is the proper, unique reality" of an existent (see Dodds, *op. cit.*, p. 235, n. 1). For example, the *hyparxis* of The One is absolute unity and supreme goodness, of the Being is limit/infinity (Prop. 102), or intelligible form (Prop. 161). The word is not synonymous with "being," "existence," "substance," or "subsistence" (on this last see J. Trouillard, *Éléments*, p. 77).

14. This fact is equivalent to the monad being at once everywhere and nowhere (see 98. 86. 27).

15. Perhaps this second fact is the explanation of how unparticipated monads are also said to be participated. See above on The One (Note 9). In 53. 52. 6–7, Eternity and Time are instanced as (presumably) monads causing participations—namely, eternities and times. On Eternity and Time, see Peter B. Manchester, "Intellectual and Sensible Time in Neoplatonism: An Introduction," (with references to studies by Sambursky and Pines, Armstrong, Whittaker, Callahan, Ford, Beierwaltes).

16. Lines 1–3: Πᾶν τὸ ἀμέθεκτον διττὰς ὑφίστησι τῶν μετεχομένων τὰς τάξεις, τὴν μὲν ἐν τοῖς ποτὲ μετέχουσι, τὴν δὲ ἐν τοῖς ἀεὶ καὶ συμφυῶς μετέχουσι.

17. Lines 11–12: ἄλλων ἐστὶν οἰστικὰ τῶν ποτὲ μετεχομένων.

18. Mediation is an important and almost universal factor in causality. The One causes only matter (57. 54. 23 sq. and 57. 56. 14–16) and the henads immediately. All else it causes through the henads and whatever else has already been caused. Mediation is required by the basic principle

that "every cause sets up things which are like it before things which are unlike" (28. 32. 10–11). Mediation, as does likeness (see Note 5), governs both procession and reversion (38. 40. 22–25). See Note 21 for discussion of a different sort of mediation.

19. See *op. cit.*, p. 234.

20. On this point a demon is in contrast with, for example, a heavenly body, which is an everlasting participant of a henad (through its soul and intelligence—129. 114. 12 sq.) and whose unity is a participation of the first sort (see Dodds., *ibid.*, p. 234). On demons and their place in the Proclian universe, see *ibid.*, pp. 294–295.

21. Prop. 81 is a description of mediation unlike that encountered previously (see Note 18, above). There it had to do with how the cause produces the effect. Here it has to do with how the effect participates the cause. Even this latter description can be made in two ways. Prop. 81 (and parallel texts) is in terms of the perfection participated: there are cases in which a participant participates a cause through a mere irradiation or power of a perfection. But other Propositions are in terms rather of the relationship between participants and the source of those perfections: a higher participant participates its cause directly, a lower participant indirectly. For example, 128. 114. 1 sq.: "Every god, when participated by what is nearer to him, is participated directly; when participated by what is more remote, through fewer or more intermediaries." Thus, a god or henad is participated directly by a being but by an intelligence through a being, by a soul through an intelligence and a being, etc. (see Prop. 129).

   As a variation of this last sort of description, see 108. 86. 9 sq. and 109. 96. 23 sq.: A member of a lower series (say, a soul) participates the monad even of a higher series (The Intelligence) through the member of the higher series it directly participates (an intelligence), as well as through the monad of its own series (the Soul).

   Incidentally, "irradiation" in Prop. 81 is identical in meaning with the same word in 64. 60. 21 and 64. 62. 6. It is not identical with the same word in 63. 60. 13; 64. 62. 11; 70. 66. 12; 137. 120. 35, in all of which it has the general meaning of "participation" (whether of the first or second sorts).

22. Apparently, Proclus' doctrine on self-constitution (Prop. 40 sq.) is parallel to and based on self-sufficiency (see 40. 42. 10–17). If so, what is and what is not self-constituted (τὸ αὐθυπόστα-τον) would roughly correspond also to the first and second sorts of participations since what is and what is not self-sufficient are parallel to these. Also, the differences he establishes between what is and what is not self-constituted match pretty well those between the two kinds of participations, as this list of differences in the former show: Prop. 41: what needs no alien seat because contained by itself and conserved in itself without a substrate *versus* what is in another and requires a substrate; Prop. 42: what can revert upon itself *versus* what cannot; Prop. 45: the *agenēton versus* the *genēton*; Prop. 46: the imperishable *versus* the perishable; Prop. 47: the indivisible and simple *versus* the divisible and composite; Prop. 49: the perpetual *versus* the transient; Prop. 51: the atemporal *versus* the entitatively temporal. See. J. Whittaker, "The Historical Background of Proclus' Doctrine of the *Aythypostata*," in ed. H. Dörrie, *De Jamblique à Proclus,* tome xxi of *Entretiens sur l'Antiquité Classique* (Vandoeuvres-Genève: Fondation Hardt, 1975), pp. 193–237.

23. One should remember (see above, Note 21, last paragraph.) that Proclus uses "irradiation" (*ellampsis*) in at least two ways. In 64. 60. 21 and 64. 62. 6, it points to a participation received intermittently by the participant (also see 81. 76. 19). But in 63. 60. 13; 64. 62. 11; 70. 66. 12; and 137. 120. 35, it has the general meaning of a "participation" (or "perfection participated"), whether permanent or intermittent.

24. Roman T. Ciapalo drew the diagram, as well as diagrams 2 and 3 below, for which I am grateful.

25. These initial members are of two sorts inasmuch as they either are themselves participants of a higher series (e.g., Being and beings 1 and 2, Intellect and intellects 1 and 2, Soul and souls 1 and 2) or are not such participants (henads 1 to 12, which are, incidentally, the traditional Greek gods). What both sorts have in common is that the members are themselves not participated.

   No significance is to be attached to there being more henads than beings, and so on: this arises simply to keep the diagram on a single page. Actually, there should be more beings than henads, more intellects than beings, more souls than intellects—see props. 62. 58. 22; 110. 98. 1; 111. 98. 18; Dodds, *op. cit.*, p. 256.

26. Lines 24 and 26–27: ἢ μὲν ὕλη, ἐκ τοῦ ἑνὸς ὑποστᾶσα. . . . ἢ μὲν γὰρ ὕλη, ὑποκείμενον οὖσα πάντων, ἐκ του πάντων αἰτίου προῆλθε.

27. The context shows that "irradiation" here is not restricted, as in Prop. 81, to the second sort of participation but indicates any sort, whether first or second. See Note 21, last paragraph.

28. The awkwardness in prop. 72, as in its two predecessors, arises from speaking of the characters, properties, attributes of causes and effects rather than directly of the causes and effects themselves. This manner of speech, though, is frequent and important in Proclus (e.g., see Props. 18, 19, 97).

29. What is the result of this participation? Body receives form (57. 56. 12–13) or, in other texts (89. 82. 1 sq.; 102. 92. 1 sq.), determination and limit (presumably through form, since the henads determine matter through unity—see 117. 112. 29 sq.).

   One should note that, in 74. 70. 22 sq., being is affirmed to be prior to forms, that every form is a being but not every being is a form: "Hence in the resultants privations are in some sense beings although they are not forms; for through the unitary power of Being they too have received some feeble reflection of being." It is not clear what that "feeble reflection of being" would be that is not form. Might it be unity? In 135. 120. 1 sq. being is closely aligned with the henad it participates. Perhaps their causality also is closely aligned so that what first results from them is the unification of the recipient. Or might it be the state of potential being which privation or matter has prior to reception of form and its state of actual being? See 138. 122. 15 sq.

30. The genesis of matter from The One is what one would expect from Prop. 71. If, in general, the irradiations from higher causes become the participant for irradiations from lower causes, then what the absolutely highest cause produces would be the participant for absolutely all other causes.

   Once the origin of matter is accounted for, that of other participants poses no problem since they are matter plus participation(s) with respect to still further participations. Obviously, "participant" is a relative notion (save with respect to matter): any recipient, however complex or perfect, is a participant in relation to further perfections received.

   Incidentally, "matter" in this article is always to be understood as the basic participant. It is identical with so-called "intelligible matter" in the transsensible world and with "prime matter" in the sensible universe.

   Proclus' interest in linking matter specially and directly with the One and the henads issues from his interest in magic and theurgy—see Dodds, *op. cit.*, pp. xxii sq., 267, 275–276. On theurgy also see E. R. Dodds, "Theurgy and Its Relationship to Neoplatonism," *The Greeks and the Irrational* (Berkeley: University Press, 1951), pp. 253 sqq.; C. Zintzen, "Die Wertung von Mystik und Magic in der neuplatonischen Philosophie," *Rheinisches Museum* 108 (1965), 71–100; J. Trouillard, *L'un et l'âme selon Proclos*, pp. 71, 171–189; Andrew Smith, *Porphyry's Place in the Neoplatonic Tradition* (The Hague: Martinus Nijhoff, 1974), pp. 111–121.

31. ἐπιτηδειότης . . . πρὸς τὴν μέθεξιν τῶν αἰτίων. The first noun also occurs in 72. 68. 22. See E. R. Dodds, *Elements*, pp. 344–345.

32. For interpretations of Proposition 72, see Dodds, *op. cit.*, pp. 238–39; L. J. Rosàn, *Philosophy of Proclus*, pp. 107, 191–192; P. Bastid, *Proclus*, pp. 239–40.

33. Lines 27–30 and 31–32: καὶ ἀπ᾽ ἐκείνων πρόεισιν, οὐχ ᾗ ἀμέθεκτόν ἐστι, ταύτῃ πρόεισιν, ἀλλ᾽ ᾗ μετέχον. ἀφ᾽ ὧν γὰρ ὥρμηται, τούτων δήπου μετέχει, καὶ ὧν μετέχε, ταῦτα οὐκ ἔστε πρώτως . . . ᾗ μὲν γὰρ ἀπ᾽ αἰτίας, μετέχον ἐστὶ καὶ οὐκ ἀμέθεκτον.

34. Lines 10–11: καὶ ᾗ μὲν ἀπὸ τοῦ ἑνὸς πᾶσαι, οὐδεμία τούτων ἀπχή ἐστιν, ἀλλ᾽ ὡς ἀπ᾽ ἀρχῆς ἐκείνης.

35. Lines 31–34 and 35 sq.: Πᾶσα ἑνὰς συνυφίστησι τῷ ἑνὶ τὸ μετέχον αὐτῆς ὄν. τὸ μὲν γὰρ ἕν, ὡς πάντων ἐστὶν ὑποστατικόν, οὕτω καὶ τῶν ἑνάδων τῶν μετεχομένων καὶ τῶν ὄντων τῶν εἰς τὰς ἑνάδας ἀνηρτημένων αἴτιον . . . . ἁπλῶς μὲν εἶναι τοῦ ἑνὸς ποιοῦντος, τὸ δὲ συμφυὲς εἶναι τῆς ἑνάδος ἀπεργαζομένης, ἥ ἐστι συμφυές.

36. "Causing by one's very being" does not demand that the cause itself be a being, obviously, since henads are such causes and they transcend being. It is, then, the same as "causing by being what they are," "causing by the very fact that they are what they are." By the very fact that a

henad is a goodness and a unity, it communicates goodness and unity. By the very fact that an intelligence is eternal and unmoved, it produces what is eternal and immutable (76. 72. 7–12; 172. 150. 15 sq.). By the very fact that a soul is self-moved and living, it communicates self-movement and life to bodies (20. 22. 9–10; 196. 170. 20–21).

Manifestly, such causality is natural (literally), inevitable, spontaneous, and necessary. See Jean Trouillard, "Agir par son être même: La causalité selon Proclus," *Revue des sciences religieuses,* 37 (Oct., 1958), 347–357; *idem, L'un et l'âme selon Proclos,* pp. 92–97.

37. Those characters seem to be what Proclus intends in 137. 122. 2–3. But they could be the participations spoken of in Props. 120–122. The former interpretation seems more likely, however.

38. Of course, if the effect is really distinct from the cause, if matter is really other than the One, if Proclus' *Weltanschauung* is not a monism, then the One would seem to create *matter* by making it actually exist.

On creation in the *Liber de Causis,* written by an anonymous Semite in the eighth or ninth century A.D., but joining a doctrine of creation to Proclus' theory of causality, see Leo Sweeney, S.J., "Doctrine of Creation in *Liber de Causis*" in ed. C. O'Neil, *Etienne Gilson Tribute* (Milwaukee: Marquette Univ. Press, 1959), pp. 274–289; also see *idem, "Esse Primum Creatum* in Albert the Great's *Liber de Causis et Processu Universitatis,"* Thomist 44 (1980), 599–646.

39. On vertical and horizontal causalities, see Note 24, above, and Diagrams One and Two.

INDEX

References to the Enneads *of Plotinus*